TM

References for the Rest of Us!®

BESTSELLING BOOK SERIES

Are you intimidated and confused by computers? Do you find that traditional manuals are overloaded with technical details you'll never use? Do your friends and family always call you to fix simple problems on their PCs? Then the For Dummies® computer book series from Hungry Minds, Inc. is for you.

For Dummies books are written for those frustrated computer users who know they aren't really dumb but find that PC hardware, software, and indeed the unique vocabulary of computing make them feel helpless. For Dummies books use a lighthearted approach, a down-to-earth style, and even cartoons and humorous icons to dispel computer novices' fears and build their confidence. Lighthearted but not lightweight, these books are a perfect survival guide for anyone forced to use a computer.

> *"I like my copy so much I told friends; now they bought copies."*
> — **Irene C., Orwell, Ohio**

> *"Quick, concise, nontechnical, and humorous."*
> — **Jay A., Elburn, Illinois**

> *"Thanks, I needed this book. Now I can sleep at night."*
> — **Robin F., British Columbia, Canada**

Already, millions of satisfied readers agree. They have made For Dummies books the #1 introductory level computer book series and have written asking for more. So, if you're looking for the most fun and easy way to learn about computers, look to *For Dummies* books to give you a helping hand.

Hungry Minds™

1/01

Microsoft® Office 2001
For Macs

FOR
DUMMIES®

Microsoft® Office 2001 For Macs FOR DUMMIES®

by Tom Negrino

Hungry Minds™

HUNGRY MINDS, INC.

New York, NY ◆ Cleveland, OH ◆ Indianapolis, IN
Chicago, IL ◆ Foster City, CA ◆ San Francisco, CA

Microsoft® Office 2001 For Macs For Dummies®

Published by
Hungry Minds, Inc.
909 Third Avenue
New York, NY 10022
www.hungryminds.com
www.dummies.com (Dummies Press Web site)

Library of Congress Control Number: 00-102508

ISBN: 0-7645-0702-8

Printed in the United States of America

10 9 8 7 6 5 4 3 2

1O/SW/QS/QR/IN

Distributed in the United States by Hungry Minds, Inc.

Distributed by CDG Books Canada Inc. for Canada; by Transworld Publishers Limited in the United Kingdom; by IDG Norge Books for Norway; by IDG Sweden Books for Sweden; by IDG Books Australia Publishing Corporation Pty. Ltd. for Australia and New Zealand; by TransQuest Publishers Pte Ltd. for Singapore, Malaysia, Thailand, Indonesia, and Hong Kong; by Gotop Information Inc. for Taiwan; by ICG Muse, Inc. for Japan; by Intersoft for South Africa; by Eyrolles for France; by International Thomson Publishing for Germany, Austria and Switzerland; by Distribuidora Cuspide for Argentina; by LR International for Brazil; by Galileo Libros for Chile; by Ediciones ZETA S.C.R. Ltda. for Peru; by WS Computer Publishing Corporation, Inc., for the Philippines; by Contemporanea de Ediciones for Venezuela; by Express Computer Distributors for the Caribbean and West Indies; by Micronesia Media Distributor, Inc. for Micronesia; by Chips Computadoras S.A. de C.V. for Mexico; by Editorial Norma de Panama S.A. for Panama; by American Bookshops for Finland.

For general information on Hungry Minds' products and services please contact our Customer Care Department within the U.S. at 800-762-2974, outside the U.S. at 317-572-3993 or fax 317-572-4002.

For sales inquiries and reseller information, including discounts, premium and bulk quantity sales, and foreign-language translations, please contact our Customer Care Department at 800-434-3422, fax 317-572-4002, or write to Hungry Minds, Inc., Attn: Customer Care Department, 10475 Crosspoint Boulevard, Indianapolis, IN 46256.

For information on licensing foreign or domestic rights, please contact our Sub-Rights Customer Care Department at 650-653-7098.

For authorization to photocopy items for corporate, personal, or educational use, please contact Copyright Clearance Center, 222 Rosewood Drive, Danvers, MA 01923, or fax 978-750-4470.

For information on using Hungry Minds' products and services in the classroom or for ordering examination copies, please contact our Educational Sales Department at 800-434-2086 or fax 317-572-4005.

Please contact our Public Relations Department at 212-884-5163 for press review copies or 212-884-5000 for author interviews and other publicity information or fax 212-884-5400.

Hungry Minds™ is a trademark of Hungry Minds, Inc.

About the Author

Tom Negrino is an author, a consultant, and a contributing editor to *Macworld* magazine. His work has also appeared in many other magazines. He is a frequent speaker at Macworld Expo and other computer trade shows.

Tom co-authored the best-selling *JavaScript Visual QuickStart Guide,* 3rd Edition, and authored *Quicken Visual QuickStart Guides* for Mac and Windows. His other books for IDG Books Worldwide are *Microsoft Office 98 For Macs For Dummies, Macs For Kids and Parents, Macworld Web Essentials,* and *Yahoo! Unplugged.*

He lives in Northern California's wine country with his wife, Dori Smith, their son Sean, Pixel the cat (you can visit Pixel's home page, at `www.chalcedony.com/pixel`), about a zillion computers, and (bliss!) a cable modem.

Please visit Tom's Web site, at `www.negrino.com`. You can take a look out of his office window at `www.negrino.com/pages/officepix.html`.

Dedication

To Patricia Negrino, for her love and her support of me as a writer. Sleep well, Sis. I miss you.

Author's Acknowledgments

I'd like to thank a bunch of people for helping out with this book:

Christian Boyce, for his excellent work on the Excel section in the previous edition, much of which survives in this edition.

IDG Books Worldwide's Mike Roney, for working to get me this project.

Colleen Esterline, my project editor, who spun straw into gold. Or at least *For Dummies* yellow.

The fine folks at Studio B, for agenting above and beyond the call: David Rogelberg, Sherry Rogelberg, and Kristen Pickens.

Microsoft's ever-helpful Irving Kwong, Product Manager of the Macintosh Business Unit, Tantek Celik and Omar Shahine of the Internet Explorer and Entourage teams, and the participants in the Office 2001 beta newsgroups. My special thanks to the fabulous Melissa Harris Thirsk, at Waggener Edstrom.

Chris Breen, for the AppleWorks screenshot.

Sean Smith, who is still the World's Best Kid™.

Finally, I could not have finished this book without the generous support of Dori Smith, my light, my partner, my love.

Publisher's Acknowledgments

We're proud of this book; please send us your comments through our Online Registration Form located at www.dummies.com.

Some of the people who helped bring this book to market include the following:

Acquisitions, Editorial, and Media Development

Project Editor: Colleen Williams Esterline

(Previous Edition: Rebecca Whitney)

Acquisitions Editor: Tom Heine

Copy Editor: Colleen Williams Esterline

(Previous Edition: Kathy Simpson, Kelly Oliver, Bill McManus)

Proof Editor: Teresa Artman

Technical Editor: Tim Warner

Senior Editor, Freelance: Constance Carlisle

Editorial Assistants: Candace Nicholson, Sarah Shupert

Production

Project Coordinator: Nancee Reeves

Layout and Graphics: Beth Brooks, Brian Drumm, John Greenough, Brian Torwelle, Julie Trippetti, Jeremey Unger, Erin Zeltner

Proofreaders: Laura Albert, Nancy Price, York Production Services, Inc.

Indexer: York Production Services, Inc.

Special Help
Richard Graves

General and Administrative

Hungry Minds, Inc.: John Kilcullen, CEO; Bill Barry, President and COO; John Ball, Executive VP, Operations & Administration; John Harris, CFO

Hungry Minds Technology Publishing Group: Richard Swadley, Senior Vice President and Publisher; Mary Bednarek, Vice President and Publisher, Networking and Certification; Walter R. Bruce III, Vice President and Publisher, General User and Design Professional; Joseph Wikert, Vice President and Publisher, Programming; Mary C. Corder, Editorial Director, Branded Technology Editorial; Andy Cummings, Publishing Director, General User and Design Professional; Barry Pruett, Publishing Director, Visual

Hungry Minds Manufacturing: Ivor Parker, Vice President, Manufacturing

Hungry Minds Marketing: John Helmus, Assistant Vice President, Director of Marketing

Hungry Minds Online Management: Brenda McLaughlin, Executive Vice President, Chief Internet Officer

Hungry Minds Production for Branded Press: Debbie Stailey, Production Director

Hungry Minds Sales: Roland Elgey, Senior Vice President, Sales and Marketing; Michael Violano, Vice President, International Sales and Sub Rights

◆

The publisher would like to give special thanks to Patrick J. McGovern, without whom this book would not have been possible.

◆

Contents at a Glance

Cartoons at a Glance

By Rich Tennant

page 129

page 37

page 287

page 323

page 7

page 181

page 247

Fax: 978-546-7747
E-mail: richtennant@the5thwave.com
World Wide Web: www.the5thwave.com

Table of Contents

Introduction

. . . .

Welcome to *Microsoft Office 2001 For Macs For Dummies!* If you've spent any time at all with Office 2001, you've seen that it consists of four main programs (and one other): Word 2001 is its word processor, Entourage 2001 is its e-mail and calendar program, Excel 2001 is its spreadsheet program, and PowerPoint 2001 is its presentation program. Office 2001 also has a Web browser, Internet Explorer 5.

All these programs add up to a great deal of power and a great deal of complexity. That's where this book comes in. When you're working in one of the Office programs and you ask yourself, "How do I . . . ?" or "How does this work?" just reach for this book. Chances are, you'll find the answers here.

A long time ago, I learned that there are two basic kinds of auto mechanics. One type is the mechanic who has been factory-trained and has had every class under the sun; the other type learned everything from just tinkering with every car that passed by. The factory-trained mechanic has all the right tools and is the one you want to rebuild your engine. The tinkerer is the one you turn to when your car breaks down in the middle of nowhere — the one who can always get your car running long enough to get you to the shop. This book is more like the tinkerer: It helps you get the job done when you need it the most. When you have a question, just look up the answer, and then get back on the road.

About This Book

I've written *Microsoft Office 2001 For Macs For Dummies* so that you can skip around in it and read just the chapters that interest you. You don't have to read Chapter 1, for example, in order to understand and enjoy Chapter 15, though it would be nice if you got around to reading Chapter 1 sometime; that chapter has some stuff that I especially like. But there's no hurry — and no requirement that you read the chapters in a particular order. The *...For Dummies* books are written as reference books, not as tutorials.

Conventions Used in This Book

Throughout this book, I use some special codes to make reading the book easier. I'll often say things like "choose File⇨New." Whenever you see something like that, it means that I'm asking you to choose a command from a menu. When you see File⇨New, I'm really saying, "Click the File menu and drag down to select the New command."

You'll also see the ⌘ symbol throughout this book. Whenever I use this symbol, I'm talking about the ⌘ key on your keyboard. This key is usually referred to as the Command key, and longtime Mac users often refer to Command-key shortcuts when they talk about performing a task from the keyboard. On some keyboards, there is a picture of an apple next to the ⌘, so you might hear some folks refer to this key as the Apple key. When I tell you to use a shortcut key, such as ⌘+P, just hold down the ⌘ key and press the P key. If you're using a USB keyboard with your Macintosh that was originally meant for use with a PC, the Command key is almost always mapped to the Alt key.

What You're Not to Read

You should read most of this book, at least the parts that interest you and that apply to the ways that you use the Office 2001 programs. But I've also added in some sections that you don't have to read at all! Those sections are set off by the Technical Stuff icon, so you can spot them fast. Why would I include stuff you don't need to read? Because the Technical Stuff sections have information that you don't absolutely need to get the job at hand done, but the information in these sections gives you a deeper and better understanding of the particular subject or gives you background information that's useful but not required. So read the Technical Stuff if you want (heck, I'd appreciate it), but you'll be able to do everything you need to do even if you skip those sections.

Foolish Assumptions

In writing this book, I've made the following assumptions about you: First and foremost, you're meeting the minimal requirements for running Office 2001. You must have a Power Macintosh, iMac, PowerPC-based PowerBook, or iBook with Microsoft Office 2001 installed on it. On that computer, you have to be running Mac OS 8.1 or later (and in my not-so-humble opinion, you really should be using Mac OS 9 or later; the benefits of using Mac OS 9 make it a must-have). You must also have at least 32MB of RAM (48MB if you're running Mac OS 9) and a CD-ROM or DVD-ROM drive (every Macintosh that Apple's shipped since 1997 does). You'll also need to set aside about 160MB of hard disk space for the suite.

I've also made the assumption that you're familiar with the basics of using a Macintosh. You don't need to be a Mac guru, although you shouldn't be stumped by concepts like selecting text, clicking and dragging, and using files and folders. If you need a refresher in the essentials, you may want to buy *Macs For Dummies,* by David Pogue (published by IDG Books Worldwide, Inc.); if you want detailed information about using the Mac OS, I suggest that you pick up a copy of Lon Poole's *Mac OS 9 Bible,* also published by IDG Books Worldwide, Inc.

How This Book Is Organized

Microsoft Office 2001 For Macs For Dummies is split into seven parts. Here's the lowdown:

Part I: Getting Started with Microsoft Office 2001

Sensibly enough, I start out by introducing you to Microsoft Office 2001. In this part, I show you what Office 2001 can do for you, why Office 2001 is a terrific Macintosh product (unlike some previous versions of Microsoft Office), and how the package stacks up against the competition.

This part also shows you how to do some things that are common to all the Office 2001 programs, such as how to start up and switch between the programs, open documents, and use the suite's help features. You also meet Max, the Office Assistant, a friendly, animated character who's great at answering your Office 2001 questions.

Part II: Using Word 2001

Microsoft Word 2001 is a superb word processor, capable of handling everything from a quick note to Mom (though I think that handwritten notes to Mom are nicer, don't you?) to reports, books, and your doctoral thesis.

Word 2001 is chock-full of features to help you wrestle your words into shape. Because most people work with words more than anything else they do, this part of the book is the longest and most detailed part.

Part II starts you off easy with the basics of creating a Word document. Then you see how Word can help you out with automatic formatting and by checking your spelling and grammar. Because the look of your work is almost as important as its content, you see how to create professional-looking documents, including fancy pieces like reports, newsletters, and even Web pages.

Part III: Organizing Your E-Mail and Time with Entourage 2001

In the early 1990s, only a few people were using the Internet, the worldwide data and information network. Only a few years later, being on the Internet and, specifically, having an electronic mail address are barely optional, whether you're a business or home user. In this part, you discover how to use Entourage 2001, the newest addition to the Office family, to tame your e-mail and communicate with others. Entourage 2001 also sports a full-featured Personal Information Manager (PIM), which lets you control your calendar, corral your contacts, and track your to-do's. You'll also see how you can carry your information with you, as Entourage 2001 knows how to transfer and synchronize its PIM data with handheld computers.

Part IV: Crunching Your Numbers with Excel 2001

This part shows you how to create your own spreadsheets with Microsoft Excel 2001. You start out in Spreadsheet Boot Camp, and, after you know the basics, discover how to add your own formulas so that Excel 2001 calculates results automatically. Excel knows how to make your spreadsheets look good, and you'll see how you can make your spreadsheets look spiffy with just a few clicks of the mouse. Because numbers can be dull, however (with apologies to our accountant friends), you discover how to use Excel 2001 to create flashy charts and graphs. With the right arsenal of pie charts and bar graphs, you'll be certain to win friends, influence co-workers, and get in the running for that next Nobel prize.

Part V: Putting on a Show with PowerPoint 2001

Giving a presentation can be the scariest thing most people do in the office (aside from asking for a big raise, of course!). In this part, you meet PowerPoint 2001, which makes creating snappy presentations a painless experience. After you see how easy it is to create a simple slide show, you find out how to improve your presentations with fancy graphics and slick animation and how you can add high-tech, interactive features to your shows. I haven't forgotten the human element, though: An entire chapter full of tips helps you deliver the presentation while simultaneously conquering stage fright.

Part VI: Working Well with Others

No man is an island, and your Mac isn't, either. You often need to share your work with other people, and Office 2001 has a zillion tools that can help. This part shows you how you can make Word, Entourage, Excel, and PowerPoint work together to create powerhouse documents that are more than the sum of their parts. You discover how to share your documents with co-workers to gather their comments and suggestions, and then you see how to ignore those suggestions (okay, and use them, too). You see how you can use Entourage to schedule follow-up tasks from any of the other Office applications, to make sure that your projects stay up to date.

Because one of the best mediums for sharing work is the Internet, this part delves into how you can embed live Internet links in your documents and create Web pages from any of the Office 2001 programs (especially from Word 2001).

Part VII: The Part of Tens

If you're hungry for hot tips and tricks to help you use Microsoft Office 2001 better, The Part of Tens is the place for you. You find out how to tame your toolbars, you get a bunch of time-saving tips, and you read about some of the best ways to customize Office 2001.

Icons Used in This Book

Throughout *Microsoft Office 2001 For Macs For Dummies,* I use little pictures, called *icons,* next to the text to get your attention. Here are the icons I use:

This icon marks pieces of information that can be helpful and that you should remember.

If you're looking for the best way, the fast way, the you-can't-top-this way of doing things, this icon tips you off. The Tip icon always points out what you can do to make your Office 2001 experience easier or faster.

Watch out! You have to be careful and follow the advice given here, or else you can have some real trouble.

You don't have to read this stuff. If you do, however, you get a deeper understanding of the subject being discussed. You may even be able to impress and amaze your friends with the depth of your incredible knowledge.

Where to Go from Here

You may want to start out by looking up some feature you've seen in one of the Office 2001 programs, or by finding out how to do something that's been puzzling you. Or you can flip through at random until a page catches your eye. If you're completely new to Microsoft Office 2001, start by browsing through Part I. You'll find the basics there.

Remember, this book is *your* guide to Office 2001. So make it your own: As you find things in the book that work for you, dog-ear that page. Jot notes in the margins. Plaster the book with sticky notes so you can find stuff again. Turn it into the personalized resource that serves you best.

I'm ready if you are. Let's go!

Part I

Getting Started with Microsoft Office 2001

The 5th Wave · By Rich Tennant

"IT'S A SOFTWARE PROGRAM THAT MORE FULLY RE-FLECTS AN ACTUAL OFFICE ENVIRONMENT. IT MULTI-TASKS WITH OTHER USERS, INTEGRATES SHARED DATA, AND THEN USES THAT INFORMATION TO NETWORK VICIOUS RUMORS THROUGH AN INTER-OFFICE LINK-UP."

In this part . . .

*E*very journey begins with a single step, and your journey into the heart of Microsoft Office 2001 is no exception. Part I gives you an overview of the Office 2001 programs and shows you how Office compares to its most popular competition. Then you find out how to create documents with the Office programs and other basics common to the whole package.

One of the best features of Office 2001 is also one of the most helpful: Max, the Office Assistant. Max can answer almost any question you have about using Office 2001, and he's fun to have around too. You meet Max in this part and find out how he's the biggest and best key to getting help with Office 2001 (except for this book, of course!).

Chapter 1

Why Office 2001?

For many people, the days of job specialization are over. The average worker today, whether he or she works as an employee or as an entrepreneur, must accomplish many tasks during the course of a day and needs many software tools to get the job done.

Imagine a typical day. You arrive at work and turn on your computer. Sipping your morning coffee, you log on to the Internet to read your electronic mail. One of the messages is a request from your boss for more details about your latest project. You start a word-processing program and write a short memo, explaining your approach. You launch your spreadsheet program and create a set of numbers to support your memo. Switching back to your e-mail, you send the memo and spreadsheet to your boss for approval. Then you go to lunch. When you get back, your boss has already replied (doesn't this guy ever take a lunch hour?), asking you to present your proposal at a meeting later that afternoon. You realize that handing copies of your memo around the table won't have the impact you want, so you fire up your presentation software and create a nice slide show.

After the smashing success of your presentation, your boss calls you into his office and offers you a huge raise. Beautiful women in evening gowns crowd around you, press bouquets of roses into your arms, and place a diamond tiara on your head. Music swells, and you begin your walk down the runway, waving to your cheering co-workers. Blinking away tears of joy, you say happily, "I owe it all to my software!"

Okay, maybe this isn't a *typical* day.

Introducing Microsoft Office 2001

To deal with all the things that come up in your workday, you need software that can handle writing, number crunching, presenting, sending e-mail, and more. You could try to find all these functions in one mammoth program — the approach taken by *integrated software* packages such as AppleWorks, and, on Windows PCs, Microsoft Works. Or you can search for a few separate, powerful, expensive programs that have been put together in one box for a cut-rate price. That arrangement is called a *suite* of programs, which is what Microsoft Office is. The Office suite includes Microsoft Word, the word processor; Microsoft Entourage, the e-mail and personal information manager; Microsoft Excel, the spreadsheet; and Microsoft PowerPoint, the presentation program. Figure 1-1 shows the icons for these four powerhouse programs.

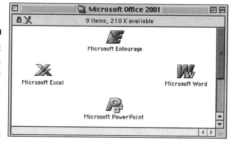

Figure 1-1:
The icons for the four main Office 2001 programs.

In addition to the four main programs, the Office 2001 CD-ROM includes another Internet program. Internet Explorer 5 is the suite's Web browser. Figure 1-2 shows Internet Explorer's desktop icon.

Figure 1-2:
The Internet Explorer icon.

Office 2001 builds on the lessons that Microsoft learned with its immediate predecessor, Office 98. That version of Office was the first to be built by a dedicated Mac team at Microsoft, one that wasn't tied to the Windows Office developers. Office 98 for the Mac pioneered features that Windows Office didn't have and sported a true Mac interface. The preceding version of Microsoft Office, Office 4.2, included Microsoft Word 6, Excel 5, and

PowerPoint 4 and was less than a resounding success. Mac users found it to be too "Windows-like" and hard to use. Office 4.2 received almost universally bad press, and many people refused to upgrade, sticking with the 1992-vintage Word 5.1 and Excel 4.0.

Microsoft learned with Office 98 that if they built real Mac programs, Mac buyers would come, and Office 98 was a big success. With the release of Microsoft Office 2001, the company has focused on making the Office suite easier to use, simplifying difficult tasks, and improving communication among the programs in the suite. The Office 2001 programs have been revised to make them look better and to work faster, smarter, and easier, yet still provide more features than you'll likely ever use. The following sections describe the individual pieces of the Office 2001 package.

Word 2001

Nothing is more important than words. It's probably no surprise that a writer would say that, but it's still true. The words you write shape the way people think about you and may even change your career. If words are so important, the means of getting those words down is vital. You should look for a writing tool that helps you get more work done with less effort.

Microsoft Word 2001 is an excellent writing tool for short memos or entire books, and it's smart: It checks spelling and grammar as you type. If you frequently type the same words, Word 2001 can remember that text and spit it back the next time you start to type it. Word watches what you do, and it can automatically format your documents. If you type the salutation of a letter, for example, Word recognizes the "Dear Oswald" part and asks whether you're writing a letter and (if so) whether you want to format your document like a letter, providing several letter styles for your formatting pleasure. New to the 2001 edition is an easier way to do form letters, a smarter spell checker and thesaurus, and more formatting help with your documents.

Word 2001 comes with terrific online help (as do Excel, Entourage, and PowerPoint) that enables you to ask questions about the program in plain English.

Word 2001 can create almost any type of document that contains words, including letters, Web pages, books, and newsletters. Figure 1-3 shows Word 2001 being used to make a newsletter.

I could go on and on singing the praises of Word 2001, but I get to do that in Part II of this book.

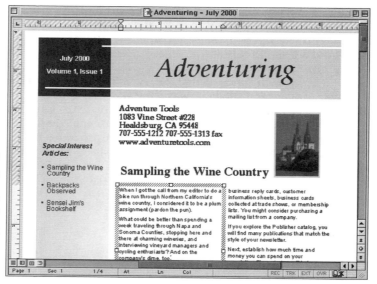

Figure 1-3:
Creating a
newsletter
from one of
the prebuilt
templates in
Word 2001.

Excel 2001

Excel is the premier spreadsheet for any computer platform, and the latest version is better than ever. What's a *spreadsheet?* Think of an accountant's ledger pad, with all the rows and columns ready to be filled in with numbers. Then imagine a pad that can do all the math for you. That's a spreadsheet. Although Excel is fine for accounting, it works well for any task that involves grinding through numbers: financial projections, statistical analysis, rocket trajectories (hey, it *is* rocket science) — you name it.

New to Excel 2001 is the List Wizard; Microsoft realized that the primary use for Excel is to make tabular lists, so they've added tools to help you make and sort lists. You'll also build formulas easier with the new Calculator.

Figure 1-4 shows an expense report written in Excel. Writing a report may not be as exciting as going to the moon, but in the grand scheme of things, isn't being reimbursed for your travel expenses just as important?

Spreadsheets also are the cannon fodder for charts and graphs. You can change the numbers in a spreadsheet into cool graphs of just about every description. Looking to make a big splash at your next meeting? Two words: pie charts. Bosses love 'em; they can't resist a piping-hot pie chart. You can bake one yourself — with the help of Excel 2001.

			Lodging –51420	Transportation		Auto Expenses (itemize below) – 51400	Local Taxi, Carfare, Tolls, etc. – 51400	Meals – 51490 (itemize below)		
				Air, Rail, etc. – 51400	Limo, Car Rental, etc – 51430			Break-fast	Lunch	Dinner

EXPENSE REPORT Name: **Tom Negrino** Number: **5655** Expense Period: **7/1/2000 – 7.**

Date	Day	City and State								
7/2/00	SUN							$18.50	$0.00	$32.87
7/3/00	MON	San Francisco	$210.00		$29.00			$4.20	$8.93	$44.81
7/4/00	TUE	San Francisco	$210.00		$29.00			$5.51	$15.22	$9.46
7/5/00	WED	San Francisco	$210.00		$29.00			$12.75	$0.00	$29.62
7/6/00	THU	San Francisco	$210.00	$247.00	$29.00			$14.22	$7.64	$36.00
7/7/00	FRI	Seattle	$100.00		$32.00					
	SAT									
		TOTALS:	$940.00	$247.00	$148.00	$0.00	$0.00	$55.18	$81.79	$152.76

Itemized Entertainment and Business Meals

Date	Person(s) Entertained: Name, Co., Title	Time and Place	Nature and Purpose of Entertainment	Amount	% Personal

Figure 1-4:
Excel 2001 can calculate your expense report!

PowerPoint 2001

When you need to persuade, you'll turn to PowerPoint 2001. It's a presentation program that enables you to create slide shows that can be shown on a computer screen (or with a projector from a computer), printed, or even transferred to 35mm slides or overhead transparencies.

PowerPoint provides powerful tools that enable you to organize your thoughts and create presentations. The program's outline mode makes building a presentation easy, and the outline converts directly into slides. You can format your slides any way you want and add animated slide transitions (as well as add animation within slides). PowerPoint 2001 also comes with dozens of templates, canned presentations, clip art, and Wizards that help you through the hassle of developing a presentation.

PowerPoint 2001 is a definite improvement over PowerPoint 98, its immediate predecessor. The new features include a three-pane view for easier presentation creation, automatic fitting of text on your slides, and more flexible presentation options. Check out Figure 1-5 to see a PowerPoint 2001 presentation being created.

Entourage 2001

Entourage 2001 is the newcomer to the Office suite. It is the Office 2001 e-mail manager and Personal Information Manager (PIM). Based on the free

Outlook Express 5, which is one of the best e-mail programs available for the Macintosh, Entourage supports the latest e-mail standards, mail filtering, and much more.

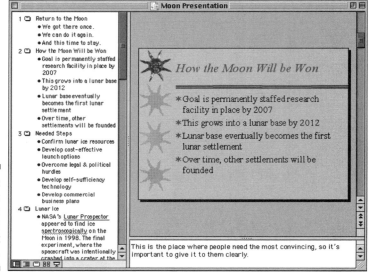

Figure 1-5:
Building a
presentation
in
PowerPoint
2001.

On the PIM side, Entourage can track your appointments in its Calendar, your to-do's in its Tasks list, and your colleagues in its Contacts manager. The program can also synchronize its PIM data (but not, oddly, its e-mail) to hand-held computers, so you can take your information on the road, make changes on your trip, and then merge the new information with your desktop machine on your return.

The Entourage Tasks list integrates other Office programs, so while creating any other Office document, you can set a reminder to follow up at a later date. Figure 1-6 shows Entourage 2001 in action.

Internet Explorer 5.0

Surfing the World Wide Web has become a core requirement of every computing platform. The Web browser that comes with Office 2001 (and that now is also the built-in browser for Mac OS, the Macintosh system software) is Microsoft Internet Explorer 5.0. When it was released in the spring of 2000, Internet Explorer 5 was the best Web browser ever released for Macintosh and arguably the best Web browser released for any computing platform. It's fast, compliant with Internet standards, and has innovative features like the Internet Scrapbook, which stores Web pages that you want to save, which is fabulous for saving receipts from online purchases. Internet Explorer does a great job of viewing Web sites, as shown in Figure 1-7, and also downloads files from the Internet.

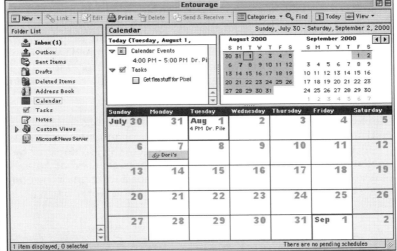

Figure 1-6:
The new Entourage 2001 manages your time, contacts, and e-mail.

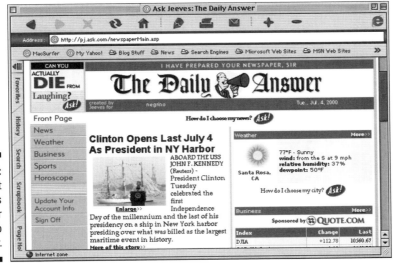

Figure 1-7:
Internet Explorer 5 is a superior Web browser.

Microsoft Office 2001 versus AppleWorks

If you haven't already bought Microsoft Office 2001, you owe it to yourself to compare Office 2001 with its closest competitor. Although several Office-like suites are available for Windows, on the Mac side AppleWorks (previously known as ClarisWorks before Apple reabsorbed its software subsidiary, Claris) is practically the only choice. This package is a suite only by courtesy — instead of being several full-featured programs bundled together, AppleWorks 6.0 is an integrated program that includes a word processor, spreadsheet, database, drawing and page layout module, painting module, and presentation module.

AppleWorks 6.0 is a fine product, with a more-than-adequate word processor and spreadsheet, and its drawing and painting modules are good, if not especially inspired. The database is basic but gets the job done for tasks such as mail merges and simple record keeping. Apple claims that AppleWorks 6.0 has all the power most people ever need, for a fraction of the complexity and price of Microsoft Office. Figure 1-8 shows AppleWorks 6.0 in action.

Figure 1-8:
Creating a newsletter in the AppleWorks drawing and page layout module.

If you have an older Mac, AppleWorks may be the better choice for you. Office 2001 requires a Power Macintosh with at least 32 megabytes (MB) of RAM (although 48MB is a more realistic figure), whereas AppleWorks 6.0 runs on any Power Macintosh and requires 24MB of RAM.

AppleWorks is also much gentler on your pocketbook than Microsoft Office 2001. A brand-new copy of Office 2001 costs around $450, whereas AppleWorks Office sets you back only about $70. Of course, Apple bundles AppleWorks with late-model iMacs and iBooks, so if you have one of those machines, the price of AppleWorks is even more attractive.

It's true that many people don't ever need more powerful software than AppleWorks 6.0. If you do, however, you'll be frustrated when AppleWorks runs out of steam. AppleWorks 6.0 uses its drawing module to create newsletters, for example — a poor substitute for the capabilities of Word. The presentation module in AppleWorks is limited to a screen resolution of 640 x 480 pixels, which is too small for many presentations, and can't compare to PowerPoint's features. The capabilities of Word 2001 far outshine those of the word processor inside AppleWorks, and the differences are big enough that if your business depends on words (ultimately, most businesses do), Word 2001 is well worth the extra investment. Also, although the AppleWorks spreadsheet isn't bad, it doesn't hold a candle to Excel 2001, the recognized world champion in spreadsheets.

Another issue you should consider is whether you need to share files with other people. AppleWorks 6.0 can only read and write RTF files (a standard Microsoft Word interchange format) but can't read Word files of any version directly and can't read Microsoft Excel files at all. Office 2001 files on the Mac and Office 2000 files on the PC are interchangeable, but if you use AppleWorks, you have to ask people who work with Office programs to resave their word processing files in RTF so that you can use those files. It's a big pain.

You can use Office files (including almost every version of Office for Mac and Windows) in AppleWorks 6.0, but you need to invest in the excellent MacLink Plus Deluxe package from DataViz (about $95; you can get more information from their Web site at www.dataviz.com). MacLink Plus Deluxe can convert almost any sort of word-processing or spreadsheet file to any other format. The program handles and converts files created in programs that have long since faded into the mists of time (such as the PC program MultiMate and the Apple II version of AppleWorks) to modern Mac formats. MacLink Plus Deluxe works well for converting recent Office files created on Macs and Windows 98 and 2000 machines to AppleWorks, and vice versa. MacLink Plus Deluxe can also handle translations between some graphics formats. Whether or not you use AppleWorks, MacLink Plus is still useful to have around for converting random PC files your friends send you.

Your decision to go with AppleWorks or Microsoft Office 2001 must be based on your unique circumstances after balancing cost, hardware and software compatibility, and features. Some people are okay with tools that are adequate for their needs. I'm the kind of person, though, who wants to know that if I ever decide to squeeze the maximum amount of power from a program, that power will be there, with no compromises. That's why I use Office 2001.

Chapter 2

Running Office 2001

In This Chapter

▶ Using the Office 2001 programs

▶ Opening documents

▶ Quitting Office 2001 programs

*I*n this chapter, you find out how to do things that are common to all Office 2001 programs, such as opening and closing programs and files, saving, and printing.

Installing Office 2001

One great feature of Office 2001 is a throwback to the early days of using the Macintosh. Way back in prehistory (in the computer world, that would be the 1980s), you never had to use any Installer programs to put programs on your Mac. You just slammed the program's floppy disk into your Mac and dragged the program's icon over to your hard disk. As time went on, programs got more complicated and required support files, called *extensions,* to be installed in your Mac's System Folder. Soon, so many of these support files were required that people couldn't keep track of them, and all programs came with Installer programs, which ensure that all the files required to make the program run are put in the right places on your hard disk.

Office 2001 enables you to return to the old way of doing installations — with a modern twist. To install Office 2001, you drag the Office 2001 folder from the CD-ROM to your hard disk's icon, as shown in Figure 2-1. This action copies the main Office 2001 programs (Word, Excel, Entourage, and PowerPoint) to your hard disk.

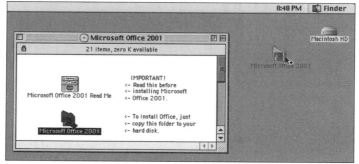

Figure 2-1: Copying the Office 2001 folder to your hard disk.

Before you drag the Office 2001 folder to your hard disk icon, make sure that you have enough available disk space. The Office suite is big: The standard installation takes more than 150 megabytes (MB) of space. To find out how much disk space you have available, look at the header of any Finder window, as shown in Figure 2-2. As long as you have at least 200MB free, you're fine. This concern is lessened on more recent Macs, which have multigigabyte hard drives, but people with older computers may have need for concern.

The amount of available disk space

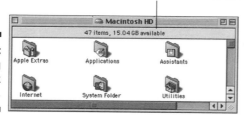

Figure 2-2: Checking your disk space.

Running any Office 2001 program for the first time takes a little extra time because Office 2001 checks your disk and automatically installs any additional files it needs. Best of all, if you later accidentally throw away any of these files, Office 2001 is smart enough to fix the installation for you. The next time you run any of the Office 2001 programs, Office knows to start up its First Run program, which copies the missing files back to your hard disk. This "self-healing" feature, introduced in Office 98, is a big improvement from previous versions of Office, which often required a bewildering amount of fiddling and saddled you with an intrusive Setup program.

Using Office 2001 Programs

After you copy the Microsoft Office 2001 folder to your hard disk, open the folder. You see the icons for the four main Office programs, plus several folders that hold additional support files. Decide which Office program you want to start, and double-click its icon. If you want to start Word, for example, just double-click the Microsoft Word icon.

Another way to start or launch any Macintosh program or document is to single-click the icon and then choose File⇨Open.

When an Office program starts, you see a brief introduction screen that displays the logo of the program; then you get the new Project Gallery, as shown in Figure 2-3.

Category list   Display area

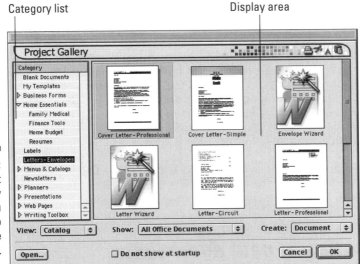

Figure 2-3:
The Project
Gallery
allows you
access to
any Office
document.

Using the Project Gallery

The Project Gallery allows you to access any Office document from any of the Office programs, even if the document you want wasn't created by the program that you're currently in. Making a selection from the category list on the left side of the Project Gallery window displays the documents and templates that you have available to you on the right side of the window. You can expand categories to see what documents or templates they contain by clicking the disclosure triangles next to the category name, much as you would do in a Finder window.

You can limit the choices displayed to documents created in just one of the Office programs by choosing one of the Office programs from the Show pop-up menu at the bottom of the Project Gallery, instead of the default All Office Documents.

If you just want a blank document from the program that you're currently using, don't choose anything from the category list; it always starts on Blank Documents. Just click the OK button, press the Enter key, or hit the Return key.

To begin creating a document using one of Office 2001's templates or Wizards, follow these steps:

1. **Choose an item from the category list.**

   The selection of templates or Wizards available in that category will appear in the display area.

2. **Click to select a specific document from one of the choices listed in the display area.**

3. **Click the OK button, press the Enter key, or hit the Return key.**

If you don't want the Project Gallery to appear when you start up one of the Office 2001 programs, you can turn it off by clicking the Do not show at startup check box at the bottom of the Project Gallery screen. You can also turn it off by choosing Edit⇨Preferences, clicking the General tab, and clearing the Show Project Gallery at startup check box. If you turn the Project Gallery off, the Office programs simply create a new blank document when they launch.

The Project Gallery is available to you in all of the Office programs at any time. You'll find it at the top of the File menu in all of the programs, or you can call it up by pressing the ⌘+Shift+P shortcut key.

Creating a new document

Whether you use the Project Gallery or not, you can always get a new document when you start one of the Office programs. What happens, however, if you're already working in an Office program and want to create a new document? You create it almost in the same way as you would in any Macintosh application: by choosing File⇨New Blank Document or pressing the ⌘+N shortcut key. Yes, darn near every other Mac program gets by with just File⇨New, but Microsoft still has their own ways of doing things.

When you press the shortcut key, the Office programs create a new, blank document based on their Normal template. If you want to create a document based on a different template, bring up the Project Gallery. (See Chapter 3 for more information about using templates.)

Saving a document

Type a line or two of text in the blank document so that you have something to save. Then follow these steps to save the document:

1. **Choose File⇨Save.**

   The Save dialog box appears, as shown in Figure 2-4. The large scrollbox shows you where the file will be saved.

Pop-up navigation list

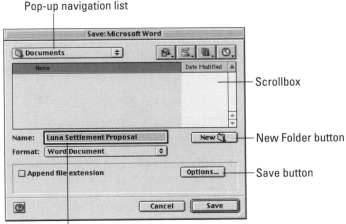

Scrollbox

New Folder button

Save button

Figure 2-4:
The Save
dialog box.

Enter file name here

2. **If you want to save the file in a different place, navigate to that place by clicking the pop-up menu at the top of the scrollbox.**

   Notice that Word has already suggested a name for the document, based on the first line of text. (Other Office programs do the same thing.) You can also choose to create a new folder — not surprisingly, by clicking the New Folder button.

3. **If that name is acceptable, click the Save button.**

   If you prefer to give the document a different name, just start typing; the new name replaces the name Word gave the document.

Closing a document

You can close a document by using any of three methods:

- ✔ **Click the close box in the top-left corner of the document window.** This method is the easiest.
- ✔ **Choose File⇨Close.** Use this method if you prefer to use the mouse.
- ✔ **Press ⌘+W.** This method works well for people who prefer to work from the keyboard.

No matter how you close the document, if you have unsaved changes, you're asked whether you want to save them. After you click Save or Don't Save, the document closes.

People commonly confuse closing a document with quitting a program. When you want to switch from one document to another that was created in the same program, always close the document by using one of the preceding methods; then choose File⇨Open to locate and open the next document. What you don't want to do is quit the program, search for the next document in the Finder, and then double-click the document, because starting a program takes much longer than simply opening another document while the program is already running.

Opening an existing document

You can open an existing document in two ways: from the Finder (the terms *Finder* and *desktop* are used interchangeably in this book) or from inside any Office application. If you're working on the desktop, just find the icon for the document you want to work with and then double-click it. The program that created the document launches and opens the document.

If you're already working in one of the Office programs, choose File⇨Open, press ⌘+O, or click the Open button (it looks like a little folder with an arrow coming out of it) on the Standard toolbar. The Open dialog box appears. If the document you're looking for is in the folder displayed in the scrollbox, select it and then click the Open button. Otherwise, navigate to the correct folder by using the pop-up navigation menu at the top of the dialog box; then open the file by clicking the Open button.

You can narrow (or expand) the files shown in the Open dialog box by choosing from the Show pop-up menu. It's normally set to All Office Documents, but you can change it to All Readable Documents to pick from all documents that Office knows how to open, or you can narrow the choices by choosing items like Text Files or Web Pages.

You also have the opportunity (using the Open pop-up menu at the bottom of the Open dialog box) to open the original file that you've selected, a Copy of the document, or a Read-Only copy that won't let you make any changes.

Printing a document

To print a document that is open on-screen, all you normally have to do is choose File⇨Print (or press ⌘+P) and then click OK in the resulting Print dialog box. If you're trying to print for the first time, however, making sure that you have selected a printer in the Chooser is a good idea. Follow these steps:

1. Choose Apple⇨Chooser.

The Chooser window appears, as shown in Figure 2-5.

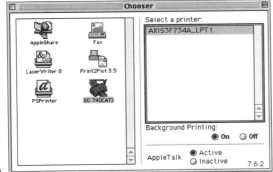

Figure 2-5:
Be sure to pick a printer in the Chooser.

2. In the left pane of the window, click the icon that corresponds to your printer.

Don't be surprised if what's on your screen isn't exactly the same as what's shown in Figure 2-5; different computers may show other things, depending on what printers are installed or available.

The software that tells your Macintosh how to use a particular printer is called a *printer driver.* By clicking one of these icons in the Chooser, you are really selecting a printer driver.

After you click a printer icon in the left pane of the Chooser window, the right pane changes. The type of change depends on whether you're using a networked printer or a directly connected printer. If you're using a networked printer, such as a LaserWriter, the right pane of the Chooser window displays a list of the printers on your network.

3. **Click to select the name of the printer you want to use.**

   If you're choosing a networked printer and no names are listed in the right pane of the Chooser window, no printers of that type are available on the network — usually because somebody switched the printer off. Or, your Mac may have been disconnected from the network. Check your network connections (the wires on the back of your Mac that connect it to the network), and then try choosing the printer again. You should also make sure that the AppleTalk Active radio button is selected at the bottom of the Chooser.

   If you choose an icon for a directly connected printer, such as a color inkjet from Epson or Hewlett-Packard, the Chooser displays the ports to which the printer can be connected (iMacs and other late-model Macintoshes will show the USB, Universal Serial Bus, port; older Macs will show icons for the printer and modem ports). Choose the appropriate port by clicking it in the right pane of the Chooser window.

Quitting Office 2001 Programs

To quit any Office program, all you have to do is choose File⇨Quit, or press ⌘+Q. If you have any open documents that are unsaved, the program asks whether you want to save your work before quitting.

Chapter 3

Help Is Everywhere You Turn

In This Chapter

▶ Using the Office Assistant

▶ Using the other Help files

*T*he Office 2001 package is big and powerful, enabling you to do just about anything you can imagine (within limits; it's just software, after all!). Powerful software means complex software, which in turn means that figuring out just how to make the programs do what you want can take some doing. Fortunately, Microsoft includes a boatload of online help that can show you how to solve even the thorniest problems.

From the Help menu on the Macintosh menu bar (see Figure 3-1), Office 2001 provides a variety of on-screen Help files, which are similar to having the Office 2001 manuals inside your computer. Using the on-screen Help system to find information is much easier than digging through the printed manuals. The Help system has an electronic index that enables you to enter a keyword. After you enter the keyword, the Help system searches thousands of pages and presents a list of (usually) relevant topics. The Office Assistant is the friendly face of the Help system; when you ask the Office Assistant a question, it displays the right topics in a Help file.

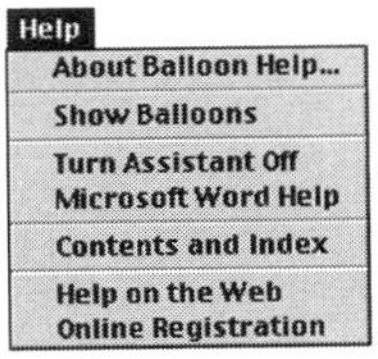

Figure 3-1:
The Help
menu from
Word 2001.

If you need even more help, Office 2001 also includes the Apple-standard Balloon Help. Finally, Microsoft provides additional help on its Web site, which you can access with one click from the Help menu.

Getting to Know the Office Assistant

The idea behind a big, integrated package such as Office 2001 is to enable people to do virtually anything they can imagine doing with a word processor, spreadsheet, or presentation program. For this reason, Microsoft has added virtually every feature that has ever been requested. Then the people in charge of Microsoft Office development noticed an odd fact: A large percentage of enhancement requests they received were for features that were already in the programs! Because the company realized that people needed an easier way to discover just what the programs can do, the Office Assistant was born.

The Office Assistant provides help in both an active and passive manner. It watches what you do (I'm not joking; the Assistant character actually turns and looks at the document while you are working on it) and offers tips, when appropriate. You can also ask the Assistant for help at any time by clicking the Assistant window. The Assistant tries to make sure that it doesn't get in your way. When you haven't used the Assistant's window for a while, it gets smaller, and if you need to type or click where the Assistant window is, it scoots out of your way. A new trick of the Office Assistant in Office 2001 is that the Assistant window is now manually resizable, so you can set the size that you want.

The Macintosh version of Office 2001 has a unique Office Assistant named Max. Max looks like the original all-in-one Macintosh, from the Macintosh Plus era, except that he has feet (made of two computer mice!), as shown in Figure 3-2.

Figure 3-2:
Max, the
Office
Assistant.

Max has a variety of whimsical behaviors, including snoring and falling over with a crash when you haven't touched the mouse or keyboard for a while. I suspect that you may get tired of Max in a hurry, but I like the little guy.

Asking the Assistant for help

To get help from the Office Assistant, follow these steps:

1. **Click the Office Assistant window. (If the Assistant window isn't visible, activate it by clicking the Office Assistant button on the Standard toolbar — the one that looks like a cartoon balloon with a question mark in it.)**

   A yellow balloon pops up, as shown in Figure 3-3. If you opened the Office Assistant by mistake, you can click the Cancel button to dismiss the yellow balloon.

Figure 3-3:
The Office
Assistant
asks you
what you
want to do.

Cancel button   Search button

2. **Type a question, such as** How do I make a table?, **and then click the Search button.**

   For best results, you should type your question in plain English, rather than trying to just enter possible search terms. Another balloon pops up, displaying a list of topics related to your question, as shown in Figure 3-4.

Topic buttons

Figure 3-4:
The Office
Assistant
shows the
Help topics
that match
your
question.

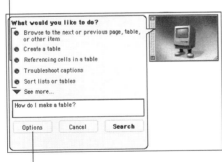

Options button

3. **Click the button that matches the appropriate topic.**

   If the balloon has a See More button, more topics are available, although they don't fit in the balloon. Click the down arrow to see the rest of the topics.

A Help window appears, displaying information about the selected topic, as shown in Figure 3-5.

4. **On the right side of the Help window, click the link of the help topic that most closely matches the task you wish to accomplish.**

The step-by-step help instructions for that topic appear.

5. **When you finish reading the Help information, close the Help window by clicking the close box in the top-left corner of the Help window.**

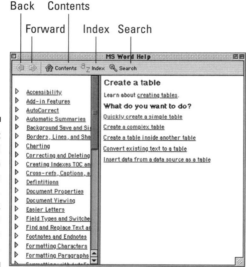

Figure 3-5:
The detailed
Help
window you
requested.
Click a link
to get to
step-by-step
instructions.

Using the Help window

The Help window in Office 2001 now uses the standard Macintosh Help system, which acts much like a familiar Web browser's window. You can resize the Help window to see more information at one time; by clicking the Zoom box at the right of the Help window's title bar, you can even expand the window to fill your screen. As you can see in Figure 3-5, the top of the Help window contains navigation buttons that let you move through the Help system. The left column of the window has a scrollable, expandable list of Help topics; click the disclosure triangle next to a topic to expand it, and click again to collapse the topic. The Help information appears on the right column of the Help window. You can display more or less of one of the columns by clicking and dragging the vertical border between the columns.

The Help window's navigation buttons do the following:

✔ The Back button brings you back to the previous Help screen.

✔ The Forward button will only be available if you have previously used the Back button; it brings you forward through the list of Help topics you've seen.

✔ The Contents button switches back to the list of topics in the left column of the Help window, if you had switched to the Index mode (see below).

✔ Clicking the Index button opens an alphabetical list of terms in the Help system.

✔ Clicking the Search button opens the Office Assistant's yellow balloon to allow you to type in a question.

Picking up tips from the Assistant

The Office Assistant pays attention to you as you're working, and when it sees an easier way of performing a particular task, it tells you so. When you see the light bulb in the Assistant window, you can click the window to get the tip, as shown in Figure 3-6.

Figure 3-6:
A tip from
the Office
Assistant —
and darn
good
advice, too.

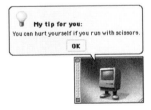

Installing and changing Assistants

In addition to Max, Office 2001 comes with 13 Assistants, as shown in Figure 3-7. You can find them in the Value Pack folder on the Office 2001 CD-ROM. Each Assistant has a different personality and displays a different set of behaviors in response to your actions. All Assistants are helpful, however.

You can choose from among these Assistants:

✔ Bosgrove, the butler

✔ The Genius, who looks and acts like a relatively famous mathematician

- Will, the bard of the group
- Earl, the high-strung cat
- Power Pup, the dog to the rescue
- Rocky, the faithful canine companion
- Scribble, the paper cat
- F1, a robot
- Hoverbot, another robot
- Clipit, the standard Assistant from the Windows version of Office
- Dot, a happy face
- Mother Nature, an Earth figure
- Office logo, for corporate types

The standard installation of Office 2001 installs only Max, although you can easily install other Assistants. Just run the Value Pack Installer inside the Value Pack folder on the Office 2001 CD-ROM. To install all the additional Assistants, click the Assistants check box in the Installer. To install individual Assistants, click the disclosure triangle next to the Assistants option so that it points down, and then select the Assistants you want.

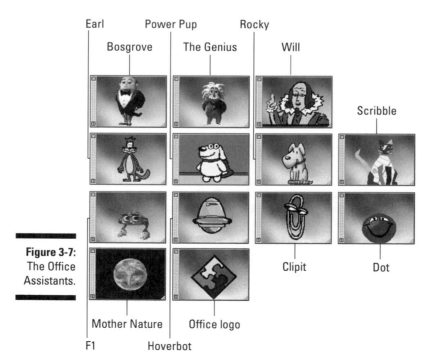

Figure 3-7:
The Office Assistants.

To change installed Assistants, follow these steps:

1. **Click the Office Assistant window.**

   The Assistant's yellow cartoon balloon appears.

2. **Click the Options button.**

   The Office Assistant dialog box appears.

3. **Click the Options tab (if it isn't already displayed).**

   This tab enables you to fine-tune the Assistant's reactions; feel free to experiment with the settings to see which ones work best for you.

   Because all the Office programs share the Office Assistant, any changes you make in the Assistant options affect the Assistant in all the Office programs.

4. **Click the Gallery tab.**

   The screen changes, as shown in Figure 3-8, displaying a description and a brief animation of each Assistant.

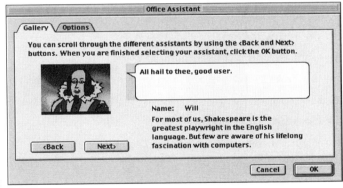

Figure 3-8:
Browsing
the choices
in the Office
Assistant
Gallery.

5. **Click the Back and Next buttons to flip through the Assistants until you find the one you want to use.**

6. **Click the OK button.**

Using the Other Help Files

Using the Office Assistant is one way to get to the Help files, although you can get to them directly too. To go straight to the Help files, follow these steps:

1. **Choose Help⇨Contents and Index.**

   The Help Contents window appears.

2. **Click the link of a subtopic that interests you.**

   A detailed Help window appears.

3. **When you're done reading the Help window, close it by clicking the close box in the top-left corner.**

You can use the Back button in the Help window to step back a level, and you can click the Contents button to get back to the top level.

Getting to the Help index

Sometimes, searching for keywords in an index is faster than drilling down through several topic levels. To search the Help file by keyword, follow these steps:

1. **Choose Help⇨Contents and Index.**

   The Help Contents window appears.

2. **Click the Index button.**

   The alphabetical index list appears.

3. **Type the first few letters of the topic you're looking for.**

4. **Click the topic you want.**

5. **Click the Show Topics button.**

   A list of appropriate topics appears at the bottom of the index window.

6. **Click the Go To button.**

7. **Read the Help topic that appears.**

Using Balloon Help

Compared with the Office Assistant, Balloon Help seems to be somewhat quaint and old-fashioned. Still, it can be useful for reminding you what toolbar buttons mean, because it gives you a more detailed explanation than the ScreenTips feature does. It displays only the name of the button, whereas Balloon Help provides a description.

To use Balloon Help, follow these steps:

1. **Choose Help▷Show Balloons.**

2. **Point at an area on-screen that you want to know more about.**

   An information balloon appears, as shown in Figure 3-9.

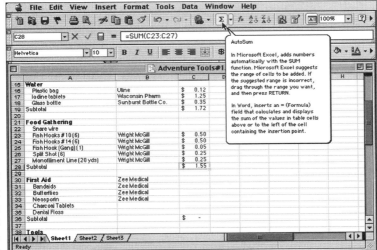

Figure 3-9:
Using
Balloon
Help.

Finding Help on the Web

In addition to providing all the Help files that come with Office 2001, Microsoft makes assistance available on its Web site. Office 2001 comes with a Web file that has links to the Microsoft Web Help page. To access this page, choose Help▷Help on the Web in any Office program. Your Web browser opens.

Click the appropriate links to get to the Help areas on the Microsoft Web site.

Part II
Using Word 2001

The 5th Wave   By Rich Tennant

In this part . . .

No matter what you do for a living, you can do it better if you write clearly and effectively. Microsoft Word 2001 is a full-featured word processor (one of the best in the world). It lets you type and revise your work, check your spelling and grammar, expand your vocabulary with a built-in thesaurus, mix your text with graphics images, and work with colleagues to revise and improve your documents.

In this part of the book, you see how to use Word 2001 to get your words on screen (and on paper); how to format your words so that they look great; and how to create terrific reports and newsletters that get your point across. This part of the book tells you everything you need to know to begin using Word 2001 effectively.

Chapter 4

Getting Friendly with Word 2001

● ●

In This Chapter

▶ Creating a new document

▶ Opening existing documents

▶ Navigating your document

▶ Working with toolbars

▶ Formatting documents

▶ Saving your files

▶ Printing

▶ Backing up your files

● ●

*M*icrosoft Word 2001 is the part of Office 2001 that enables you to work with words. With Word 2001, you can write letters, memos, books, newsletters, Web pages, and virtually any other document that depends on words. You can use Word to write your dissertation. You can use Word to create brilliant ad copy. You can use Word to write down your list of non-negotiable demands. After several revisions, Microsoft has given Word 2001 an amazing amount of power, and chances are that you'll never use more than a fraction of that power. Who cares? Getting your work done with Word 2001 is all that counts.

Creating a New Document

To write in a document, you first must create one. In Word 2001, you create a document in one of these four ways:

✔ Start Word 2001. Doing so automatically brings you to the Project Gallery (if you haven't turned it off). Clicking the OK button (or pressing the Return or Enter keys) creates a blank document, ready for you to begin typing.

✔ Choose File⇨New Blank Document.

> ✔ Press ⌘+N.
>
> ✔ Click the New Blank Document button on the Standard toolbar.

Opening an Existing Document

Most people work with documents that they've already created even more than they create new documents, and Word 2001 provides four ways to open an existing document:

> ✔ Choose File➪Open.
>
> ✔ Press ⌘+O.
>
> ✔ Click the Open button on the Standard toolbar.
>
> ✔ Choose from the bottom of the File menu one of the last four files you opened.

You can increase or decrease the number of files Word 2001 displays on the File menu. Choose Edit➪Preferences to display the Preferences dialog box; then click the General tab. In the text box labeled Recently Used File List, type a number ranging from 0 through 9.

No matter which method you use to open a file, you see the standard Macintosh Open dialog box, as shown in Figure 4-1. Navigate the folders until you find the file you want; then click the Open button.

File list

File Type Menu

Find File button

Show Preview button

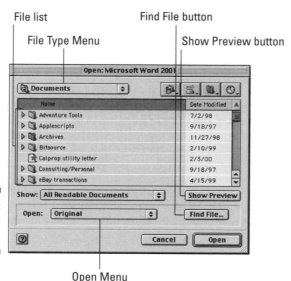

Figure 4-1:
The Open
dialog box.

Open Menu

Besides the usual Mac OS features, there are some controls special to Office 2001 at the bottom of the Open dialog box:

✔ The Show pop-up menu lets you filter the documents shown in the file list. Whatever choice you make here will increase or limit the documents you can open; it's useful if you already have an idea of what kind of file you want to open. For example, the broadest practical choice is All Readable Documents, so you'll see any file that Word knows how to read, even things like Excel spreadsheets and graphic documents. Actually, there's one broader choice, All Documents, which will make Word attempt to open up any document on your hard disk. The upshot of this is usually a display of unreadable gibberish characters, but it can occasionally be useful, as when it allows you to salvage usuable text out of damaged or otherwise unreadable documents. You can narrow the choices by choosing All Office Documents or All Word Documents. Other choices include Text Files or Web Pages.

✔ The Show Preview button is useful for looking at some graphic files, which are often saved with preview images — a thumbnail image of the document.

✔ The Open pop-up menu allows you three choices: You can open the Original of the document you've chosen; you can open a Copy of the document; or you can open the document in Read-Only mode, which won't allow you to save any changes to the document.

✔ Clicking the Find File button opens the Search window, as shown in Figure 4-2. Enter the file's name (or part of it) in the File name field, then select from the File type and Location (that is, the hard disk) pop-up menus.

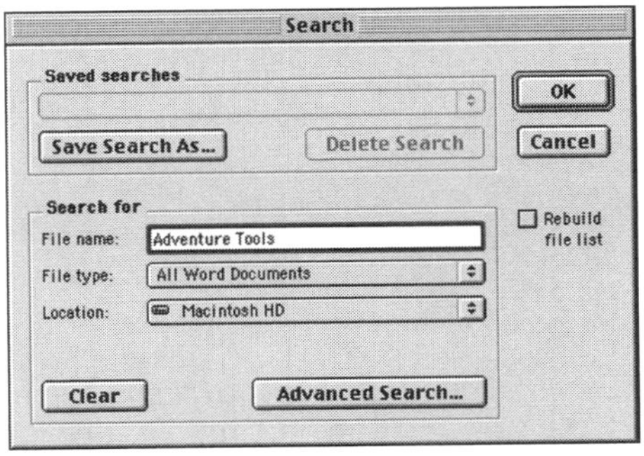

Figure 4-2:
You can find documents you want to open using the Search window.

Navigating Your Document

After you open a document, take a minute to give it a good look. Although the document looks a little confusing at first, you soon get used to it. Figure 4-3 gives you a rundown of the parts of the Word 2001 screen.

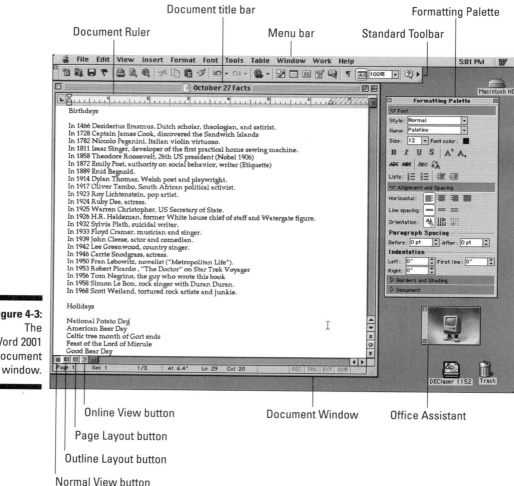

Figure 4-3:
The Word 2001 document window.

Document Ruler
Document title bar
Menu bar
Standard Toolbar
Formatting Palette
Online View button
Page Layout button
Outline Layout button
Normal View button
Document Window
Office Assistant

Taking a different view

Word 2001 enables you to view your document in four ways. Each view gives you a different perspective of the organization and appearance of your document. To change the view of your document, choose one of these options from the View menu:

✔ **Normal:** The standard view you work in most of the time, providing the cleanest screen and the fewest distractions. Just click in the document area and type.

- **Online Layout:** Changes the layout of the document in an effort to make it easier to read on-screen. Text is larger and wraps to fit the window rather than as it would actually print. The headings you use in your document are used by the Document Map, a separate pane in the document window. When you click headings in the Document Map, you jump to the corresponding area in the document. Online Layout view is also the only view that displays certain features (such as background colors and textures) you use when you create Web pages.

- **Page Layout:** Shows the document exactly as it will appear when you print it, including headers, footers, and page numbers.

- **Outline:** Outline view shows you the document's structure. Each heading in your document is a topic or subtopic. Subtopics are indented below topics. Outline view is a good way to organize your thoughts before you begin writing the body of the document. (Some people love working with outlines; others hate it. Me, I'm an outline kind of guy.)

The other way to switch views is to click the View buttons on the horizontal scrollbar (refer to Figure 4-3).

Zooming in and out

Although the views Word 2001 provides are useful, sometimes you need to see your document closer — or farther away. You may want to use the 12-point Times font for your letter, for example, because it looks good when you print the document. For many people, however, 12-point Times is not a good screen font because it's a little too small. Word 2001 enables you to magnify the document for greater comfort. In the same manner, you can shrink the document to get an overview of the document's structure or just to fit more words on your screen.

To zoom in or out of your document, follow these steps:

1. **Choose View⇨Zoom.**

   The Zoom dialog box appears.

2. **Click the radio buttons to set the document magnification you want.**

   If you don't like one of the button choices, you can type any number you want (between 10 and 500) in the Percent box.

   Clicking the Page Width radio button is a fast way to get the document to zoom up to fit comfortably in the document window, no matter how you may have resized that window.

3. **Click the OK button.**

You can also zoom in or out of your document by using the Zoom pop-up menu at the right end of the Standard toolbar. Because the menu provides more preset magnification choices, using it may be more convenient for you than using the Zoom dialog box.

Much Ado about Toolbars

The Office 2001 programs try, whenever possible, to give you multiple ways to accomplish a task so that you're not forced to memorize one particular way to get your work done. Quite often, you have three ways to do something: You can choose a command from a menu, press a shortcut key, or click a button on one of the many toolbars.

Although Word 2001 has 19 preset toolbars, most of the time you use only one of them: the Standard toolbar. This toolbar appears when you start Word 2001; as with any of the other toolbars, you can hide or display this toolbar whenever you want.

Hiding and showing toolbars

To hide or show a toolbar, follow these steps:

1. **Ctrl+click any visible toolbar.**

   The Toolbar pop-up menu appears, as shown in Figure 4-4.

2. **Click the name of the toolbar you want to hide or show.**

Figure 4-4:
Hiding or showing toolbars with the Toolbar pop-up menu.

You can also hide or display toolbars by choosing View➪Toolbars and then choosing a toolbar from the hierarchical menu. If you prefer to work with dialog boxes, you can choose Tools➪Customize to display the Customize dialog box and then put a check in the appropriate check boxes to activate certain toolbars.

Introducing the Standard toolbar

The Standard toolbar enables you to control the core features of Word 2001 — the ones you'll probably use most often. Figure 4-5 shows the Standard toolbar.

Figure 4-5:
The buttons on the Standard toolbar don't remain mysterious for long.

From left to right, here's what each of the buttons on the Standard toolbar does:

- ✔ **New Blank Document:** Creates a new blank document.

- ✔ **Open:** Opens an existing document.

- ✔ **Save:** Saves the current document to disk.

- ✔ **Flag for Follow Up:** Creates a task in Entourage 2001's Task list and sets a reminder to work on the document again at a future date and time you select.

- ✔ **Print:** Prints the current document to whatever printer is selected in the Chooser.

- ✔ **Print Preview:** Shows you what your document will look like when you print it.

- ✔ **Web Page Preview:** Shows you (in your preferred Web browser) what your document would look like as a Web page.

- ✔ **Cut:** Moves the selected text to the Clipboard.

- ✔ **Copy:** Copies the selected text to the Clipboard.

- ✔ **Paste:** Puts the contents of the Clipboard in the current document, where the insertion point is blinking.

- **Format Painter:** Copies the formatting of the selected text and enables you to apply that formatting to whatever text you select next.

- **Undo:** Reverses your last action; click this button to recover from mistakes.

- **Redo:** Reverses an Undo action; click this button to repeat your mistakes.

- **Insert Hyperlink:** Creates a link to a Web page, a different file on your hard disk, or another place in the current document.

- **Tables and Borders:** Shows the Tables and Borders toolbar; hides it if it is open.

- **Insert Table:** Inserts a table into your document, at the insertion point.

- **Columns:** Formats your text in one to six columns.

- **Drawing:** Shows the Drawing toolbar; hides it if it is open.

- **Dictionary:** Opens the Word dictionary for quick definitions; closes it if it is open.

- **Show/Hide Paragraph Marks:** Shows or hides the characters for tabs, spaces, carriage returns, and hidden text.

- **Formatting Palette:** Toggles the Formatting Palette on or off.

- **Zoom menu:** Changes the screen magnification of your document.

- **Office Assistant:** Activates the Office Assistant.

- **More Buttons pop-up menu:** Shows additional features, plus customized items that you may have created.

To activate any function, just click a button. The buttons on toolbars require only a single click.

If you're wondering, "How will I ever remember what all those little toolbar buttons mean?" — don't worry. Point at any button and hold the mouse still for a moment. A small yellow label, called a ScreenTip, pops up, showing you the name of the button.

Whipping text into shape with the Formatting Palette

In an ideal world, the content of your document would be all that matters. The look and format of the document would be of only secondary importance, if they were noticed at all. Welcome to the real world. Looks matter, and you have to make sure that your document is pretty as well as shining with inner brilliance.

Your chief weapon for making your documents look good is the Formatting Palette, a new feature in Office 2001, which contains controls for commands that change the fonts, text alignment, borders, and document layout. Figure 4-6 shows the Formatting Palette.

Figure 4-6:
The Formatting Palette allows you to make your document look the way you want. The Font section is expanded here.

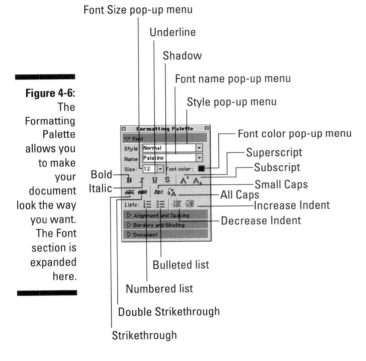

Font Size pop-up menu

Underline

Shadow

Font name pop-up menu

Style pop-up menu

Font color pop-up menu

Superscript

Subscript

Small Caps

All Caps

Increase Indent

Decrease Indent

Bold

Italic

Bulleted list

Numbered list

Double Strikethrough

Strikethrough

The Formatting Palette consists of four sections:

- ✔ The **Font** area lets you set the font, font size, font color, and the font style (such as bold and italic) of your text.

- ✔ In **Alignment** and **Spacing,** you'll control text justification (left, center, and right), as well as paragraph indentation, and line and paragraph spacing.

- ✔ The **Borders** and **Shading** section allows you to surround paragraphs with lines and borders, and highlight paragraphs with colored shading.

- ✔ The **Document** area gives you control over margins and some miscellaneous other formatting.

Each of these sections can be hidden, so that the Formatting Palette takes up less room on your screen. To hide or show a section, click on the section's name.

Here's what each of the controls on the Font section of the Formatting Palette does (other sections will be covered later in this book):

- ✔ **Style:** Sets the *style* — the predefined blueprint, including font, font size, type style, paragraph spacing, and so on — for the paragraph the insertion point is in.
- ✔ **Name:** Sets the *font* — the type style — of the selected text.
- ✔ **Size:** Sets the size of the selected text. The numbers are in *point sizes,* which are common measurements printers use.
- ✔ **Font Color:** Changes selected text to a different color.
- ✔ **Bold:** Makes selected text **bold.**
- ✔ **Italic:** Makes selected text *italic.*
- ✔ **Underline:** Underlines selected text.
- ✔ **Shadow:** Adds a shadow format to selected text.
- ✔ **Superscript:** Lets you superscript text, such as in scientific notation (for example, 10^2).
- ✔ **Subscript:** Subscripted text is used in chemical formulas, such as H_2O.
- ✔ **Strikethrough:** Text that is crossed out is ~~struck out~~.
- ✔ **Double strikethrough:** If you really don't like some text, give it a ~~double strikethrough~~.
- ✔ **Small Caps:** Small caps are another way to EMPHASIZE YOUR TEXT.
- ✔ **All Caps:** Using all caps can make your text feel LIKE YOU'RE SHOUTING.
- ✔ **Numbered List:** Adds automatic numbering to or removes automatic numbering from paragraphs.
- ✔ **Bulleted List:** Adds or removes bullets from paragraphs.
- ✔ **Increase Indent:** Moves selected paragraphs one tab stop to the right.
- ✔ **Decrease Indent:** Moves selected paragraphs one tab stop to the left.

Formatting Documents with the Ruler

The *ruler* shows you the margins, indents, and tab stops in your document. You can use the ruler to set any of these features, and if you have multiple columns in your document, the ruler can also set column width.

Setting margins

To set the margins of your document, follow these steps:

1. **Choose Format⇨Document.**

2. **Click the Margins tab, as shown in Figure 4-7.**

3. **Type in the margin numbers you wish, or use the up and down arrow buttons next to each margin to set the number.**

4. **Click OK.**

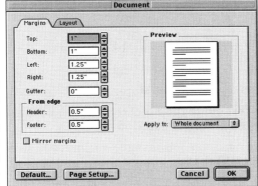

Figure 4-7:
Setting
margins
in the
Document
window.

Double-clicking in the margin area on the ruler is a faster way of opening the Document window, set to the Margins tab.

Setting tabs

Tabs are incredibly useful to format your text. Pressing the Tab key enters an invisible Tab character, which Word interprets according to how you've set up the tab stops. Word 2001 enables you to set five kinds of tabs, as shown in Figure 4-8.

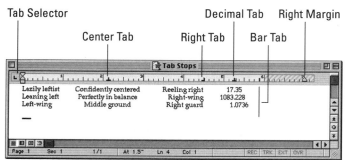

Figure 4-8:
The five
kinds of
tabs.

Word 2001 lets you use the Tab Selector to switch between the five sets of tabs:

- ✓ **Tab Selector:** Clicking the button switches between the five tab types.
- ✓ **Left Tab:** The regular tab stop. Text is aligned at the stop on its left edge.
- ✓ **Center Tab:** Centers text on the tab stop.
- ✓ **Right Tab:** Pushes text out to the left of the tab stop so that the right edge of the text lines up with the tab stop.
- ✓ **Decimal Tab:** Perfect for columns of numbers; lines up the decimal points of the numbers at the tab stop.
- ✓ **Bar Tab:** What you have to pay at the end of an evening on the town. Actually, in Word, it produces a vertical line at the tab stop, which is useful for creating dividers between columns of text or figures.

To put a tab on the ruler, follow these steps:

1. **Click anywhere in the paragraph in which you want to insert a tab.**
2. **Click the Tab Selector button on the ruler until it shows the kind of tab you want to use.**
3. **Click on the ruler where you want to put the tab.**

Word 2001 maintains the formatting of the current paragraph when you press the Return key to begin a new paragraph. So the new paragraph will have all of the same tabs as the one you set up by hand.

To move an existing tab, follow these steps:

1. **Click anywhere in the paragraph in which you want to modify a tab.**
2. **On the ruler, drag the tab marker to its new location.**

To remove a tab, follow these steps:

1. **Click anywhere in the paragraph in which you want to modify a tab.**

2. **Drag the tab you want to delete off the ruler.**

Indenting paragraphs

You also use the ruler to indent paragraphs. Four controls on the ruler help you set indents, as shown in Figure 4-9:

First Line Indent

Hanging Indent

Right Indent

Figure 4-9:
The paragraph indenting controls. The paragraph shown has a first line indent.

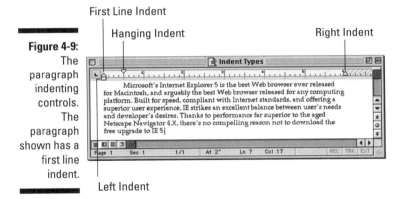

Left Indent

✔ **First Line Indent:** Use this to have the first line of each paragraph indent, relative to the left margin.

✔ **Hanging Indent:** This sets the position of all lines of the paragraph *except for the first line* relative to the left margin. So the first line is not indented, and all other lines are. Moving the Hanging Indent marker also moves the Left Indent marker.

✔ **Left Indent:** This sets the position of all lines of the paragraph relative to the left margin.

✔ **Right Indent:** This controls the right indent position of all of the paragraph's lines relative to the right margin. A paragraph that is indented on both the left and right is block indented, as shown in Figure 4-10.

Double-clicking any indent marker in the ruler opens the Paragraph window so that you can make adjustments numerically, rather than dragging the marker.

Figure 4-10: This paragraph is block indented. Note the position of the indent markers.

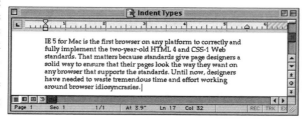

TIP

It's possible to give paragraphs a negative amount of indenting (also known as an *outdent*). Hanging paragraphs are outdented, for example, as shown in Figure 4-11.

Figure 4-11: This paragraph has a hanging indent.

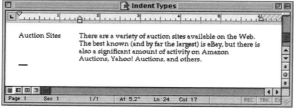

To indent (or outdent) paragraphs by using the First Line Indent, Left Indent, Right Indent, or Hanging Indent controls, follow these steps:

1. **Select the paragraphs you want to indent.**

2. **On the ruler, drag the indent control you want to use to where you want to indent the paragraph.**

TIP

In order to add, delete, or move tabs, or change indents in several paragraphs at the same time, select the paragraphs first. Changes made on the ruler will affect all of the paragraphs.

Don't Lose It: Saving Your Files

If you've gone to all the time and trouble of creating a document, you're going to want to save it. Word 2001 gives you several ways to save a file by yourself, and it provides two other ways to save your files automatically. Get the impression that saving is *really* important?

Saving your file

To save the document that's on your screen, use any of these methods:

- Choose File⇨Save.
- Click the Save button on the Standard toolbar.
- Press ⌘+S.
- Close the document. Word will ask you if you want to save it. Click the Save button.

When a computer crashes, it almost always does so without warning. Anything you've written since the last time you saved the document in Word 2001 is lost. To be on the safe side, get into the habit of frequently saving your files. Learn to love the shortcut-key combination for saving, which is ⌘+S. Then teach your left hand to press ⌘+S at every opportunity. If you take a momentary break from typing, press ⌘+S. If you sneeze, press ⌘+S. If you stop for a moment to gather your thoughts while writing, press ⌘+S. Ingrain this habit; you'll be happy that you did.

The first time you save a file, Word 2001 asks you to give the file a name. Macintosh file names can be as long as 31 characters and must not contain a colon (:) or begin with a period (.).

Saving a file under another name

Here's the fifth way to save a file by yourself. The Save As command, which is available in almost all Macintosh programs, saves a copy of the current document under a different name. You want to do that when you base a new document on an existing document. You start the older document, make any changes you need, and then save the edited document under a new name.

To save a file under a different name, choose File⇨Save As; then give the new file a name in the Save As dialog box.

Saving a file in a different format

As great as Office 2001 is, you probably have many co-workers who haven't upgraded, who are using Windows 95 machines, or who simply prefer to use other products. The Office 2001 programs enable you to open and save files in other file formats, including older Macintosh Office files and most Microsoft PC document formats.

To save a Word 2001 document in a different file format, choose File⇨Save As; then choose a file format from the Save File As Type pop-up menu in the Save As dialog box.

If you don't find on the pop-up menu the file format you need, don't despair. You can always save a file in either of two almost universally supported formats: RTF (Rich Text Format) or plain text. Virtually any word processor running on any kind of computer can read files saved in one of these two formats. Using RTF preserves most of your document's text formatting, such as font, size, and character styles. Plain text is the lowest common denominator, and you have to reformat your document — but that's still better than having to type the entire thing again.

Saving a file automatically

Few computer events are more frustrating than realizing immediately after your computer crashes that the last time you saved your document was about two hours ago. With older versions of Word, you could pretty much wave happy trails to all the work you had done since the last save. Word 2001, on the other hand, is determined to be smart, even if you weren't. The program has two ways to rescue you: automatic file backup and AutoRecover.

Automatic file backup is just what it sounds like: Word 2001 saves a copy of your document at preset intervals. AutoRecover tries to resurrect your document in the event of a system crash or power failure.

To have Word 2001 save your files for you automatically, follow these steps:

1. **Choose Edit⇨Preferences.**

   The Preferences dialog box appears.

2. **Click the Save tab.**

   The Save tab appears, as shown in Figure 4-12.

3. **If you want to have Word 2001 save a backup copy of your document, click the Always create backup copy check box.**

   Automatically saving a backup copy has one drawback: You end up with twice as many files on your hard disk as you need. You have your original file (World Domination Plan, for example) and the extra backup file (Backup of World Domination Plan).

4. **To have Word 2001 protect you against crashes, click the Save AutoRecover info every check box and fill in the number of minutes you want to wait between saves.**

5. **Click the OK button.**

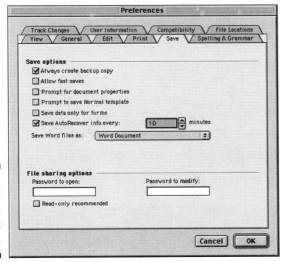

Figure 4-12:
The Save
tab in the
Preferences
window.

Printing a Document

Even in this brave new world, in which we all live in the paperless office (ha — we have more paper than ever in the office; so much for pompous prognostications by the so-called "experts"), you want to print your documents. Before committing your masterpiece to paper, however, looking at it in the Word 2001 Print Preview window is a good idea. If the document needs to be tweaked to look right, you can change it before you print it. You have little reason to print a document before it's really done.

Previewing before you print

To preview a document with Print Preview, follow these steps:

1. **Choose File⇨Print Preview.**

   Word 2001 displays a miniature view of your document, as shown in Figure 4-13.

Magnifer

One Page

Multiple Pages

Zoom

View Ruler

Shrink to Fit

Top Margin

Full Screen

Horizontal Ruler

Print

Close Preview

Right Margin

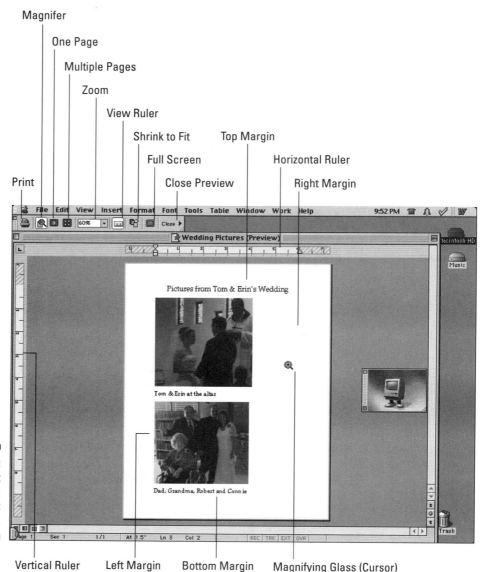

Figure 4-13:
A document
displayed in
Print
Preview.

Vertical Ruler   Left Margin   Bottom Margin   Magnifying Glass (Cursor)

2. **To view your document in full size, click the magnifying glass anywhere on the document; to zoom back out again, click the mouse
   again.**

You can change the margins of your document in Print Preview mode. Just click the margin markers in the rulers and drag them to set the margins you want.

3. Click Close to exit Print Preview mode.

Common problems when printing are documents where the last few sentences land on a separate page. Having a last, mostly blank page doesn't look great, so you probably want to get rid of it. Don't start deleting words; all you have to do is click the Shrink to Fit button in Print Preview. This will reduce your document by one page, by shrinking the font sizes in the document. Usually this works well, but you should page through your document in the Print Preview window to make sure that it suits you before you print.

Printing a document

To print a document, follow these steps:

1. Choose File⇨Print or press ⌘+P.

The Print dialog box appears.

2. Specify how many copies you want to print.

3. Click the Print button.

Printing a range of pages

The main pop-up menu in the Print dialog box has a Microsoft Word 2001 option. Choosing this option shows you the Word 2001 special print options. You can choose to print the document, document properties, comments, styles, AutoText entries, or shortcut-key assignments. You can also choose to print just the odd-numbered pages or just the even-numbered pages in your document. The Range button enables you to print different ranges of pages, as shown in Figure 4-14.

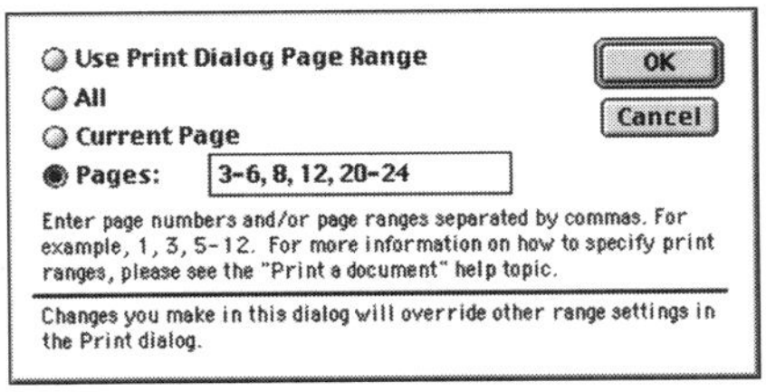

Figure 4-14:
The Print
Range
dialog box.

○ **Use Print Dialog Page Range**
○ All
○ Current Page
● Pages: `3–6, 8, 12, 20–24`

[OK]
[Cancel]

Enter page numbers and/or page ranges separated by commas. For example, 1, 3, 5–12. For more information on how to specify print ranges, please see the "Print a document" help topic.

Changes you make in this dialog will override other range settings in the Print dialog.

Printing in reverse order

Have you ever printed a long document and then had to manually reverse the pages so they are in the correct order? In a program as smart as Word 2001, surely there's a way to avoid wrestling with a stack of paper, and there is.

Choose Edit⇨Preferences and click the Print tab. Select Reverse Print Order under Printing Options, and Word will begin with your last page and work its way toward the front. When you collect the stack from your printer, your first page will be on top, right where it should be.

Creating a Backup Strategy

Here's a hard fact of life: Computers crash. Although they don't crash that often, it happens. In fact, they always seem to happen at the worst possible time, such as when you're almost ready to print — a scant ten minutes before your deadline — the report on which your entire future career rests.

More often, your computer doesn't crash, but a document file does become corrupted and unreadable. This situation can occur for any number of reasons: a hardware failure, a problem with your system software, or other software incompatibilities.

Computer problems aren't the only reason that you should be thinking about backups. Plenty of other things can go wrong, including fires, floods, theft, earthquakes, hurricanes, plagues of locusts, and — well, you get the idea.

One possible solution is to pray nightly to the Computer Gods, but this approach has a spotty success rate. A better idea is to keep backups of your files. A *backup* is a recent copy (or better yet, multiple copies) of your documents. You can copy the files to removable cartridge disks (such as the Iomega Zip or Jaz disks) or to a second hard disk, or you can buy a specialized backup device called a *tape drive.* You can even back up your files to remote storage facilities over the Internet, though you'll want to have a fast Net connection, such as a DSL line or a cable modem.

For many people, the Iomega Zip disk is the perfect balance between cost and convenience. The disk holds 100 or 250MB (megabytes) of data and costs between $10 and $15, and the drive costs well under $200. Those prices are relatively economical, especially if you back up only your documents, which don't take up much space on your hard disk compared with your applications and the system software. Although having a full backup of your entire hard disk is nice, these days, when computers often come with 10GB (gigabyte) hard disks, you would need dozens of Zip disks. You're better off to back up only your documents, which shouldn't take more than a few Zip disks, if that many. If the worst happens, you can restore your system software and applications from their original disks and then restore your documents from your backup disks.

Depending on how much money you want to spend on backing up, you can make your backup chore easier. You can get an Iomega Jaz drive, which has a removable cartridge that holds as much as 2GB worth of data. One or two cartridges could back up all your stuff.

The ultimate in backup convenience — and cost — is a tape drive. Tape backups are fast, backing up your data at as much as 70MB per minute. Because the tapes themselves hold at least 8GB worth of data, you don't have to worry about changing tapes very often. Tape drives come with backup software that enables you to back up your hard disk automatically, even if you're not around. The drawback is that a good tape drive costs $600 or more.

Following a Backup Strategy

No matter which backup medium you choose, you should get into the habit of backing up regularly. Have a schedule. Get into the habit of backing up your files before you shut down your Mac, for example. If you keep all your documents in a single folder on your desktop, dragging that folder to a Zip disk and copying the files is a simple matter.

Having multiple backup copies is the extra-safe way to go. You can easily rotate your backup copies so that you always have three good backups of your work. Many people use the idea of a "family" of backups. You start on Monday with a backup disk and copy your files to it. On Tuesday, you take a fresh, second disk and back up all your files again. On Wednesday, you repeat the process with a third new disk. Now you have three backup disks, each with a progressively older set of backed-up files. Wednesday's disk is the child disk. Tuesday's disk is the parent disk. Monday's backup — the oldest backup — is the grandparent disk. On Thursday, rotate the grandparent disk back to the front of the lineup (making it the new child disk), and use it to back up your files. Keep repeating the process, and you'll always have three days' worth of backups.

For even more protection, keep an extra backup off the premises in a safe place, such as a safe-deposit box. Bring in that backup and update it periodically — once per month, for example. Then take the backup off-site again. Having multiple backups does you no good if all your backup disks are destroyed along with your computer.

Chapter 5

Working with Words

*W*riting well is difficult, and a good word processor makes it easy to deal with drudgery such as checking your spelling and grammar, formatting your words correctly, and moving text around.

Word 2001 has intelligence under the hood that automates some of these tasks, and it gets others done with the least amount of effort.

Selecting and Editing Text

Word 2001 can't do anything with your text until you select it. Selecting text tells Word 2001 that whatever you do next, this text is what you want to do it to. You select text by using either the mouse or the keyboard.

Selecting text with the mouse

Selecting text with the mouse is a basic Macintosh skill — and one you probably already have. Just click at the beginning of the text you want to select, hold down the mouse button, and drag to the end of the text, which highlights everything in between. When you get to the end of the text you want to select, release the mouse button. This list describes a few text-selection tips:

- Double-click a word to select it.

- Select an entire sentence by holding down the ⌘ key and clicking anywhere in the sentence.

- Triple-click inside a paragraph to select the entire paragraph.

- If you want to select a large block of text, clicking and dragging it can be difficult to do. Instead, click at the beginning of the selection, scroll to the end of the selection, and then hold down the Shift key and click. All the text between the two clicks is then selected.

- To select a line of text, place the mouse pointer to the left of the line of text until the mouse pointer changes to a right-pointing arrow; then click.

- Double-click when the mouse pointer is a right-pointing arrow to select an entire paragraph.

- Triple-click when the mouse pointer is a right-pointing arrow to select the entire document.

- Cancel a selection by clicking anywhere other than on the selected text in the document window, or press any arrow key.

Selecting text with the keyboard

Yeah, I know: Mac users are mouse-oriented. We want to do *everything* with the mouse. Mouse, mouse, mouse. Well, here's my secret shame as a Mac user since 1984: I like to use the keyboard. Lots of times, using the keyboard is just faster. I like using shortcut keys, using keyboard macro programs such as QuickKeys and Keyquencer, and even selecting text with the keyboard. Try it a few times, and you probably will too. The keyboard shortcuts listed in Table 5-1 get you started, but the list is not exhaustive; if you want to know more, ask the Office Assistant.

Table 5-1	Shortcut Keys for Selecting Text
Shortcut Key	*Selects*
Shift+→	One character to the right of the insertion point
Shift+←	One character to the left of the insertion point
⌘+Shift+→	To the end of the word
⌘+Shift+←	To the beginning of the word
Shift+↓	One line down

Shortcut Key	*Selects*
Shift+↑	One line up
⌘+Shift+↓	To the end of the paragraph
⌘+Shift+↑	To the beginning of a paragraph
⌘+A	The entire document

Moving and copying text

To move or copy text from one place in a document to another, follow these steps:

1. **Select the text.**

2. **Cut or copy the selected text.**

   To cut the text, choose Edit➪Cut, press ⌘+X, or click the Cut button on the Standard toolbar. To copy the text, choose Edit➪Copy, press ⌘+C, or click the Copy button on the Standard toolbar.

3. **Click where you want the text to go.**

4. **Paste the text by choosing Edit➪Paste, pressing ⌘+V, or clicking the Paste button on the Standard toolbar.**

You can also use the *contextual menu* to move or copy text. A contextual menu is a menu that pops up at the mouse pointer's location when you press the Control key and click. The reason the menu is called contextual is that the items in the menu will change, depending on where the pointer is (in other words, depending on the pointer's context).

To move or copy text with the contextual menu, follow these steps:

1. **Select the text.**

2. **Make sure the mouse pointer is over the selected area, then Control+click.**

   The contextual menu pops up, as shown in Figure 5-1.

3. **Click where you want the text to go.**

4. **Paste the text by Control+clicking and then choosing Paste on the con-textual menu.**

Rank	Title	Total Box Office
1	Titanic (1997)	$600,743,440
2	Star Wars (1977)	,655
3	Star Wars: Episode I - Th	,444
4	E.T. the Extra-Terrestrial	,539
5	Jurassic Park (1993)	,175
6	Forrest Gump (1994)	,287
7	Lion King, The (1994)	,367
8	Star Wars: Episode VI -	,373
9	Independence Day (1996	,800
10	Sixth Sense, The (1999)	,675
11	Star Wars: Episode V - T	,751
12	Home Alone (1990)	,243
13	Jaws (1975)	,000
14	Batman (1989)	,924
15	Men in Black (1997)	$250,147,615
16	Toy Story 2 (1999)	$245,823,397
17	Raiders of the Lost Ark (1981)	$242,374,454
18	Twister (1996)	$240,233,000
19	Ghostbusters (1984)	$238,600,000
20	Beverly Hills Cop (1984)	$234,760,478

Contextual menu items shown: ✂ Cut ⌘X, 🗐 Copy ⌘C, 📋 Paste ⌘V, A Font..., ¶ Paragraph... ⌘⌥M, ≔ Bullets and Numbering..., Define, Hyperlink... ⌘K

Figure 5-1: You can move or copy text with the contextual menu.

Wonder where the text goes when you cut or copy it? It goes to an invisible holding area called the *Clipboard*. The Clipboard can also hold graphics.

Introducing the Office Clipboard

In most Macintosh programs, the Clipboard can hold only one item at a time, so cutting or copying a second item replaces the contents of the Clipboard. But the Office 2001 programs (except for Entourage 2001) extend the standard Clipboard so that it can now hold multiple items. You can show the new Office Clipboard by choosing View➪Office Clipboard. Cutting or copying text, a graphic, or a QuickTime movie places the item on the Office Clipboard. You can also drag and drop items from a document window to the Office Clipboard, and vice versa. Each item goes into a small box in the Clipboard's window. At the bottom of the Office Clipboard windows are four buttons that let you manage the Clipboard's contents, as shown in Figure 5-2.

The four buttons are

- ✔ **Paste Selected:** Pastes the contents on the selected Clipboard box at the insertion point
- ✔ **Paste All:** Pastes the contents of all Clipboard boxes at the insertion point
- ✔ **Clear Selected:** Deletes the contents on the selected Clipboard box from the Clipboard
- ✔ **Clear All:** Deletes the entire contents of the Clipboard

Be careful using Clear All, because it doesn't give you any warning or ask for confirmation before it wipes out everything on the Office Clipboard.

Figure 5-2:
The new
Office
Clipboard
lets you
store and
paste many
snippets of
text and
pictures at
once.

Clear All

Clear Selected

Paste All

Paste Selected

Dragging and dropping

Rather than cut and paste text, you can move text easily by dragging and dropping it with the mouse.

All of the Office 2001 programs are compatible with the Macintosh Drag-and-Drop feature. You can drag items (including formatted text and graphics) from any Office program to any other Office program, or to any other Macintosh program that is compatible with Macintosh Drag-and-Drop (that's most programs, these days). Because one of those programs is the Finder, you can drag text clippings to and from the desktop into your Office 2001 document.

To drag and drop text to a new location, follow these steps:

1. **Select the text and hold down the mouse button.**

   The mouse pointer now has a dashed box above it the size of the selection, and a vertical line shows you where the text will end up when you release the mouse button.

2. **Drag the text to its new location.**

3. **Release the mouse button.**

To copy the text rather than move it, hold down the Option key as you drag the text.

Deleting text

Not much can be said about deleting text. Just select the offending text and press the Delete key on your keyboard. (Some older keyboards call this key Backspace.) You can also select the text and choose Edit⇨Clear, although that technique is more work than it's worth, if you ask me.

You don't have to delete text before you begin replacing it with new text. Just select the text and begin typing. The new text replaces the old.

Searching for Text

When your company changes the name of its main product from Whizbang Thing to WonderWidget and you have to make the changes in the 200-page annual report, you'll be glad that Word 2001 can search for text throughout a document and replace it with other text.

Finding text

To find a bit of text in your document, follow these steps:

1. **Choose Edit⇨Find, or press ⌘+F.**

   The Find and Replace dialog box appears, set to the Find tab, as shown in Figure 5-3.

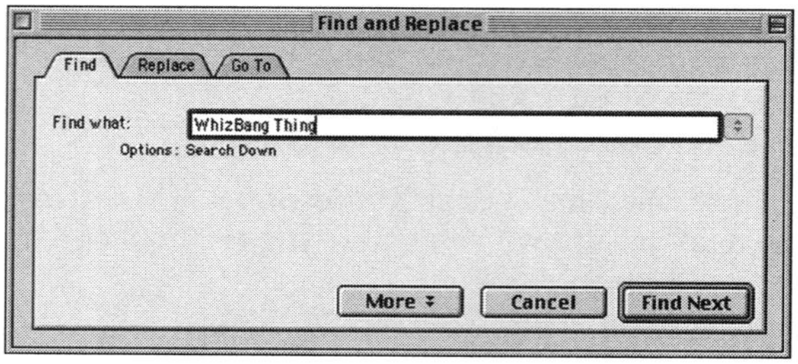

Figure 5-3:
The Find tab
in the Find
and Replace
window.

Find and Replace
Find / Replace / Go To
Find what: WhizBang Thing
Options: Search Down
More ↕   Cancel   Find Next

2. **In the Find what box, type the text you want to find.**

3. **Click the Find Next button.**

   Word 2001 finds the text and highlights it in your document.

4. **To find the next occurrence of the text, click the Find Next button again.**

5. **When you're done finding text, click the Cancel button.**

Finding and replacing text

To find a word or a phrase and replace it with other text, follow these steps:

1. **Choose Edit➪Replace, or press ⌘+H.**

   The Find and Replace dialog box appears, set to the Replace tab, as shown in Figure 5-4.

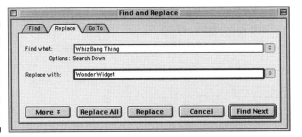

Figure 5-4:
The Replace tab in the Find and Replace window.

2. **In the Find what box, type the word or phrase you want to find.**

3. **In the Replace with box, type the word or phrase you want to substitute for the found text.**

4. **Click the Find Next button.**

   Word 2001 finds and selects the next instance of the text you're searching for.

5. **Click the Replace button.**

   Word 2001 inserts the replacement text and then finds the next instance of the search text.

To replace all instances of the search text with the replacement text in one step, click the Replace All button instead.

6. **When you're done replacing text, click the close box.**

Advanced finding and replacing

Word gives you many more options than simply finding and replacing strings of text. You can search and replace styles, text formatting, or invisible characters like tabs and paragraph marks. You can even use *wildcards* to search for a variety of criteria at once. Wildcards are placeholders that can stand for one or more characters. For example, you use the wildcard character * to stand for one or more characters. With this, searching for "w*e" would find both "whole" and "whale."

To search and replace text styles or other formatting, follow these steps:

1. **Choose Edit⇨Replace, or press ⌘+H.**

   The Find and Replace dialog box appears, set to the Replace tab.

2. **If the More button is visible, click it.**

   The Find and Replace dialog box expands, as shown in Figure 5-5.

Figure 5-5:
Advanced options for finding and replacing. You can replace formatting by specifying what you want with the Format menu.

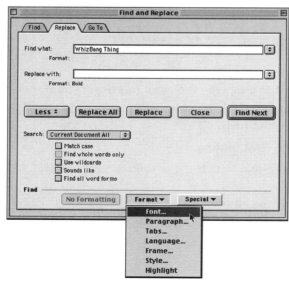

3. To search for text with specific formatting, enter the text in the Find what box. Or to search for specific formatting only, delete any text in the Find what box.

4. Click the Format button, and then choose the formatting you want to search for.

5. In the Replace with box, repeat Steps 3 and 4.

6. Click Replace All, Replace, or Find Next.

Don't think that you're limited to searching or replacing on only one attribute; you can have as many as you want. So if you want to search for text that is in the Palatino font, bold, in 18 point, with the Heading 1 style, and replace it with 27 point italicized Olde English font in purple, you can do that. The Taste Police may give you a call, but Word doesn't care.

To replace paragraph marks, tabs, and other special characters:

1. Choose Edit⇨Replace, or press ⌘+H.

2. If the More button is visible, click it to expand the Find and Replace box.

3. Click into the Find what or Replace with boxes, depending on what you want to accomplish.

4. Click the Special button, and choose the special item you want, such as Paragraph Mark or Tab Character.

   Word places its code for the special character into the Find what or Replace with boxes.

5. Click Replace All, Replace, or Find Next.

Some of the other choices in the Special pop-up menu are very useful. For example, when you want to search for numbers, the Any Digit choice comes in handy. Similarly, the Any letter choice works well, on occasion.

To use wildcards in a search:

1. Choose Edit⇨Find, or press ⌘+F.

2. If the More button is visible, click it to expand the Find box.

3. Click the Use wildcards check box.

4. In the Find what box, type in your search string, using one of the wildcard characters (see Table 5-2).

5. Click the Find Next button.

Table 5-2	Wildcard Characters	
Wildcard	*What It Does*	*Example*
*	Finds any string of characters	w*e finds "whale" and "whole"
?	Finds any single character	th?ng finds "thing" and "thong"
[ ]	Finds one of the specified characters	r[ai]ce finds "race" and "rice"
<	Finds the beginning of a word	<(ex) finds "excited" and "explosion" but not "vexed"
>	Finds the end of a word	(th)> finds "death" and "wealth" but not "thesaurus"

Many other wildcard characters are available; the ones above are just the ones I think are most useful. To see the entire list, search Word Help for wildcards.

Using Browse Objects

Word 2001 gives you a quick way to browse through your document by page, table, graphic, section, or other locations. On every document's vertical scroll bar, you'll find the Select Browse Object button, as seen in Figure 5-6.

Figure 5-6:
The Select Browse Object button is often overlooked, but it can be a powerful helper.

Document Scroll buttons
Next
Select Browse Object
Next

Clicking on the Select Browse Object button brings up a pop-up menu with 13 items, as shown in Figure 5-7.

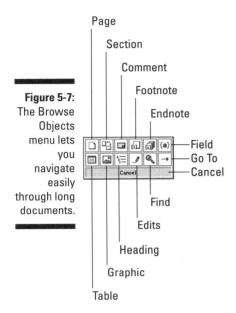

Figure 5-7: The Browse Objects menu lets you navigate easily through long documents.

When you choose one of the Browse Objects, the Previous and Next buttons jump you to the previous or next occurrence of that item. For example, if you choose the Graphic item, the Next button becomes Next Graphic, and clicking it moves you to the next image in your document. You can tell that Browse Objects is active because the double arrows in the Previous and Next buttons turn blue.

By default, Browse Objects is set to Page, so if you don't choose anything from the Select Browse Object button, the Previous and Next buttons will be Previous Page and Next Page.

Using the Spelling and Grammar Checkers

Even if you are a good speller, using the Word 2001 spelling checker is a good idea because it usually catches typographical errors in addition to true spelling mistakes. The grammar checker tries to find mistakes in sentence structure and capitalization as well as misused words.

Word 2001 points out a potential spelling error by putting a wavy red line below the suspect text. Suspected grammar problems get a wavy green underline.

If you don't see the wavy red or green lines, chances are they've been turned off. Choose Edit⇨Preferences, then click the Spelling & Grammar tab. Make sure that the Check Spelling As You Type and Check Grammar As You Type boxes are checked.

Checking as you type

If you prefer, Word 2001 can watch your typing and immediately point out a possible mistake. When the telltale wavy red or green underline appears, you can fix the problem right away.

To fix a spelling error that Word 2001 flags, follow these steps:

1. **Control+click a word that has a wavy red underline.**

   A contextual menu appears, as shown in Figure 5-8. The contextual menu contains suggestions for the spelling error.

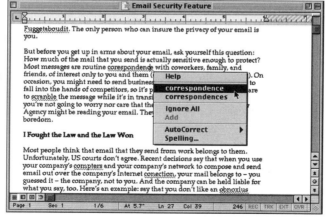

Figure 5-8:
Fixing spelling on the fly with the spell-checking contextual menu.

2. **If the correct spelling appears on the contextual menu, choose it.**

   The incorrect version is replaced by the correct version.

If the suspect word is spelled correctly, the word may simply not be in the built-in dictionary. You can add the word to your own custom dictionary by choosing Add from the contextual menu. If the word is correct but you don't want to add it to your custom dictionary, choose Ignore All from the contextual menu.

To check grammar as you type, follow these steps:

1. **Control+click a word or phrase that has a wavy green underline.**

   A contextual menu appears, containing suggested corrections for the grammar error.

2. **If you like one of the suggestions, choose it from the contextual menu.**

   The text is replaced by a Word 2001 suggestion.

   If you complete this step, you can skip the remaining steps.

3. **If you need more information about the grammar error, choose Grammar from the pop-up menu.**

   The Grammar dialog box appears, as shown in Figure 5-9. The top box shows you the error in context, labeled with the type of error it is. The bottom box contains suggestions for replacement. Because many grammar rules need explaining, the Office Assistant also appears, with a rundown of the violated grammar rule and grammatically correct examples.

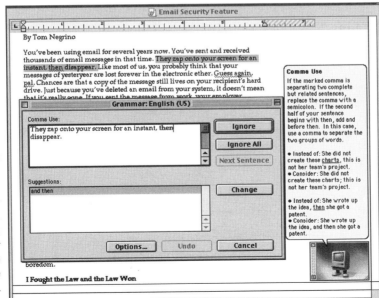

Figure 5-9:
The Grammar dialog box, with grammar tips from the Office Assistant.

4. **Click the Ignore or Replace button to deal with the grammar error.**

5. **Repeat Steps 1 through 4 as necessary until you deal with all the grammar errors.**

6. **Click the Cancel button to dismiss the Grammar dialog box.**

Some people think that it's kind of creepy to have your word processor always looking over your shoulder for mistakes. If you're in that camp, follow these steps to turn off this feature:

1. **Choose Edit⇨Preferences.**

   The Preferences dialog box appears.

2. **Click the Spelling & Grammar tab.**

3. **Clear the check boxes labeled Check Spelling As You Type and Check Grammar As You Type.**

4. **Click the OK button.**

Checking everything at the same time

To check the spelling and grammar of your document at the same time, follow these steps:

1. **Choose Tools⇨Spelling and Grammar.**

   Word 2001 displays the Spelling and Grammar dialog box, as shown in Figure 5-10, and begins to check the document.

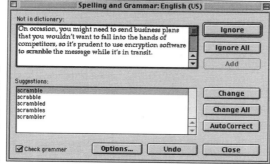

Figure 5-10: The Spelling and Grammar dialog box.

2. **Do one of the following things (remember that because Word is just a software program, it could be wrong):**

- Click Ignore to skip this instance of the error.

- Click Ignore All to skip all instances of the error.

- Click one of the suggestions displayed in the Suggestions box; then click Change or Change All.

When all the errors have been dealt with, the Office Assistant pops up a message to tell you that the spelling and grammar check is complete.

You can also fix errors in the top box of the Spelling and Grammar dialog box and then click the Change button.

3. **Click the OK button to go back to your document.**

The other buttons in the Spelling and Grammar dialog box give you other options:

✔ The Add button adds the flagged word to your custom dictionary, which is shared by Excel, PowerPoint, and Entourage. Use this button when the word is spelled correctly yet not recognized by Word 2001, such as a proper name or a technical word.

✔ The AutoCorrect button adds the word to the AutoCorrect list — a list of errors that Word 2001 fixes automatically (see the section "Correcting mistakes with AutoCorrect," later in this chapter).

This fact will come as a shock to fourth-grade teachers everywhere, but many people don't like to use a grammar checker. To turn off grammar checking (without turning off spell checking), follow these steps:

1. **Choose Edit⇨Preferences.**

   The Preferences dialog box appears.

2. **Click the Spelling & Grammar tab.**

3. **Clear the check box labeled Check Grammar with Spelling.**

4. **Click the OK button.**

If you want to turn off grammar checking for just the current check, clear the Check grammar check box in the Spelling and Grammar dialog box (refer to Figure 5-10).

Using the Built-In Dictionary

One of the new features in Office 2001 is the included Encarta World English Dictionary, which is available in all of the Office programs. It pops up and allows you to get the definition for any word in your document, without leaving your document.

To look up words:

1. **Place the insertion point anywhere within the word you want to define.**

2. **Control+click the word.**

3. **From the resulting contextual menu, choose Define.**

   The Dictionary window appears, as shown in Figure 5-11.

4. **When you're done reading the word's definition, click the Dictionary window's close box.**

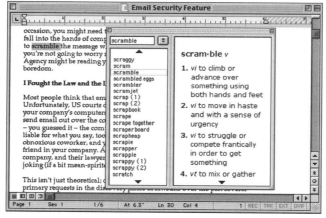

Figure 5-11:
Looking
up the
definition of
a word with
the Encarta
World
Dictionary.

Using the Built-In Thesaurus

A huge difference exists between the right word and the wrong word for any occasion, and Word 2001 has a tool that helps you pick the right word at the right time. The thesaurus provides synonyms for words you select. The thesaurus in Office 2001 is new, and Microsoft claims that it will now offer many more synonyms and make better suggestions than the Office 98 thesaurus. To use the thesaurus, follow these steps:

1. **Select a word for which you want to find a synonym.**

2. **Choose Tools⇨Thesaurus.**

   The Thesaurus dialog box appears, as shown in Figure 5-12.

Using Quick Thesaurus

Word 2001 has a faster way to pick synonyms: the Quick Thesaurus. The Quick Thesaurus first lived in the early Jurassic period, when he spent most of his time dodging the larger, slower thesauruses. A Quick Thesaurus that wasn't quick enough became, of course, a Dead Thesaurus. After millions of years, the Quick Thesaurus became an employee of Microsoft, where he happily lives inside Office 2001 for the Macintosh.

To use the Quick Thesaurus, follow these steps:

1. **Control+click a word for which you want to find a synonym.**

   The contextual menu appears.

2. **Choose Synonyms.**

   You see a hierarchical menu of synonyms.

3. **If you like one of the synonyms, choose it from the pop-up menu.**

   The original text is replaced by the synonym.

Figure 5-12: Finding synonyms with the thesaurus.

3. **In the Can mean box, click the desired meaning of the word you selected.**

   A list of synonyms appears in the box on the right.

   Was the Thesaurus dialog box empty when it appeared? If so, you forgot to select some text first. Just click the Cancel button to dismiss the Thesaurus dialog box; then try again.

4. **In the box on the right, click the synonym you want to use.**

5. **Click the Replace button.**

   Word 2001 replaces the original word with the selected synonym.

Having Word 2001 Do the Work for You

If you've read the first part of this chapter, you've seen the ways you can get Word 2001 to correct your mistakes. Microsoft built more intelligence into Word 2001, however, so that the program can actively seek out and fix some errors. Word 2001 can also help you by remembering standard or repeatedly used text and then spilling it out on command.

Correcting mistakes with AutoCorrect

AutoCorrect is already programmed with a list of common spelling mistakes and typographical errors. When you make one of these mistakes (such as typing *teh* rather than *the* or *compair* rather than *compare*), AutoCorrect automatically replaces the misspelling immediately. Often, you don't even realize that you made a mistake.

You can add your personal list of typing annoyances to the AutoCorrect list. I tend to type *instread* for *instead,* for example, but the mistake never reaches my documents anymore.

To add your own entries to the AutoCorrect list, follow these steps:

1. **Choose Tools⇨AutoCorrect.**

   The AutoCorrect dialog box appears, as shown in Figure 5-13.

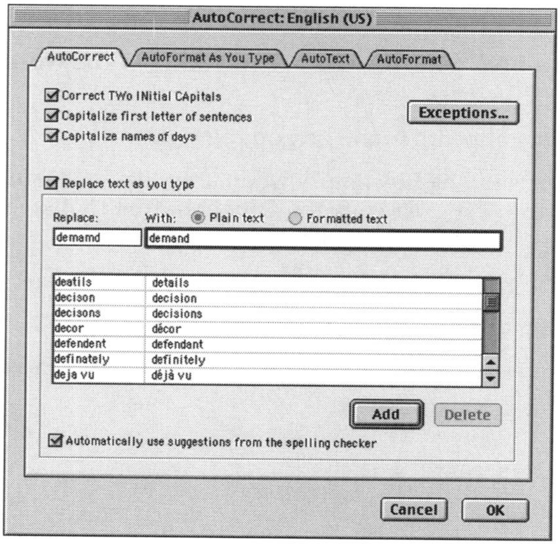

Figure 5-13:
The AutoCorrect dialog box.

2. **In the Replace box, type a word you often misspell.**

   You can also type a shortcut word to represent a longer phrase. You could type **NYC**, which would be replaced by *New York City,* or you could use your initials, which would expand to your entire name.

3. **In the With box, type the correct spelling of the word or type the phrase you want AutoCorrect to use to replace the shortcut word.**

4. **Click the Add button.**

5. **Click the OK button.**

Removing a word from AutoCorrect

To remove a word from the AutoCorrect list, follow these steps:

1. **Choose Tools⇨AutoCorrect.**

   The AutoCorrect dialog box appears.

2. **Select the word you want to remove from the list.**

3. **Click the Delete button.**

4. **Click the OK button.**

Turning AutoCorrect off

If AutoCorrect bugs you, you can turn it off. Follow these steps:

1. **Choose Tools⇨AutoCorrect.**

   The AutoCorrect dialog box appears.

2. **Clear the check box labeled Replace text as you type.**

3. **Click the OK button.**

Inserting text automatically with AutoText

Although AutoCorrect is cool, AutoText can really save you some time. If you think about your writing for a moment, you'll probably realize that many of the words and phrases you use are common to many of your documents. Elements such as salutations and signatures in letters and the formats of headers and footers tend to be standardized. Some people regularly use the same paragraphs or groups of paragraphs in their writing. This type of standard text is called *boilerplate.* You can store it in AutoText and insert it by choosing a single menu command, without having to copy and paste it from older documents.

Word 2001 comes with several AutoText entries, and you can easily add your own. You may well be able to create entire letters by using AutoText.

Because AutoText can handle graphics as well as text, you can also use it to store the images you use most often. You could save your company logo as an AutoText entry, for example, and then squirt it into your document in a flash.

In previous versions of Word (before Word 98), AutoText was called the Glossary. The feature has gained the capability to hold more boilerplate text and has also garnered its own toolbar. AutoText is now more like glossaries on steroids.

To create your own AutoText entry, follow these steps:

1. **Select the text or graphic you want to save as AutoText.**

2. **Choose Insert⇨AutoText⇨New.**

   The Create AutoText dialog box appears. Word 2001 proposes a name for the AutoText entry.

3. **Accept the name or enter your own.**

4. **Click the OK button.**

To insert an AutoText entry into your document, follow these steps:

1. **Click where you want to insert the AutoText.**

2. **Choose Insert⇨AutoText.**

   A submenu appears.

3. **Choose the category you want.**

4. **From the appropriate submenu, choose the AutoText entry you want to use.**

AutoText entries can contain virtually any formatting, including paragraph styles. To include the style of your selected text in the AutoText entry, first click the Show/Hide Paragraph Marks button on the Standard toolbar to display paragraph marks in your document. Select the paragraph mark at the end of the text you want to use as an AutoText entry. (The paragraph mark contains the formatting information for the paragraph.) Then choose Insert⇨AutoText⇨New.

Useful Stuff to Know

Hey, it's Word 2001 Grab Bag time! Although the topics in this section don't exactly belong in this chapter, I think that they're important things to know how to do in Word 2001, so they ended up here. You'll want to perform each of these tasks sooner or later, so here they are, sooner.

Printing envelopes

Word 2001 has a nifty built-in envelope-printing utility, which actually works! You can use this utility to print almost any kind of envelope that fits into your printer.

To print a single envelope, follow these steps:

1. **Choose Tools⇨Envelopes.**

    The Envelopes dialog box appears (see Figure 5-14).

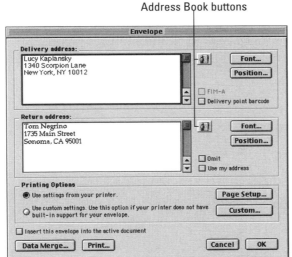

2. **In the Delivery Address box, type the recipient's address, or click the Address Book button to look up a name from Entourage's Address Book. Select the name from the Address Book, then click Insert Address.**

3. **In the Return Address box, type your address, or click the Address Book button to insert your name from Entourage's Address Book.**

4. **Click the Custom button (optional).**

    Word 2001 normally uses the envelope settings from the printer you have selected in the Chooser. But if the printer doesn't have built-in information about your envelope size, you need to tell Word how to handle the envelope. The Custom Page Sizes dialog box appears.

6. Set the necessary options, then click OK (optional).

The most important option is the envelope size; choose one from the pop-up menu.

7. If you want to print the envelope immediately, click the Print button. Otherwise, click OK.

Word creates a new document the size and shape of the envelope, with the address information filled in.

8. Choose File⇨Print to print your envelope.

Printing mailing labels

Word 2001 handles the printing of mailing labels and envelopes in a similar manner. To print mailing labels, follow these steps:

1. Choose Tools⇨Labels.

The Labels dialog box appears, as shown in Figure 5-15.

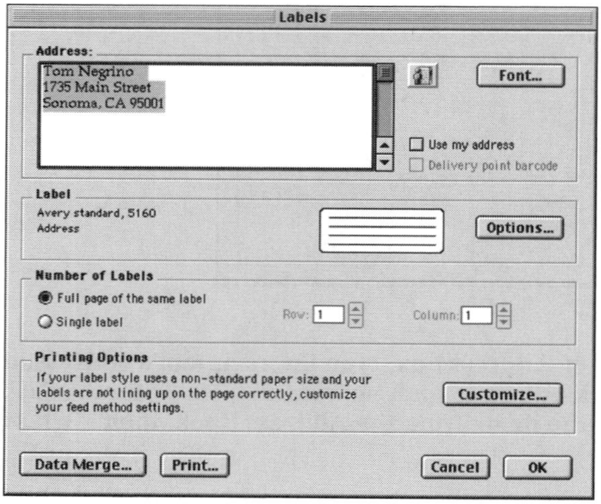

Figure 5-15:
The Labels
dialog box.

2. In the Address box, type the name and address you want on the label, or click the Address Book button to look up a name from Entourage's Address Book. Select the name from the Address Book, and then click Insert Address.

3. Click the Options button.

The Label Options dialog box appears, as shown in Figure 5-16.

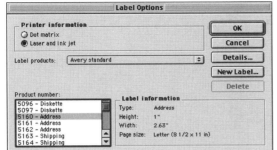

Figure 5-16:
Setting the
Label
Options.

4. **In the Printer information box, select Dot matrix or Laser and ink jet.**

5. **Use the Label products pop-up menu and text box to specify the kind of label you plan to use.**

6. **Click the OK button to return to the Labels dialog box.**

7. **To print an entire page of labels that contain the same text (such as return-address labels), click the Full Page of the Same Label button, and then skip to Step 9.**

8. **To print a single label from a sheet of labels, click the Single Label button and then set the row and column numbers of the next free label on your sheet.**

9. **Click the Print button.**

To print a bunch of different names on mailing labels, you have to have a data source that contains the names. This data source can be the Word 2001 internal Address Book, an Excel spreadsheet, another Word document, or the Address Book from Entourage 2001.

Counting your words

For some people (especially professional writers!), counting the number of words in a document is a useful capability. Word 2001 counts the pages, words, paragraphs, characters, and number of lines in your document.

To count the words in your document, choose Tools➪Word Count. The Word Count dialog box appears, as shown in Figure 5-17. When you're done looking at the statistics, click the OK button to dismiss the dialog box.

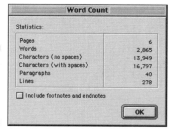

Figure 5-17:
The Word
Count dialog
box.

If you select some text before you choose Tools⇨Word Count, Word 2001 counts just the words in the selection.

Live Word Count

Another of Word 2001's new features is Live Word Count, which displays (in the status bar at the bottom of the document window) the total current word count of your document and also the position of the cursor in the document, as shown in Figure 5-18. You turn on Live Word Count by choosing Edit⇨ Preferences, then clicking the View tab. In the Window area, click the Live Word Count check box.

Figure 5-18:
Live Word
Count
constantly
updates you
on the
length of
your
document.

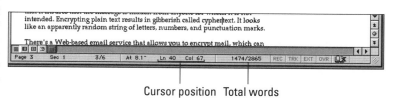

Cursor position   Total words

Inserting the date or time into your document

Can't remember what the date is? Word 2001 can (at least it can if the Mac's clock is set correctly). To insert the date or time into your document, choose Insert⇨Date and Time; then choose one of the many date and time formats. If you want the date or time to change whenever the document is opened or printed, click the Update Automatically check box. If you prefer that the date remain the one you put in when you wrote the document, clear that check box.

Numbering pages

To add page numbers, follow these steps:

1. **Choose Insert⇨Page Numbers.**

   The Page Numbers dialog box appears.

2. **Choose the page-number position and alignment from the appropriate menus.**

3. **Click the OK button.**

Chapter 6

Looks Matter: A Guide to Attractive Formatting

A well-written document is like a good musical performance. In music, the singer delivers the meaning of the song, and backup musicians provide the context that lets you appreciate the singer. In a document, the meaning of your words is enhanced by the format of the document. Just as people appreciate a singer more if he or she is backed by a good band, your audience is more receptive to your words if they are presented attractively.

Making Text Look Good

Word 2001 provides many tools to change the appearance of your text. You can control the fonts and font sizes, styles, text colors, and character spacing. Word 2001 lets you apply any of these controls on a character-by-character basis so that you have complete mastery over the look of your document.

On the other hand, restraint is important too. Just because you *can* make every character look different doesn't mean that you *should*. Documents with too much formatting look amateurish, so find a happy medium.

Choosing fonts and font sizes

Because the Macintosh was the first personal computer to come with a variety of fonts, having (and using) many fonts is practically the birthright of a Macintosh user. Every Macintosh is shipped with a variety of attractive fonts, and most Mac users quickly add more. Installing Office 2001 adds even more fonts to your Macintosh.

To change the font of some text, follow these steps:

1. **Select the text you want to change.**

2. **From the Font menu, choose the new font.**

   If you prefer, you can use the Font menu on the Formatting Palette (it's quicker), as shown in Figure 6-1.

Figure 6-1:
Use the
Formatting
Palette to
make quick
font
formatting
changes.

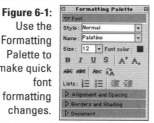

To change the font size of text, follow these steps:

1. **Select the text you want to change.**

2. **Choose a new size from the Size menu on the Formatting Palette.**

Picking character styles

Character styles add emphasis to your words. Words in *italics,* **boldface,** UPPERCASE, and <u>underlined</u> words draw the reader's attention.

Try to avoid underlining text. Underlining is a technique left over from the use of typewriters, which didn't have italics. Use italics for emphasis or to denote things like the titles of books. Another problem with underlined words in the age of the World Wide Web is that they are easily mistaken for hyperlinks. Likewise, when uppercase letters are used to emphasize text, they aren't as readable as lowercase letters, and uppercase letters break up the visual flow of a document.

To add character styles to text, follow these steps:

1. **Select the text you want to change.**

2. **Choose one or more of the following:**

   • Click the Bold button on the Formatting Palette, or press ⌘+B.

   • Click the Italic button on the Formatting Palette, or press ⌘+I.

   • Click the Underline button on the Formatting Palette, or press ⌘+U.

If you need to make many changes to text, you can do it all in one step by using the Font dialog box, as shown in Figure 6-2. You can change the font, font style, font size, color, and several other text attributes. It includes some lesser-used font formatting options not found on the Formatting Palette.

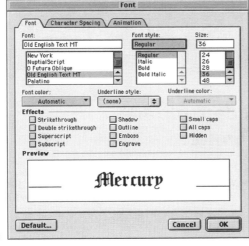

Figure 6-2:
The Font dialog box gives you the most complete control over character styles.

To make many changes at a time to text, follow these steps:

1. **Choose Format⇨Font.**

   The Font dialog box appears.

2. **Make the changes you want.**

   You can see the effects of your changes in the Preview box at the bottom of the Font dialog box.

If you apply any character formatting without selecting text first, Word 2001 applies that formatting to the next text you type.

A sense of style

The difference between a good-looking document and an amateurish-looking one is in both the broad strokes and the details. Type is used in both good and bad ways. The following list includes a few tips to help you improve your documents — all the fonts mentioned are either part of the standard Macintosh complement or installed with Office 2001:

- A formal message requires a formal font. If you're writing a report for the board of directors, for example, use an authoritative font, such as Times or Palatino. If you're writing an invitation to a beach party, a fun font like Comic Sans MS is appropriate.

- Try not to use more than two different fonts per page. The use of a sans serif font like Helvetica for headlines and a serif font like Times for body text is common. *Serifs* are the small, decorative strokes that are added to the end of a letter's main strokes; *sans serif* text doesn't have the decorative strokes.

- Left justification (the lines of text are lined up on the left) is usually easier to read and doesn't look as formal as full justification (where the right margin is also straight).

- Use headings and subheadings to help your readers easily find information in your document.

- Keep your document simple and clean. Visual clutter is the enemy of readability.

Copying character formats with Format Painter

After you format a text block the way you like it, you can use the terrific Format Painter tool to copy the text format and apply it to other text. Using Format Painter saves you time because you have to format a text block only once.

To use Format Painter, follow these steps:

1. **Select the text that is formatted the way you like it.**

2. **Click the Format Painter button on the Standard toolbar.**

   The insertion point turns into an I-beam with a plus sign next to it.

3. **Select the text to which you want to apply the formatting.**

   The text changes to the formatting of the text you selected in Step 1.

To copy the selected formatting to more than one location, double-click the Format Painter button. This action "locks on" the button. Click the button again after you finish formatting.

Changing case

If you've ever typed an entire sentence without realizing that the Caps Lock key on your keyboard was accidentally turned on, you'll appreciate the Word 2001 Change Case feature. You can use it to change the capitalization of selected text in the following five ways:

- **Sentence case:** The selected text has an initial capital letter.
- **Lowercase:** The selected text has no capital letters.
- **Uppercase:** The selected text has all capital letters.
- **Title case:** Each word in the selected text begins with a capital letter.
- **Toggle case:** Each letter in the selected text is reversed from normal, sentence case (upper-/lowercase) capitalization: for example, i LIVE IN lOS aNGELES.

To change case, follow these steps:

1. **Select the text you want to change.**
2. **Choose Format⇨Change Case.**

   The Change Case dialog box appears.
3. **Choose the capitalization option you want.**
4. **Click OK.**

Using Wizards and Templates to Jump-Start a Document

One of the key goals of the Microsoft team that created Microsoft Office 2001 was to make programs that would save you time by doing as much work for you as possible. What could be more helpful than documents that format themselves? The Office 2001 programs have two features that give you prefor-matted documents. *Wizards* ask you a series of questions and then create a document based on your responses. *Templates* are documents that Microsoft provides with formatting already in place; you simply fill in the templates with your own text.

Besides the Wizards and templates that come with the usual installation of Office 2001, you can find more Wizards and templates in the Value Pack folder on the Office 2001 CD-ROM.

We're off to see the Wizard

Wizards are amazing. When you use a Wizard, Word 2001 presents you with dialog boxes that ask you questions about the document you want to create. The Wizard then uses your answers to create a custom document. Word 2001 comes with Wizards that help you create agendas, newsletters, envelopes, faxes, letters, mailing labels, memos, Web pages, and more.

The following example uses the Letter Wizard, and other Wizards work in much the same way.

To create a document with the Letter Wizard, follow these steps:

1. **Choose File⇨New Blank Document.**

   A blank document appears.

2. **Choose Tools⇨Letter Wizard.**

   The Letter Wizard dialog box appears, as in Figure 6-3. The Wizard opens to the Letter Format tab.

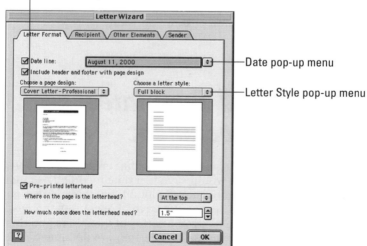

Figure 6-3:
The Letter
Format tab
of the Letter
Wizard.

3. **Click Date line, then choose a date format from the date pop-up menu.**

4. **Pick one of the page designs.**

The Choose a page design menu lists the letter templates that Word 2001 knows about. To add more items to this menu, save Word templates in the Templates folder inside your Office 2001 folder. In order to be used by the Letter Wizard, the templates must also have "letter" or "ltr" somewhere in their names.

5. **Choose one of the three letter styles from the Choose a letter style pop-up menu.**

    The Full Block choice justifies all text to the left. Modified block indents the date line and signature to about two-thirds of the way across the page. The Semi-block choice also indents the date and signature, but also applies a first line indent to each paragraph in the body of the letter.

6. **If you'll be printing on pre-printed letterhead, click the Pre-printed letterhead check box, then tell the Wizard the location of the letterhead on the page and how much space to reserve.**

7. **Click the Recipient tab of the Letter Wizard window.**

    The Recipient screen appears, as shown in Figure 6-4.

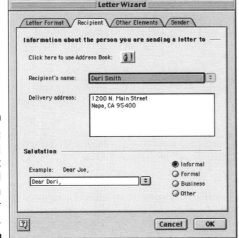

Figure 6-4: Choosing the recipient and salutation for your letter.

8. **To look up a contact from the Entourage Address Book, click the Address Book button. Otherwise, type in the recipient's name and address.**

9. **Choose the type of salutation you prefer.**

10. **Click the Other Elements tab of the Letter Wizard window (optional).**

    The Other Elements screen appears. This screen has optional items you can add to your letter, such as a reference line, a subject line, or mailing instructions. Click the check boxes next to the items you want to include. You can also add Courtesy Copies (cc) addresses here, again picked from the Address Book.

11. Click the Sender tab of the Letter Wizard window.

Type in the Sender's name, or again, look it up in the Address Book, as shown in Figure 6-5. Then add any of the other, optional choices, such as the closing salutation or the writer's/typist's initials.

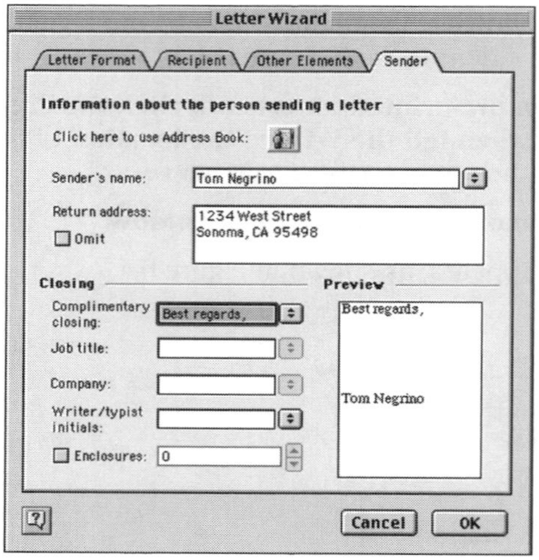

Figure 6-5:
Entering the Sender information.

12. Click OK.

Word creates the letter and places the cursor where you can begin entering the body of your text.

Using templates

Unlike with Wizards, when you use a template, you don't have to step through a dialog box. Microsoft creates the document template for you, and it comes complete with appropriate character formatting, styles, and sometimes even graphics. You only have to fill in the template with your own words.

The following example uses one of the letter templates; the other templates work in a similar manner.

To use a template to start a document, follow these steps:

1. **Choose File➪Project Gallery.**

   The Project Gallery appears.

2. **From the list on the left side of the window, click a category you want to use.**

3. **On the right side of the window, click the icon for the template you've chosen, and then click OK.**

   Word 2001 creates the document, based on the template you chose, as shown in Figure 6-6. Placeholder text is included where you enter your information.

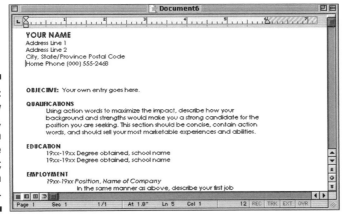

Figure 6-6:
A new document, fresh from the template; this one is a résumé.

4. **Replace the placeholder text in the template with your own text.**

Do It with Styles

Of all the candidates for the prize of Most Underused Word 2001 Feature, I give the nod to *styles,* which define the appearance of text in your document. You can store a whole set of character and paragraph formats under a style name. After a style is created, you can select a paragraph and use that style to apply its set of formats in one step.

Suppose that you want the headlines in your document to be Helvetica 14-point boldface, centered on the page. You can format your headline manually just once and then assign the formats to a style you name Heading 1.

When you want to apply that formatting to other parts of your document, you can select the text you want to format and apply the Heading 1 style by using the Formatting toolbar. Boom! — the selected text gets formatted in the same style as the original text.

One of the nicest things about styles is that when you want to change the formatting of all the text in a particular part of your document, you can simply change the style definition. If you decide, for example, that your headlines look better in Times 18-point font and left-justified, just change your Heading 1 style definition, and all the text in your document that is formatted as Heading 1 also changes. This feature is incredibly cool because formatting is the dog work of word processing. The longer a document is, the better the use of styles is. Imagine having a 100-page document with lots of pictures and your boss telling you to change the typeface of all the picture captions. You could go through and change each caption separately, or, if you defined a Caption style, you could use just one dialog box to change the Caption style, which would then ripple throughout the entire document.

Word 2001 has two kinds of styles. A *character style* is a combination of any of the character formats in the Font dialog box that is then given a style name. A *paragraph style* is a set of character formats and paragraph formats (including justification, indents, and line spacing) stored under a single name. Paragraph styles tend to be used more than character styles because styles are most useful for formatting the structure of a document, and that structure is made up of paragraphs.

Creating styles

The fastest way to create a new paragraph style is to format a paragraph in your document the way you like it and then store that formatting as a style by using the Formatting toolbar. Follow these steps:

1. **Select some text you want to use as an example for a style.**

2. **If necessary, format the text the way you want.**

3. **Make sure that the text is still selected.**

4. **On the Formatting Palette, click the Style box.**

   The style name in the Style box is highlighted.

5. **Type over the existing style name to create your new style name.**

6. **Press Enter.**

Applying styles

To apply a different paragraph style, follow these steps:

1. **Select the text you want to change.**

2. **Select from the Style pop-up menu on the Formatting toolbar the style you want to apply.**

3. **Press Return.**

Paragraph styles almost always include character attributes, such as bold or italic. You can apply the character attributes of a paragraph style to specific text within a paragraph, without changing the style of the entire paragraph the text is in: Simply select a portion of text in a paragraph, and then apply the paragraph style. The selected text changes to the character attributes of the newly applied paragraph style, and the rest of the paragraph retains the original paragraph style. If you select the entire paragraph and apply the paragraph style, the entire paragraph changes, of course, to the new style definition.

Modifying styles

Sometimes you want to change a style you've already defined or modify a style predefined in an Office 2001 template. To change or modify a style, follow these steps:

1. **Choose Format⇨Style.**

   The Style dialog box appears, as shown in Figure 6-7. Notice that the Style dialog box contains preview areas that show how the paragraph will look and how characters in the paragraph will look.

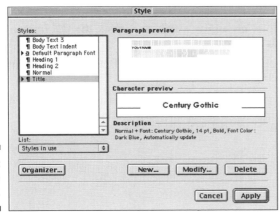

Figure 6-7:
The Style
dialog box.

2. **In the Style dialog box, click the style you want to modify.**

   The preview of that style appears in the Paragraph preview and Character preview boxes.

3. **Click Modify.**

   The Modify Style dialog box appears, as shown in Figure 6-8.

Figure 6-8:
The Modify Style dialog box.

4. **Click Format, and then choose from the pop-up menu the attribute you want to change (such as Font, Paragraph, or Tabs).**

   The dialog box for the attribute you chose appears.

5. **Make whichever changes you want, and then click OK.**

   You return to the Modify Style dialog box.

6. **Continue choosing from the Format pop-up menu the attributes to change.**

   Note that you can use the Shortcut Key button to let you apply the style from the keyboard.

7. **When you're done changing attributes, click the OK button in the Modify Style dialog box.**

8. **If you want to apply the modified style, click the Apply button. Otherwise, click the Cancel button.**

   The modified style is saved in the style template of the current document.

AutoFormat Steps In

The Word 2001 AutoFormat feature makes formatting your documents even easier by doing the work for you. AutoFormat analyzes your document and then applies paragraph styles to make your document look good. AutoFormat works in two main ways:

- ✔ The AutoFormat command formats your entire document in one pass.
- ✔ The AutoFormat As You Type feature watches what you're typing and automatically formats headings, numbers, symbols, and bulleted and numbered lists.

AutoFormatting entire documents

When you use the AutoFormat command, Word 2001 first scans your document and tries to figure out which parts of your document are headings, which are body text, and so on, and then it applies paragraph styles. You can choose to have AutoFormat make all the changes at one time, or you can review each change as it is made. To automatically format an entire document, follow these steps:

1. **Choose Format⇨AutoFormat.**

   The AutoFormat dialog box appears.

2. **Choose either AutoFormat now or AutoFormat and review each change.**

3. **Select a document type from the pop-up menu.**

   AutoFormat uses this document type as a starting point for the formatting process.

4. **Click the Options button to set AutoFormat options (optional).**

   The AutoCorrect dialog box opens, set to the AutoFormat tab, as shown in Figure 6-9.

5. **Turn on or off any AutoFormat options, and then click OK (optional).**

6. **Back in the AutoFormat dialog box, click OK.**

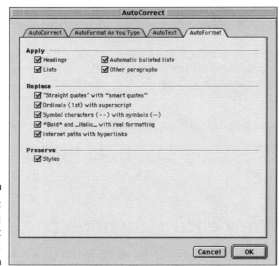

Figure 6-9:
Setting
AutoFormat
options.

AutoFormatting as you type

To have the Word 2001 AutoFormat feature help you format your document as you write it, follow these steps:

1. **Choose Tools⇨AutoCorrect.**

   The AutoCorrect dialog box appears.

2. **Click the AutoFormat As You Type tab.**

   The dialog box now looks like Figure 6-10.

3. **Set the AutoFormat options you want.**

4. **Click OK.**

You need to set these options only once; after you do so, Word 2001 remembers your settings and automatically formats your text as you type it.

To turn off all automatic formatting, clear all the options on the AutoFormat As You Type tab in the AutoCorrect dialog box.

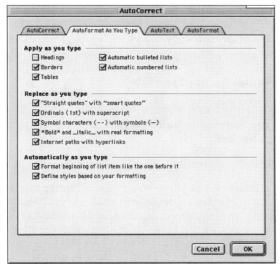

Figure 6-10:
Setting the
AutoFormat
As You Type
options.

Using AutoFormat for numbered and bulleted lists

AutoFormat As You Type makes creating numbered or bulleted lists easy.
You simply start the list with a bullet or number and then press Return.
AutoFormat inserts the next number or bullet for you.

Here's an example of a numbered list:

1. **Call florist**

2. **Buy candy**

3. **Beg forgiveness**

This list is a bulleted list:

- **Call lawyer**

- **Serve papers**

- **Move out**

To have Word 2001 format your lists for you, follow these steps:

1. **Choose Tools⇨AutoCorrect.**

   The AutoCorrect dialog box appears.

2. **Click the AutoFormat As You Type tab.**

   Refer to Figure 6-10.

3. **Make sure that the Automatic bulleted lists and Automatic numbered lists options are checked.**

4. **Click OK.**

Word 2001 creates a numbered list when you type a number followed by a period, hyphen, closing parenthesis, or greater-than sign (>) followed by a space or a tab and then text. A bulleted list is created when you type an asterisk, one or two hyphens, or a greater-than sign followed by a space or a tab and then text.

To stop the automatic numbering or bulleting while you're typing a list, press the Return key twice.

If you don't like the format of the numbered or bulleted list Word 2001 creates, you can change it by following these steps:

1. **Select the numbered or bulleted list you want to change.**

2. **Choose Format⇨Bullets and Numbering.**

   The Bullets and Numbering dialog box appears, as shown in Figure 6-11.

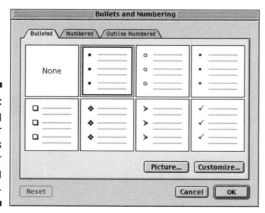

Figure 6-11:
Changing your document's bullet or numbering format.

3. **Click either the Bulleted or Numbered tab.**

4. **Choose one of the eight styles of bullets or numbers.**

The Picture button in Figure 6-11 is another new feature in Word 2001. It allows you to use images as bullets, and Office comes with eight pictures you can use as bullets. You're more likely to use this feature in a Web page or on a PowerPoint slide than in a letter, but you now have the capability.

5. **Click OK.**

By using the Bullets and Numbering dialog box, you can change a bulleted list to a numbered list or vice versa. You can also turn a group of selected paragraphs into a bulleted or numbered list.

Instant hyperlinks

AutoFormat can also help you create instant hyperlinks in your documents. *Hyperlinks* are colored and underlined text you click to jump to a file or a particular location in a file on your hard disk, to an e-mail address, or to a page on the World Wide Web.

To automatically format hyperlinks, follow these steps:

1. **Choose Tools➪AutoCorrect.**

   The AutoCorrect dialog box appears.

2. **Click the AutoFormat As You Type tab.**

   Refer to Figure 6-10.

3. **In the Replace As You Type section, make sure that the option labeled Internet paths with hyperlinks is checked.**

4. **Click OK.**

Whenever you type an e-mail or Web address, Word 2001 now automatically converts it into a hyperlink.

Hyperlinks can also take you to FTP sites, newsgroups, or Telnet.

Using the Style Gallery

After you use AutoFormat to apply styles throughout your document, you can then apply a style template to change the entire look of your document in one step. Because Word 2001 includes many style templates, giving your document a facelift is easy. Follow these steps to apply a style template:

1. **Choose Format⇨Theme.**

2. **Click the Style Gallery button.**

   The Style Gallery dialog box appears, as shown in Figure 6-12.

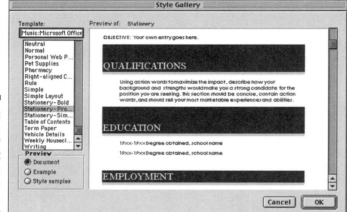

Figure 6-12: Choosing a new document format from the Style Gallery.

3. **In the Template area on the left, click the name of a template.**

   The Preview area shows what your document will look like if you apply the template you've selected.

4. **Click OK.**

Working with Tables

Tables are great for presenting complicated information in simple ways. Tables enable you to organize columns of numbers, produce forms, and format reports.

Tables consist of rows and columns. *Rows* are the horizontal divisions of the table; *columns* are the vertical divisions. A row and a column intersect to form a *cell.* You can put either text or a graphics image into a cell. When you type text in a cell, the text wraps within the cell, and the cell enlarges as you enter more text.

When you add a table to your document, you need to define the number of rows and columns in the table. After the table is added, you can modify the table and its contents by formatting the text, adding borders, and changing the size of the table.

Creating a table

Word 2001 gives you three ways to create tables:

- ✔ Use the Insert Table button on the Standard toolbar.
- ✔ Use the Insert Table dialog box from the Table menu.
- ✔ Use the Draw Table feature.

Using the toolbar

The fastest way to create a table is from the Standard toolbar, by following these steps:

1. **Click the Insert Table button on the Standard toolbar.**

   A table appears below the toolbar, as shown in Figure 6-13.

Figure 6-13: Building a table with the Insert Table button.

3 x 4 Table

2. **Drag the mouse down and to the right to choose the height and width of your table.**

3. **Release the mouse button.**

   Word 2001 draws the table.

Using the Insert Table dialog box

Using the Insert Table dialog box to create a table isn't as quick as using the Standard toolbar, although the dialog box gives you a little more control. Follow these steps to create a table with the Insert Table dialog box:

1. **Choose Table⇨Insert Table.**

   The Insert Table dialog box appears, as shown in Figure 6-14.

Figure 6-14:
The Insert
Table
dialog box.

2. **In the box labeled Number of columns, enter the number of columns you want in the table.**

3. **In the box labeled Number of rows, enter the number of rows you want in the table.**

4. **Leave the box labeled Initial column width set to Auto, or click the up and down arrow to set the column width. If you want the table to automatically resize, click one of the two AutoFit options.**

5. **Click the AutoFormat button (optional).**

   If you don't want to use AutoFormat for your table, skip to Step 8.

   The Table AutoFormat dialog box appears, as shown in Figure 6-15.

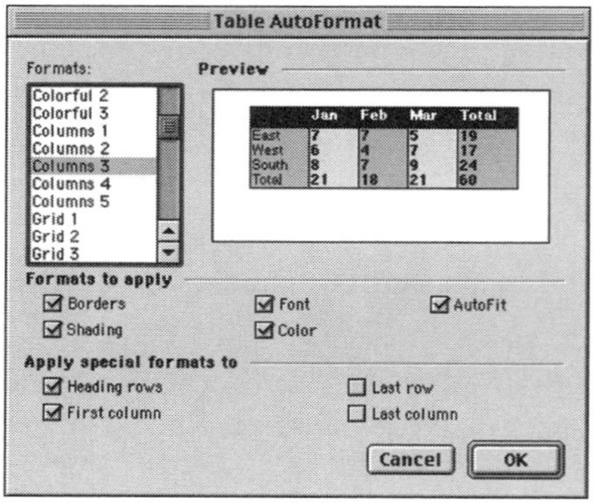

Figure 6-15:
The Table
AutoFormat
dialog box.

6. **Click one of the predefined table formats in the Formats list.**

   Experiment with the different formats and formatting options available in the dialog box. The Preview area shows what your table will look like.

7. **Click OK.**

The Insert Table dialog box reappears (refer to Figure 6-14).

If you want the table settings you just created to be used every time you make a table, click the Set as default for new tables button.

8. **Click OK.**

Using the Draw Table feature

The Draw Table feature enables you to create complex tables just by drawing rows and columns with a Pen tool. Follow these steps to use the Draw Table feature:

1. **Click the insertion point where you want to create the table.**

2. **Click the Tables and Borders button on the Standard toolbar.**

The Tables and Borders toolbar appears, and the mouse pointer turns into a pen.

3. **Drag diagonally to create the outer borders of the table.**

4. **Draw horizontally and vertically with the pen tool to create the rows and columns of your table.**

5. **To erase a line, click the eraser tool and drag over the offending line.**

The drawing method enables you to create complicated tables, as shown in Figure 6-16.

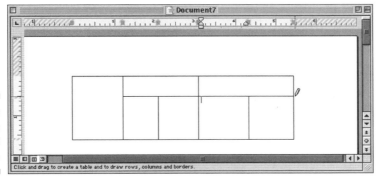

Figure 6-16:
Drawing a complex table.

While you're drawing a table, pressing the Shift key toggles between the pen and eraser tools.

Changing table size

After you work with a table, you may realize that you made a mistake and want to change the number of rows or columns in the table. You can add or delete rows or columns and change the height and width of cells.

To add a row or column, follow these steps:

1. **Put the insertion point in any row or column.**
2. **Choose Table⇨Select Row (or Select Column).**

   Word 2001 highlights the row or column.
3. **Choose Table⇨Insert Rows Above (or Rows Below, Insert Columns to the left, or Insert Columns to the right).**

   Word 2001 inserts the new row next to the row the insertion point is in or adds a new column next to the column where the insertion point is.

To delete a row or column, follow these steps:

1. **Put the insertion point in any row or column.**
2. **Choose Table⇨Delete Rows (or Delete Columns).**

   Word 2001 wipes out the row or column that is selected.

To change the height or width of a table's cells, follow these steps:

1. **Put the insertion point over the column line or row line you want to move.**

   The insertion point turns into a two-headed arrow.
2. **Drag the column line or row line to where you want it located.**

Merging and splitting table cells

You may want to join one or more cells (or split them apart). The heads of columns often stretch across more than one column, for example.

To merge table cells, follow these steps:

1. **Select the cells you want to join.**
2. **Choose Table⇨Merge Cells.**

To split table cells, follow these steps:

1. **Select the cells you want to split.**

2. **Choose Table⇨Split Cells.**

Cleaning up your tables

If you've drawn a table or moved row or column lines around, your table may not look as neat as you want because the spacing is usually off between row or column lines. Word 2001 has two tools to deal with this problem: the Distribute Rows Evenly and Distribute Columns Evenly buttons. Follow these steps to clean up your tables:

1. **Click multiple rows or columns inside a table.**

2. **On the Tables and Borders toolbar, click either the Distribute Rows Evenly or Distribute Columns Evenly button (or click both of them).**

   Word 2001 evens out the amount of space between rows or columns.

To automatically resize a table, follow these steps:

1. **Click inside a table.**

2. **Choose Table⇨AutoFit, and then choose from the hierarchical menu.**

   • AutoFit to Contents resizes the table to make it fit snugly around the contents of each column.

   • AutoFit to Window makes the table fit between the left and right margins.

Sorting a table

Although Word 2001 doesn't have the data-manipulation capabilities that Excel 2001 does, you can still do some simple sorts and calculations on the data in tables.

To sort the data in a table, follow these steps:

1. **Select the columns or rows you want to sort.**

   The data is highlighted.

2. **Choose Table⇨Sort.**

   The Sort dialog box appears.

3. Choose the sort options you want.

4. Click OK.

Word 2001 sorts the table, with results similar to those shown in Figure 6-17.

Figure 6-17:
The sorted table.

Variety	Winery	Vintage
Cabernet Sauvignon	Kendall-Jackson	1996
Chardonnay	Mill Creek	1997
Merlot	Mil Creek	1996
Pinot Noir	Simi	1997
Zinfandel	Clos de Bois	1996

Doing table calculations

Word 2001 is no spreadsheet like Excel 2001, but you can still do some calculations in tables. Most often, you'll use table calculations to sum up a column of numbers, but you're not limited to that.

To perform a calculation on a table's contents, follow these steps:

1. At the bottom of a table, create a new row.

2. Click in the cell at the bottom of the column you wish to calculate.

3. Choose Table⇨Formula.

The Formula dialog box appears, as shown in Figure 6-18. By default, it has =SUM(ABOVE) in the Formula box (which is what you would want if you just wanted to add up the column), but let's change that.

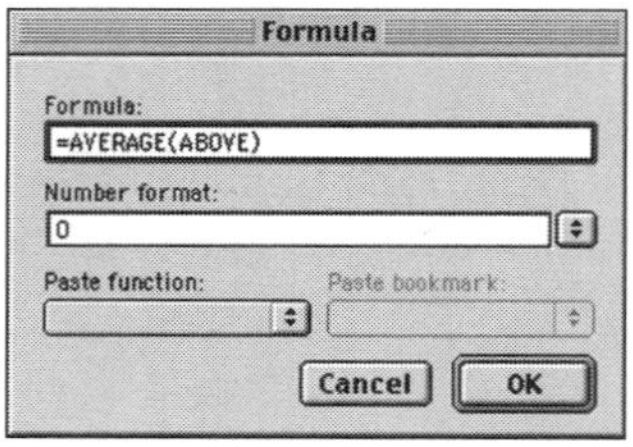

Figure 6-18:
The Formula dialog box.

4. Replace SUM with AVERAGE in the Formula box.

5. Choose a number format from the pop-up menu.

6. Click OK.

Figure 6-19 shows the result.

Figure 6-19:
Word has
calculated
the average
vintage of
our wine
collection.

Variety	Winery	Vintage
Cabernet Sauvignon	Kendall-Jackson	1994
Chardonnay	Mill Creek	1997
Merlot	Mill Creek	1995
Merlot	Dry Creek	1995
Pinot Noir	Simi	1997
Syrah	Zaca Mesa	1993
Viognier	Hawley	1998
Zinfandel	Clos de Bois	1989
Average vintage in collection:		1995

If you change the values in a table, it's easy to get Word to recalculate the results of the table's formulas. Simply place the cursor anywhere in the table, choose Edit⇨Select All (or press ⌘+A), then press F9. Word will recalculate all the formulas in the table.

Deleting a table

To delete a table (and its contents), follow these steps:

1. **Click anywhere inside the table.**

2. **Choose Table⇨Delete⇨Table.**

To delete the contents of the table (but not the table itself), follow these steps:

1. **Click anywhere inside the table.**

2. **Choose Table⇨Select Table.**

3. **Press the Delete key.**

Chapter 7

Creating Reports and Newsletters

· ·

· ·

*O*ver the years, Microsoft Word has gained more and more of the features previously found only in desktop publishing programs. With Word 2001, you can create complicated documents such as newsletters and reports with a high degree of control.

In this chapter, you find out how to use Word 2001 to create longer and more complex documents. You also see that although Word 2001 won't be replacing Adobe InDesign or QuarkXPress (the big-name desktop publishing programs designers use to make books, brochures, reports, and so on) on professional designers' desktops, it's more than capable enough for most of us.

Creating Reports

Reports come in many varieties: financial reports, reports to the board of directors, reports to your boss, and even your kids' book reports for school, for example.

Reports can seem like deceptively simple documents when you first look at them. But a closer look shows that many longer reports have quite a bit of complex formatting, including the following:

- A title page
- Multiple sections, each with its own format
- Headers and footers, which may or may not be different on even and odd pages
- Footnotes or endnotes

Pat yourself on the back: Adding a title page with Click and Type

Title pages have formatting that is usually different from the rest of your document. Typically, a title page has the title of the document centered vertically on the page and the author's byline either directly below the title or in a block of text at the bottom of the page.

The best way to create a title page in Word 2001 is to use the new Click and Type feature, which lets you put text or graphics anywhere on a blank page. All you need to do is to double-click on a blank area of the page, and Click and Type will attempt to apply the correct formatting needed to put the text or graphic where you clicked. For example, if you double-click in the middle of a title page, Word will center the text both horizontally and vertically.

Click and Type only works in Page Layout or Online Layout views, and you should make sure that it has been turned on by choosing Edit➪Preferences, clicking the Edit tab, then clicking the Enable Click and Type check box.

When you use Click and Type, Word 2001 applies the kind of formatting that it thinks will best accomplish your task, and it figures that out by noticing where on the page that you clicked. But Word also warns you what sort of formatting it will apply by changing the cursor to one of six choices, as shown in Figure 7-1:

✓ **Left Aligned:** Applies a left-aligned tab

✓ **Right Aligned:** Applies a right-aligned tab

✓ **Centered:** Applies a centered tab

✓ **Left Text Wrap:** Will wrap text around the left side of a graphic

✓ **Right Text Wrap:** Will wrap text around the right side of a graphic

✓ **Left Indent:** Will place a left indent where you click

Figure 7-1:
The Click and Type cursor changes to let you know what will happen when you use it.

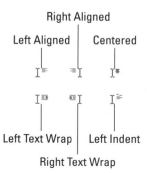

To create a title page with Click and Type, follow these steps:

1. **Press ⌘+N to create a new blank document.**

2. **Click in a blank space in the document where you want to begin typing.**

   The cursor turns into one of the Click and Type cursors, depending on where on the page you have clicked.

3. **Double-click, and then type the text you want to appear on the title page.**

   In this example, I use a document title and an author's byline, but you can type as much or as little on the title page as you want. The text appears on the page, as shown in Figure 7-2.

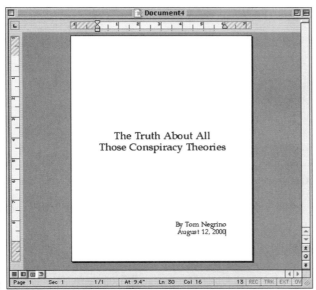

Figure 7-2:
Clicking and
Typing on a
blank page.

4. **Select the text that you typed in Step 2.**

5. **Using the Formatting Palette, format the text to your satisfaction.**

   Titles are usually in a large point size and are often centered on the page.

6. **Format any other text on your title page.**

Give your document a break!

A *page break* is the point at which one page ends and the next page begins. You've seen page breaks already; Word puts them in automatically when you fill a page with text and/or graphics. These types of page breaks are automatic, or "soft" page breaks. If you know that you don't want anything else on a page you've been working on, you can insert a manual, or "hard" page break. You do this by choosing **Insert⇨Break⇨Page Break**, or by pressing **Shift+Enter.** In the Page Layout view, you'll see a page break at the end of the page, just as it would appear in the real world. In the Normal view, a manual page break appears as shown in Figure 7-3.

Figure 7-3:
How a page
break
appears in
Normal
view.

Using sections

Sections are extremely useful in formatting longer documents because each section of a Word document can have entirely different formatting. For example, one section can have a single column of text, and the next section can have multiple columns. The margins, headers, and footers of one section can differ from the next. Different sections can have opposite page orientations, so you can mix both portrait and landscape pages in the same document.

To tell Word that you are about to create a different section, you must insert a section break into your document. Word 2001 has four types of section breaks:

- ✓ **Next page:** Inserts the section break, breaks the page, and starts the new section on the next page

- ✓ **Continuous:** Inserts a section break and starts the new section on the same page

- ✓ **Odd page:** Inserts a section break and starts the new section on the next odd-numbered page

- ✓ **Even page:** Inserts a section break and starts the new section on the next even-numbered page

To insert a section break, follow these steps:

1. **Click where you want to insert the section break.**

2. **Choose Insert➪Break, and then choose the sort of section break you want from the hierarchical menu.**

Using headers and footers

A *header* is an area of text at the top of each page that repeats itself on every page of your document. Similarly, a *footer* is an area of text at the bottom of the page that also repeats itself.

Typical things to put in a header or footer are

- ✔ The date
- ✔ Page numbers
- ✔ The document's title
- ✔ A chapter title
- ✔ Your name

When deciding what information to put in the header and footer, keep in mind that you probably don't want to put the same information in both the header and the footer. In fact, most documents have either a header or a footer, but not both.

To add a header or a footer, follow these steps:

1. **Choose View➪Header and Footer.**

   Word 2001 switches to Page Layout view, displays the Header and Footer toolbar, and displays Header and Footer text boxes, where you insert the text you want to appear (see Figure 7-4).

2. **Type your header text in the Header text box (or if you're creating a footer, type in the Footer text box), or click a toolbar button to insert the page number, the date, or the time.**

   If you want the word *Page* to appear before the page number, type the word **Page** and leave a space before you click the Insert Page Number button on the toolbar.

   If you want to have one bit of information appear at the left end of the header, one in the center, and one on the right end, press Tab between them. The header and footer have separate paragraph formatting from the rest of your document, and you can change the tabs and other formatting to adjust the appearance of the header and footer as you like.

Different Odd and Even Pates

Show/Hide Document Text

Same as Previous

Header and Footer toolbar

Switch Between Header and Footer

Inserted AutoText

Show Previous

Header text box

Show Next

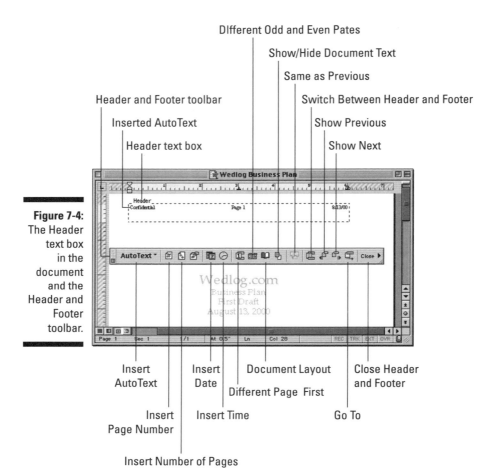

Figure 7-4:
The Header text box in the document and the Header and Footer toolbar.

Insert AutoText

Insert Date

Document Layout

Close Header and Footer

Different Page First

Insert Page Number

Insert Time

Go To

Insert Number of Pages

3. Click the Document Layout button on the Header and Footer toolbar.

The Document dialog box appears, set to the Layout tab, as shown in Figure 7-5.

4. Click the Different odd and even check box if you want to have different headers and footers for odd and even pages.

For example, you may want to have page numbers appear at the left end of the header on even-numbered pages and at the right end of the header on odd-numbered pages, as in this book.

5. Click the Different first page check box if you want a different header or footer for your first page.

You usually don't see page numbers on the first page in a document. You probably want to leave the header and footer blank on the first page.

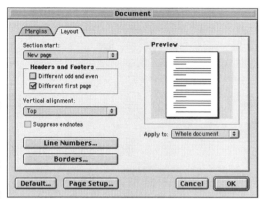

Figure 7-5:
Setting
header and
footer layout
options.

6. **Click OK.**

   The Document dialog box disappears.

7. **Click Close on the Header and Footer toolbar to leave Page Layout view.**

While you're thinking of headers, footers, and other things at the margins of your document, note that the Document dialog box has a new Borders button that brings you to the Borders dialog box and allows you to add borders in many different styles around any or all edges of your pages.

Adding footnotes and endnotes

Word 2001 lets you bolster your arguments with footnotes and endnotes. A *footnote* appears at the bottom of a page and contains snippets of text citing sources of information, comments, explanations, or other references. *Endnotes* are similar, except that they appear at the end of your document. If you want, you can have both footnotes and endnotes in the same document; for example, you may use footnotes for comments and endnotes to cite your references.

A footnote or endnote consists of two linked parts — the note itself and the *note reference mark.* You can number note reference marks yourself, but Word can do it for you automatically. Word also automatically renumbers the marks if you delete, move, or add new ones.

To add a footnote or endnote, follow these steps:

1. **Click in your document where you want to insert the note reference mark.**

2. **Choose Insert⇨Footnote.**

   The Footnote and Endnote dialog box appears, as shown in Figure 7-6.

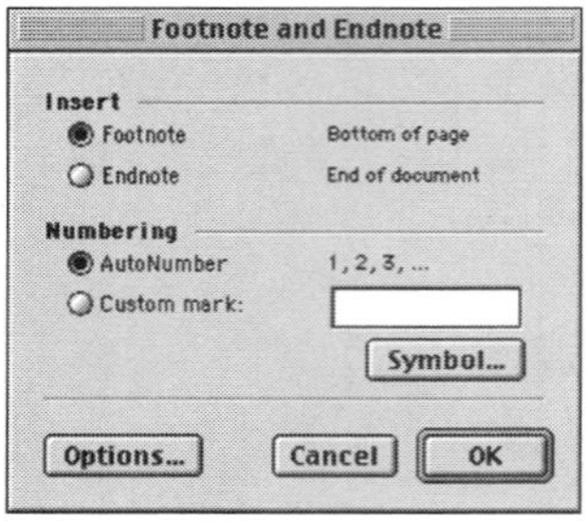

Figure 7-6:
Adding a
footnote or
endnote.

3. **In the Insert area, choose either Footnote or Endnote.**

4. **In the Numbering area, choose AutoNumber or Custom mark.**

5. **Click OK.**

   The document window splits to show a Footnotes pane, as shown in Figure 7-7.

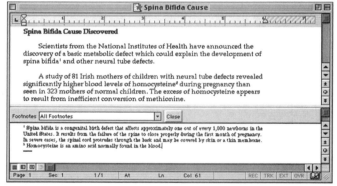

Figure 7-7:
Entering the
footnote.

6. **Type your footnote or endnote text into the Footnotes pane.**

7. **Click back into the document pane to continue writing your document.**

   If you don't want to keep the Footnotes pane open, click the Close button.

A Nose for Newsletters

Before the introduction of the Macintosh launched the desktop publishing revolution, newsletters were produced by ink-stained wretches and paste-up artists. Now, anyone can create a newsletter with a word processor, and Word 2001 has some great tools that help you get your newsletter done in a jiffy (okay, maybe two or three jiffies).

Newsletters can have almost any layout you want, from simple single-column pages to complex multicolumn behemoths with tables of contents, continued-on-page-12 text runs, and embedded images on the page.

Starting with the Newsletter Wizard

Rather than try to lay out the newsletter yourself, I suggest that you let the Word 2001 Newsletter Wizard do the heavy lifting. This Wizard lets you choose from three basic styles of newsletters, and the results are just fine for most people.

To create a newsletter with the Newsletter Wizard, follow these steps:

1. **Choose File⇨Project Gallery.**

   The Project Gallery appears.

2. **Click the Newsletters category.**

3. **From the list of newsletter designs that appear on the right, click the icon for the design you want to use.**

4. **Click OK.**

   A new document window opens, as does the Newsletter Wizard, as shown in Figure 7-8.

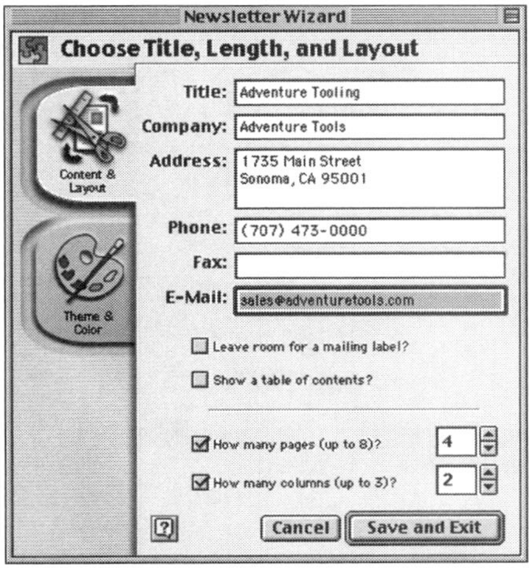

Figure 7-8:
The Content & Layout tab of the Newsletter Wizard.

7. **In the Content & Layout tab of the Newsletter Wizard, enter the information you want to include on the front page of your newsletter. Then decide if you want to leave room for a mailing label, have a table of contents, and set the number of pages and columns for the newsletter.**

8. **Click the Theme & Color tab, and change the Theme and the Color Scheme for the newsletter (optional).**

   Themes are preset font and color schemes that Word 2001 can apply to your documents. Unlike templates, themes can't provide custom toolbars, macros, or shortcut keys; a theme concentrates on changing the look of your document with character and paragraph styles, graphics, and colors. Themes, because they rely so much on colors and background images, tend to be more useful for Web pages than printed documents.

   You can apply Themes to any document, not just ones created by the Newsletter Wizard. Choose Format➪Theme to bring up the Theme dialog box.

9. **Click Save and Exit.**

   Word creates the newsletter, as shown in Figure 7-9.

   In terms of placing items on the page, Word gets things mostly right. But don't be at all surprised if you have to tweak things like font sizes and text boxes to get things exactly where you want them. The Wizards can give you a leg up, but they can't do all the work for you.

Figure 7-9:
The completed newsletter template, as created by the Newsletter Wizard.

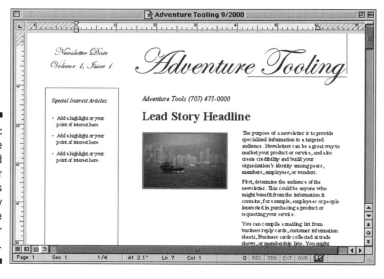

The newsletter consists of a headline, several text boxes where your stories will go, and a few pictures. Notice that the pre-inserted text in the text boxes tells you what to put in each of the text boxes. All you need to do is select the text and replace it with your own headlines, bylines, and stories.

Working with text boxes

For newsletters, Word 2001 uses *linked text boxes* to contain the text in columns. Linked text boxes allow articles to flow continuously across pages. For example, you can have a text box on the first page of your newsletter with the beginning of the story that is linked to another text box on the fourth page that continues and ends the story.

When you add words to the text box, any words in the following text box flow forward. When you delete words from a text box, the words in the following text box move backward.

Think of the text boxes as pipes and the words as water in the pipe. When you add more water to the beginning of the pipe, the water that's already in the pipe flows farther down the pipe.

 You can only see text boxes and their contents in the Page Layout or Online Layout views, so make sure that you've switched to one of those views using the View menu or the buttons at the bottom of the document window.

Creating text boxes

To create a text box, follow these steps:

1. **Choose Insert⇨Text Box.**

   The cursor changes into a crosshair.

2. **Click and drag in the document window to draw a text box.**

   The text box appears, with a thick border and square white handles (the white squares that appear at the corners and the sides of the text box).

3. **Type inside the text box to use it.**

Linking text boxes

To link two text boxes, you must already have two existing text boxes. Follow these steps to link the two boxes:

1. **Click the border of the first text box to select it.**

   A thick border and handles appear around the text box.

2. **Choose View⇨Toolbars⇨Text Box.**

   The Text Box toolbar appears.

3. **Click the Create Text Box Link button on the Text Box toolbar.**

   The cursor changes into a pitcher.

4. **Click in the text box that you want the text to flow to.**

5. **Type in the first text box.**

   As your text fills the box, the excess text flows into the second box, as shown in Figure 7-10.

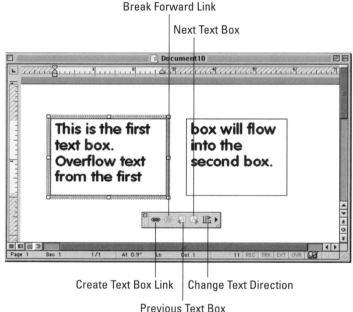

Break Forward Link

Next Text Box

Figure 7-10:
Linking two
text boxes
with the
Text Box
toolbar.

Create Text Box Link Change Text Direction

Previous Text Box

Changing text direction in text boxes

If you've ever wondered how to create vertical text in Word, you've just seen the tool that you need. The Change Text Direction button on the Text Box toolbar changes the orientation of text in 90-degree increments. Just select a text box with some text in it, and click the Change Text Direction button. The text will rotate and flow down from the top of the text box. Clicking the button again makes the text flow up. Check out the different orientations in Figure 7-11.

Deleting text boxes

To delete a text box, click the box's border to select it, and then press the Delete key. The box disappears, along with any text it contains. Deleting a text box that is the destination for a link also deletes that link.

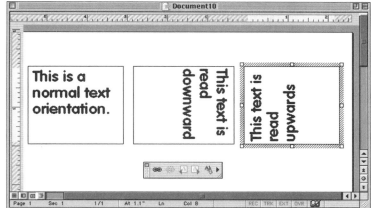

Figure 7-11:
You can
change the
text
direction
using text
boxes.

Sizing and moving text boxes

To resize a text box that you've drawn, follow these steps:

1. **Click inside the text box you want to resize.**
2. **Click and drag one of the text box handles until the text box is the size that you want.**
3. **Release the mouse button.**

To move a text box, follow these steps:

1. **Click inside the text box that you want to move to select it.**
2. **Click and drag on the gray border of the text box, dragging the box to where you want to move it.**

   When you're moving a text box, the cursor becomes a grabber hand. If it is a small box with a two-headed arrow, it means that the mouse is over one of the text box handles. If you drag a text box handle, you resize the text box. Make sure that you see the grabber hand on-screen.
3. **Release the mouse button.**

Adding pictures to your newsletter

Newsletters have more impact with pictures, and Word 2001 allows you to use several kinds of pictures. In fact, Word takes advantage of the graphic filters provided by QuickTime, so Word 2001 can open any sort of graphic file that your version of QuickTime can handle. These file types include

- ✔ A picture from the clip art gallery that comes with Office 2001
- ✔ Graphic formats such as TIFF (often created by scanners), EPSF (Encapsulated Postscript), Photoshop, FlashPix, MacPaint, or PICT

✔ Windows and other computer platform graphic formats such as BMP, DIB, WMF, EMF, SGI, and TGA

✔ Web graphic formats such as GIF, JPEG, or PNG

To add a picture to your document, follow these steps:

1. **Choose Insert⬄Picture.**

2. **Choose one of the following:**

   - **Clip Art:** Lets you choose a picture from the Office 2001 clip art gallery.

   - **From File:** Inserts a graphic from your hard disk.

   - **Horizontal Line:** Inserts a graphic file from a folder of line pictures installed with Office 2001.

   - **AutoShapes:** Lets you choose from the shapes found on the Word 2001 Drawing toolbar.

   - **WordArt:** Lets you add special effects to text.

   - **From Scanner or Camera:** Lets you acquire images directly from a scanner or digital camera hooked up to your computer.

   - **Chart:** Inserts a chart, such as a pie or bar graph.

   Word inserts the picture.

Wrapping words around the pictures

By default, Word inserts pictures as *inline graphics,* which means that the pictures take up space just as lines of text would. You may sometimes want the text near the picture to wrap around the picture rather than have the picture breaking up the text.

To wrap words around pictures, follow these steps:

1. **Put the cursor over the picture around which you want to wrap text.**

2. **Ctrl+click the picture.**

   A pop-up menu appears.

3. **Choose Format Picture from the pop-up menu.**

   The Format Picture dialog box appears, as shown in Figure 7-12.

4. **Click the Layout tab.**

5. **Click one of the options in the Wrapping style area.**

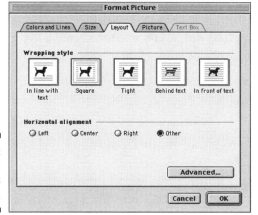

Figure 7-12:
Formatting a
picture's
text wrap.

6. **Click one of the options in the Horizontal alignment area.**

   If you need more control over the amount of text wrap, click the Advanced button, which takes you to a dialog box where you can set the exact distance of the text from the graphic.

7. **Click the Top, Left, Bottom, or Right boxes, and set the amount of distance between the picture and the text that is wrapped around it.**

8. **Click OK.**

   The Format Picture dialog box disappears, and text now wraps around your picture, as shown in Figure 7-13.

Figure 7-13:
Text
wrapped
around a
picture.

Using drop caps

Drop caps are large, initial capital letters you often see in the first word of a paragraph. Drop caps are used for emphasis and to set apart the text on a page. For example, the first letter of the regular text in this chapter is a drop cap.

To create a drop cap, follow these steps:

1. **Click in the paragraph in which you want to create a drop cap.**
2. **Choose Format⇨Drop Cap.**

   The Drop Cap dialog box appears.
3. **Choose a style for the drop cap.**
4. **Click OK.**

   Word creates the drop cap, as shown in Figure 7-14.

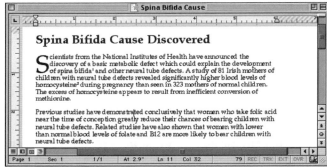

Figure 7-14: The completed drop cap.

Part III
Organizing Your E-Mail and Time with Entourage 2001

The 5th Wave   By Rich Tennant

"I ALWAYS BACK UP EVERYTHING."

In this part . . .

*E*ntourage 2001 is the new program in the Office suite, and it's there to handle your e-mail, calendar, and contacts. Handling e-mail has become a major chore for many people; it's not unusual to meet folks who get hundreds of e-mail messages every day. It's too hard (not to mention time-consuming) to sort all that mail manually, and Entourage provides the tools to speed e-mail handling, allowing you to automatically get rid of junk mail, sort mail you want into folders for easy reading, and manage your Address Book.

E-mail is only one part of time management, and Entourage is ready to handle the rest of the job. You can use Entourage to track your calendar, and prioritize your to-do list. You don't even have to be at your computer to take advantage of Entourage's management; it has two-way synchronization with handheld devices, so your data travels with you.

This part of the book shows you how to use Entourage 2001 to tame your e-mail and handle your time and contacts.

Chapter 8

E-Mail Basics: Reading, Writing, Replying

In This Chapter

▶ Setting up Entourage 2001 for e-mail

▶ Reading your e-mail

▶ Replying to e-mail

▶ Creating and sending new e-mail

▶ Attaching files to your e-mail

▶ Scheduling your e-mail

*A*lthough the World Wide Web is the Internet service that gets all the attention, the true killer application of the Net is *electronic mail,* also known as *e-mail.* The almost instant communication e-mail provides has revolutionized the business world to an even greater extent than the adoption of fax machines in the 1980s. For many businesses, not having access to e-mail is now nearly unthinkable. Personal use of e-mail has lagged behind that of businesses, but not by much. In my family, for example, nearly everybody has access to e-mail at home or at work, and my son can exchange e-mail with two of his three grandparents. Even my cat has an e-mail address (and a Web page, but we're more than a little extreme).

The newest addition to Office 2001, Microsoft Entourage, recognizes the importance of e-mail and time management in today's offices. The program enables you to send and receive e-mail for multiple Internet accounts (but not America Online accounts), and you can also use it to read Usenet newsgroups. In addition, Entourage is a full-featured Personal Information Manager (PIM), allowing you to track your contacts, appointments, tasks, and notes (for more information about Entourage's PIM features, see Chapter 10). If you share your computer with a co-worker or with another family member, each person can have his or her own setup in Entourage.

Entourage 2001 is built on the sturdy bones of Outlook Express 5.0, Microsoft's popular (and free) e-mail program. Entourage shares most of Outlook Express's e-mail capabilities (adding relatively minor improvements), beefing up the free program with a better Address Book, and adding Calendar, Tasks, and Notes sections.

Setting Up Entourage for E-mail

The main Entourage window makes reading and managing your e-mail easy, as you can see in Figure 8-1. Starting from the left side of the window and moving clockwise, you first see the *Folder list,* which contains your Inbox, Outbox, and the folders you create to file your e-mail. Also in the Folder list, you'll find icons for the Address Book, Calendar, Tasks list, and Notes. At the top of the window is the *toolbar,* which has buttons that enable you to perform common tasks. The *Message list,* below the toolbar, shows the messages in the Inbox or any other folder you're viewing. Below the message list is the *Preview pane.* Clicking the title of a message in the Message list displays the contents of the message in the Preview pane.

Before you can start getting your e-mail, you have to tell Entourage about your e-mail account (or accounts, if you have more than one). If you're accessing the Internet by using the company network, you can get this information from your network administrator. If you're logging on from home, your Internet Service Provider (ISP) should give you this information when you sign up for your account. Here's the information you need:

- ✔ **Your name.** You know what it is. If not, check your driver's license.

- ✔ **Your e-mail address.** People use this address to send e-mail to you — usually some form of your name, followed by @, and then followed by the domain name of your company or organization, which is something like microsoft.com or pbs.org.

- ✔ **The name of your organization or company.** (This information is optional.)

- ✔ **The SMTP server name.** The *SMTP server* is the computer that gets mail from you and sends it to other computers on the Internet.

- ✔ **Your account ID.** This information is the name of your e-mail mailbox. The ID is usually (but not always) the same as the first part of your e-mail address (the part before the @).

- ✔ **The POP server name.** The *POP server* is the computer that receives mail for you and holds it until you pick up the mail.

- ✔ **Your e-mail password.** Your password is the secret word that identifies you to the POP server.

Standard mail folders

Folder list

PIM icons   Toolbar   Message list

Figure 8-1:
The main
Entourage
window.

Hotmail icon   Preview pane

Custom mail folders

Choose your password carefully because anyone who has your password can pick up your e-mail. Good passwords are at least six characters long, and they contain, ideally, both letters and numbers. Make sure that you don't choose easy-to-guess passwords — the names of your spouse or children, your address, or the like. And for goodness sake, don't use *secret* as your password; hackers in grade school know that one. Changing your password from time to time is also a good idea.

Follow these steps to set up your e-mail account:

1. **Launch Entourage by double-clicking its icon on the desktop.**

2. **Choose Tools⇨Accounts.**

    The Accounts window appears.

3. Click New.

The New Account dialog box appears. Choose POP from the Account type pop-up menu.

4. Click OK.

The Edit Account dialog box appears, as shown in Figure 8-2.

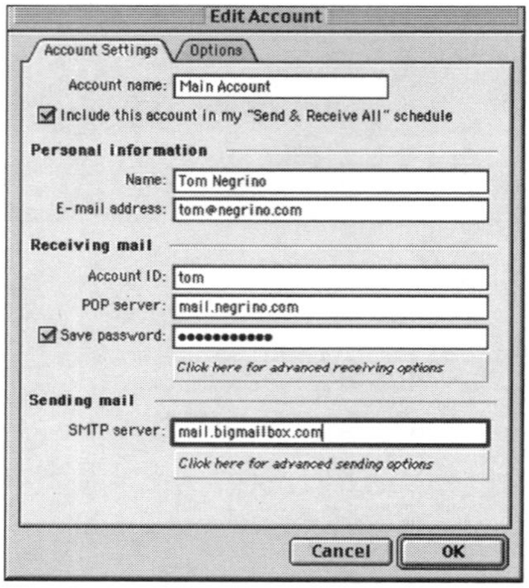

Figure 8-2: Setting up your e-mail account in the Edit Account dialog box.

5. Enter the Account name.

The Account Name box gives this mail setup a name so that you can easily switch between different accounts (if you have more than one).

6. In the Personal information section, enter your Name. If the Name box is blank, type your first and last name in it; if another name appears in the box, highlight that name and replace it with your name.

Your name may be in this box already because Entourage is smart enough to get the name from your Macintosh's Users and Groups control panel.

7. Type your e-mail address (with the @ sign in it) in the E-mail address box.

If you don't know your address, refer to the account information you got from your network administrator or ISP.

8. In the Receiving mail area, type your account name in the Account ID box.

9. **Type the name of your POP server in the POP server box.**

POP stands for *Post Office Protocol.* The POP server is the machine that accepts mail from other people and holds it for you. Although it may seem strange that one machine sends mail and another machine receives mail, that arrangement is just part of the inexplicable weirdness of the Internet.

10. **If you want Entourage to remember your password, click the Save Password check box and then type your password in the adjacent text box.**

To shield your password from potentially prying eyes, a line of bullets appears in the text box rather than what you type.

If you don't enter your password in the Preferences dialog box, you'll be asked for your password every time you get your e-mail.

If you share your computer with other people or work in a place where your computer isn't secure, *not* saving your password probably is a good idea. By saving your password, you're making it easy for anyone who sits at your computer to send and receive e-mail in your name. Imagine the mischief that someone could cause by sending a nastygram to your boss from your e-mail account.

11. **In the Sending mail section, type the SMTP server information in the text box.**

SMTP stands for *Simple Mail Transfer Protocol;* the SMTP server is the machine that takes mail from you and sends it to the rest of the Internet.

12. **Click the OK button to save the information.**

Congratulations! You're done setting up your e-mail account.

Working with E-Mail

Now that you've set up an e-mail account in Entourage, it's time to get to work. To work with your e-mail, you don't have to be connected to the Internet (although, of course, you have to connect to send and receive your mail) — you can read incoming mail, create outgoing messages, and save those messages in your Outbox until you're ready to connect. Then Entourage connects to your Internet Service Provider (ISP) and fires off all the messages. If you work in an office and your Macintosh is on a network, you don't have to worry about dialing up the Internet, because your network is always connected.

Where are my e-mail and calendar files?

Unlike some other e-mail programs, Entourage 2001 doesn't keep each of your e-mail messages as separate files on your hard disk. For technical reasons, that approach makes handling e-mail too slow to be practical. Instead, Entourage keeps all of your messages as entries in a big mail database. Similarly, that same database holds all of your Calendar, Tasks, and Notes entries.

Entourage keeps its data files inside a folder called Microsoft User Data, which is inside the Documents folder on your hard disk. When you arrange to back up your hard disk, you should always make sure that the Microsoft User Data folder is contained in the backup set.

Reading your e-mail

E-mail that other people send to you is stored on your mail server (the POP server) until you tell Entourage to retrieve it. Entourage dials up your ISP, retrieves your mail, and places it in your Inbox, ready for you to read.

To retrieve and read your e-mail, follow these steps:

1. **Do one of the following things:**

   • Choose Tools⇨Send & Receive⇨Send & Receive All.

   • Click the Send & Receive toolbar button.

   If you connect to your ISP via a modem, you should hear the modem dial and connect (though it's possible to mute the modem's sound with a setting in the Modem control panel). When you're connected, you should see a brief progress dialog box as Entourage retrieves your mail from the mail server. If you have mail, the name of your Inbox in the Folder list appears in boldface, indicating that you have unread mail.

2. **Click the Inbox in the Folder list.**

   In the Message list, Entourage displays the subjects of the messages, the senders, and when the messages were sent.

3. **Click one of the messages to read it in the Preview pane.**

   If the Preview pane isn't big enough, you can resize the window or double-click a message title to display the message in its own window.

4. **To move to the next message, click that message's title or press the down-arrow key on the keyboard.**

When you read an e-mail message in the Preview pane, a bar appears at the top of the pane, showing the sender's name and sometimes his e-mail address (the From field), the recipient's names and e-mail addresses (the To field), and the message subject (the Subject field). Below the bar is the body of the message, as shown in Figure 8-3. If you display the message in a separate window, you see similar address information.

If the e-mail is from someone with whom you think you'll be corresponding with in the future, now is a good time to add that person's name and e-mail address to the Entourage Address Book. To add the sender's address of the opened e-mail message to your Address Book, choose Tools⇔Add to Address Book, or press ⌘+= (⌘ and the equal sign).

Replying to your e-mail

After reading an e-mail message, you will often want to reply. To reply to an e-mail message, follow these steps:

1. **In the Folder list, click the folder that contains the message to which you want to reply.**

   Usually, this folder is your Inbox. The titles of the messages in the folder appear in the Message list.

Subject field · Message body · Sender's name · Recipient's name

Figure 8-3: Reading an e-mail message in the Preview pane.

2. **In the Message list, click the e-mail message to which you want to reply.**

3. **Click the Reply or Reply All toolbar button.**

   You should use Reply All when the original message was also sent to other people and you want everybody to get a copy of your reply. Clicking the Reply button sends your reply to only the person listed in the From field.

   The Message dialog box appears, displaying a copy of the original message in the message window, along with the recipient's e-mail address.

4. **Type your reply.**

5. **Click the Send Now button.**

Entourage sends your e-mail. If you click the Send Later button, Entourage stores your message in its Outbox, and the message will be sent the next time you choose Send & Receive All.

 If you begin writing a message, and then want to save your incomplete work and continue writing it at a later time, you want to save the message as a Draft. To do this, choose File⇨Save while you have the incomplete message's window open. The message will be saved in the Drafts folder. Later, you can open up the message, complete it, and click Send Now or Send Later.

Forwarding e-mail

If you receive a message you want to send on to someone else, Entourage enables you to forward it. To forward your e-mail, follow these steps:

1. **Select a message in the Message list.**

   The text of the message appears in the Preview pane.

2. **Click the Forward toolbar button, choose Message⇨Forward, or press ⌘+J.**

   A new message appears, with the contents of the message you are forwarding already entered in the message body.

3. **Enter the recipient's e-mail address in the Address box.**

4. **In the message body, add any text you want to send along with the forwarded message.**

5. **Click the Send button.**

   The next time you send and receive e-mail, the message is forwarded.

Creating and sending new e-mail

To write a new e-mail message, follow these steps:

1. **Choose File⇨New⇨Mail Message, click the New toolbar button, or press ⌘+N.**

   An untitled Message dialog box opens, as shown in Figure 8-4. The insertion point is in the To field, ready for you to begin addressing the message.

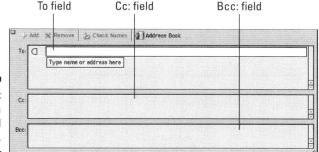

Figure 8-4: Creating a new e-mail message.

2. **Begin typing the name of the person to whom you are sending the e-mail.**

   As you type, Entourage pops up a list of e-mail addresses that match what you have typed so far. You can continue typing to narrow the list, or you can use the arrow keys to make a selection. People with multiple e-mail addresses will show an arrow at the right border of the list, and selecting that will pop out a hierarchical menu with the rest of their e-mail addresses. Press the Return or Enter keys to accept an e-mail address and enter it into the To field.

3. **If you want to send a copy of your message to someone other than the primary recipient, type that person's name in the Cc (carbon copy) field.**

   If you want to send a copy of a message to a person without that person's name or address appearing in the recipient list, you can make an entry in the Bcc (blind carbon copy) field. In other words, the people listed in the To and Cc fields won't know that you sent a copy of your message to anybody listed in the Bcc field.

4. **Enter the names of your Bcc recipients (if any).**

5. **In the Subject field, type the subject of your e-mail message.**

6. **Type your message in the message body.**

   As you type, Entourage automatically checks your spelling. If you make a mistake, the incorrect word gets marked with a wavy red underline. To correct the error, hold down the Control key and click the incorrect word. A list of suggestions appears, as shown in Figure 8-5. Choose one of the suggestions, or choose Add to add a correct but unknown word to your custom user dictionary (which is shared by the other Office 2001 applications, by the way).

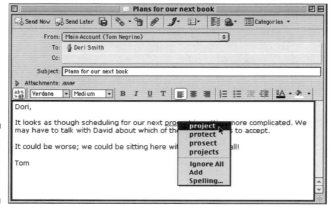

Figure 8-5:
Correcting a
spelling
error.

7. **Use the Formatting toolbar to change the appearance of the text in your message, if you want.**

   The text is formatted as HTML, which has its good and bad points. The good part is that you can format your message in much the same way as you would in a word processor, with fonts, in bold, italic, or even colored type. The bad part is that your nicely formatted message looks horrible to any recipient whose mail program doesn't understand HTML-formatted text, because your words are surrounded by the HTML formatting tags. My advice: Unless you're sure that all your recipients can handle HTML-formatted e-mail, turn off the formatting by making sure there's no check mark next to Format⇨HTML.

8. **Send or save your mail.**

   To send your message immediately, click the Send Now button, choose Message⇨Send Message Now, or press ⌘+K. Entourage connects to the Internet and sends your mail on its way.

   If you prefer to save your message and send it later, click the Save button, choose File⇨Save, or press ⌘+S.

9. **When you finish writing all your messages, click the Send & Receive toolbar button to have Entourage send all the mail in your Outbox and receive any e-mail that's waiting for you.**

Attaching a file

You can send any sort of a Macintosh file along with an e-mail message by attaching the file to the message. If you're working on a report in Word 2001 and want to share that report with a co-worker, you can e-mail the Word document to your friend. To attach a file to an e-mail message, follow these steps:

1. **Create a new e-mail message.**

2. **Write and address a new message as you normally would.**

3. **Click the disclosure triangle to open the Attachments area.**

4. **Click the Add button.**

   The Open file dialog box appears. Navigate to the file's location, select it, then click the Choose button.

   You can also add file attachments by dragging their icons from the Finder into the Attachments area.

5. **Repeat Step 4 until you have added all the files you want to attach.**

6. **Click the Done button.**

   The icons of the files you attached appear in the Attachments area.

7. **Send the message.**

Encoding and compressing

Clicking the button underneath the Attachments area allows you to set the encoding for the attached file and whether or not it is compressed, as shown in Figure 8-6. Encoding is the format that the file must be translated into in order to be sent over the Internet. Because Macintoshes and Windows machines encode files differently, you are best off to click the button marked Any computer (AppleDouble). The AppleDouble format is specifically designed to be read easily by both Mac and Windows e-mail programs.

The Compression area gives you the choices of None (no compression of the files) or Macintosh (using the popular StuffIt compression format, created by Aladdin Systems). Compression uses a mathematical algorithm to shrink the size of files, thereby making them take less time to

transmit. If you add or drag files into the Attachments area separately, they will be encoded, but not compressed (unless you specifically turn compression on). If you add or drag a Macintosh folder into the Attachments area, compression will be automatically turned on. Although the StuffIt format is primarily a Mac format, Windows users can use it too, by downloading the free Aladdin Expander from www.aladdinsys.com.

The Compatibility & Efficiency area has a check box that lets you add Windows file extensions to the names of Mac files, so that they will be more likely to be openable on Windows machines. There's also another check box that lets you choose whether you want to send the file attachments to the Cc and Bcc recipients.

Figure 8-6:
Setting
encoding
and
compression
options for
your file
attachments.

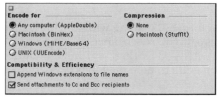

Receiving file attachments

You can recognize an e-mail message with an attached file because the Attachments symbol, which looks like a paper clip, appears next to the message title in your Inbox. The Attachments pane of the e-mail message will include a list of files attached to the message. The list will detail the file name and size for each attachment. From the Attachments pane, you can open the attachment, save it to a folder on your computer, or remove it from the e-mail message.

To handle a received file attachment, follow these steps:

1. **Open the message that contains the attachment.**

   If the Attachments pane is hidden, click its disclosure triangle to open it.

2. **Click once on the attachment to select it.**

3. **Depending on what you want to do, click the Open, Save, or Remove buttons.**

   Open will launch a program capable of reading the attachment; Save will open a dialog box that will allow you to specify where you want to put the attachment; Remove will delete the attachment.

Deleting e-mail

By default, Entourage saves (in the Sent Mail folder) a copy of every message you send. After awhile, that folder can accumulate a huge number of messages, and you may want to get rid of some of them. To delete messages you no longer want, follow these steps:

1. **In the Folder list, click the folder that contains the messages you want to delete.**

   The messages in the folder appear in the Message list.

2. **Select the messages you want to delete.**

   To select a range of messages, Shift+click the messages. To select discontiguous messages in the list, ⌘+click each message.

3. **Click the Delete toolbar button (it looks like a trash can).**

   Entourage moves the message to the Deleted Messages folder.

The message isn't irretrievably gone yet, however. If you made a mistake and want to get a message back, click the Deleted Messages folder, click the title of the message you want to retrieve, and then drag the message back to the folder it came from.

By default, Entourage empties the Deleted Messages folder when the messages in them are seven days old (but you can change that by modifying the Empty Deleted Items Folder item in the Schedules window). After that folder has been emptied, you have no way to get your mail back.

Using Schedules

Entourage 2001 uses Schedules to automate the sending and receiving of e-mail. You can also set up schedules for certain tasks, such as emptying the Deleted Items folder. Entourage comes with three schedules already created for you:

- ✔ **Send & Receive All:** Sends all e-mail in the Outbox and receives e-mail from all active e-mail accounts.
- ✔ **Send All:** Sends all e-mail in the Outbox.
- ✔ **Empty Deleted Items Folder:** Gets rid of deleted mail messages.

You can also set up schedules that you only activate when you're traveling. For example, if you have a fast Internet connection at home, but on the road you're limited to a slower modem connection, you can set up a travel schedule that will not download large files, saving on connect time.

Modifying an existing schedule

Before showing you how to create a new schedule, let's get started by changing one of the existing schedules. We'll change the Empty Deleted Items Folder schedule to allow deleted items to hang around a little longer, and to get rid of deleted items when you quit Entourage.

To modify a schedule, follow these steps:

1. **Choose Tools⇨Schedules.**

   The Schedules window opens, as shown in Figure 8-7.

Figure 8-7:
The
Schedules
window.

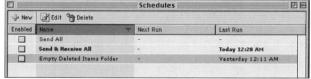

2. **Double-click the Empty Deleted Items Folder schedule.**

   The Edit Schedule dialog box appears, as shown in Figure 8-8.

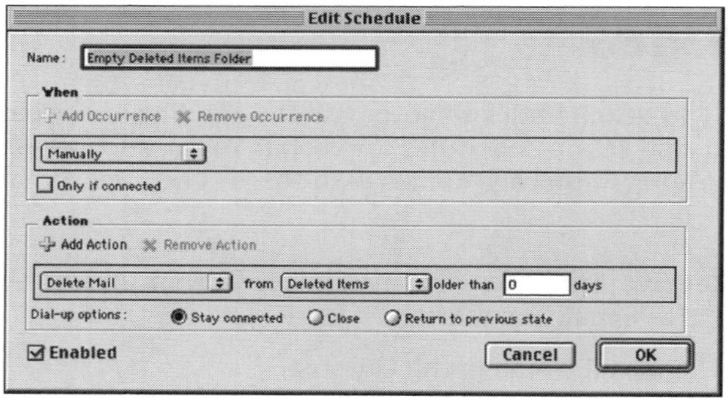

Figure 8-8:
Modifying a
schedule in
the Edit
Schedule
window.

3. **In the When section, change the pop-up menu from Manually to On Quit.**

4. **In the Action section, leave the pop-up menus set to Delete Mail and Deleted Items, but in the field next to days, change the 0 to 10.**

5. **If it isn't already checked, click the Enabled button.**

6. **Click OK.**

Changing the timing of a schedule

In the When section of the Edit Schedule dialog box, there are six choices under the Occurrence pop-up menu:

- ✔ **Manually:** The schedule executes only when triggered via Tools⇨Run Schedule.
- ✔ **At Startup:** The schedule executes when Entourage starts up.
- ✔ **On Quit:** The schedule executes when Entourage quits.
- ✔ **Timed Schedule:** The schedule executes at specified days, hours, and times, as shown in Figure 8-9.
- ✔ **Repeating Schedule:** The schedule executes at a specified interval of minutes, hours, or days.
- ✔ **Recurring:** The schedule uses Entourage's Recurring Schedule interface (the same as recurring calendar events).

Figure 8-9:
The Timed Schedule options. Click the buttons to set the days and times that you want the schedule to run.

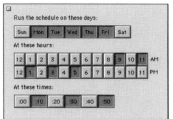

Chapter 9

Taming Your E-Mail with Folders and Rules

*T*he blessings of e-mail are many: almost instant communication with colleagues, family, and friends; easy ability to plan and run business events; and, of course, endless opportunities for workplace humor. One of the drawbacks to e-mail is the sheer amount of it; it can be horrifyingly difficult to find a particular piece of e-mail when you want to retrieve it. One of the ways that Entourage allows you to sort and categorize your mail is by classifying it into folders (and subfolders). Entourage also has good search tools that can help you find e-mail based on any number of criteria.

Another blight upon e-mail is unsolicited commercial e-mail (UCE), often known as *spam.* Practically as soon as you open an e-mail account, you can expect to start getting unwanted and unasked-for pitches for exciting (and bogus) business opportunities, offers to sell you a trillion e-mail addresses (so you can become a spammer yourself), and come-ons for steaming hot pornography (which turn out to be, well, pornography). You might think that it would be easy to block this deluge, but it can be surprisingly tricky. After all, this is e-mail that is addressed to you, and that's what e-mail programs are supposed to do — deliver the mail. The trick is to try to screen out the mail that you want from the mail that you detest. Better e-mail programs let you apply rules (also called *filters* in some programs) to incoming mail; these rules test each message to see if it passes. If it does, the mail drops into your Inbox or is sorted into your mail folders. Rejected mail ends up in the trash, or if you prefer, in a holding cell, ready for you to pass final judgment.

Microsoft Entourage has an arsenal of weapons to help you handle your onslaught of e-mail. This chapter shows you how to employ folders, filters, and search tools to effectively manage the mail flow.

File Messages in Folders

Just as file folders on your desk help you organize your paper documents, folders in Entourage organize your e-mail messages. Entourage gives you a head start by automatically creating the following folders:

- **Inbox:** Incoming mail goes here by default.
- **Outbox:** Mail waiting to be sent takes a pit stop in this folder.
- **Sent Items:** Entourage automatically puts mail that you send here.
- **Drafts:** Partially written e-mail that you've saved to finish later waits for its big moment in this folder.
- **Deleted Items:** Messages that you have thrown away rest here before they are thrown away for good.

Entourage also allows you to create custom folders (and subfolders) so that you can file your mail in categories that make the most sense to you and the way that you work. Regardless of whether the folders are ones you created or ones that Entourage created, all folders appear in the Folder list on the left side of the Entourage window, as shown in Figure 9-1.

Creating a custom mail folder

To create a custom mail folder, follow these steps:

1. **Choose File⇨New⇨Folder, click and hold the New button on the tool-bar and choose Folder from the resulting pop-up menu, or press ⌘+Shift+N.**

   The new folder will appear in the Folder list, with the name "untitled folder."

2. **Type in the name of the new folder.**

Custom folders

Figure 9-1:
The
Entourage
window,
with the
Folder list at
the left.

Subfolders

3. **Press the Return key.**

   Folders will appear in the Folder list in alphabetical order but below the folders automatically created by Entourage.

   Just as in the Finder, you can make custom mail folders float to the top of the Folder list (but still below the folders automatically created by Entourage) by using tricks such as adding a blank space before the name of the folder, or using an asterisk as the first character in the folder name.

Creating a subfolder

To create a subfolder of an existing mail folder, follow these steps:

1. **Select the folder for which you want to make a subfolder.**

2. **Choose File➪New➪Subfolder, or click and hold the New button on the toolbar and choose Subfolder from the resulting pop-up menu.**

   The new subfolder will appear in the Folder list indented under its parent folder, with the name "untitled folder."

3. **Type in the name of the new folder.**

4. **Press the Return key.**

Moving folders

To make a custom mail folder into a subfolder, drag it to another folder. If you want to turn a subfolder into a top-level folder, drag the subfolder up to the Folder list header and release the mouse button. The subfolder will be promoted up a level to a top-level folder.

Renaming and deleting folders

To rename a folder, click to select it, click into the folder name to highlight it, type the new name, and then press the Return key. To delete a folder, click to select it, then click the Delete button on the toolbar, or choose Edit⇨Delete Folder.

Filing mail in folders

The easiest way to file your incoming mail is to simply drag it from the Inbox to one of your custom mail folders. Dragging a message from one folder to another moves the entire message (including any attachments the message has). If you would prefer for some reason to copy a message into a second folder, leaving the original message in the original folder, hold down the Option key while dragging the message from the first folder to the destination folder.

Don't be afraid to create as many custom folders as you need to properly organize your e-mail. There's obviously a point of diminishing returns if you have too many mail folders, because you can actually have so many subcategories that you begin to forget where you want each kind of your mail to go. However, a reasonable amount of organization can be a tremendous help. For example, I have a main folder called Book Projects, and every time I start writing a new book, I create a new subfolder inside Book Projects, labeled with the name of the new book. Then I create a set of mail Rules that automatically sort incoming mail from my book's editor into the book's subfolder. And I also put all the mail I send to my editor into the same folder. You'll see how to create mail Rules in the next section.

Ruling Your E-Mail

One of the most useful capabilities in Entourage is its facility for filtering e-mail, called Rules. *Mail filters* enable you to automatically trash unwanted mail, sort and prioritize mail as it comes in, and even add people to your Address Book. Entourage also lets you apply Rules to your outgoing mail, which is great for automatically filing messages you send. After you start using Rules, you'll wonder how you ever got along without them. Trust me. This section shows you how to create several useful Rules and how to use Entourage's other filtering tools to make your e-mail life easier.

Using the Junk Mail Filter

The first line of defense in controlling your e-mail should be to try to get rid of junk mail so that it doesn't bother you and waste your time. To do so, you should enable Entourage's Junk Mail Filter. This feature scans the *headers* (the normally hidden routing information) of incoming e-mail to try to figure out whether the mail is spam. For example, spammers don't want to be tracked down, so most mail that comes from spammers puts false information in the From field of the e-mail. The Junk Mail Filter looks for telltale signs of a forged From header (as well as other spam spoor) and nabs offending messages.

To enable the Junk Mail Filter:

1. **Choose Tools⇨Junk Mail Filter.**

   The Junk Mail Filter window opens, as shown in Figure 9-2.

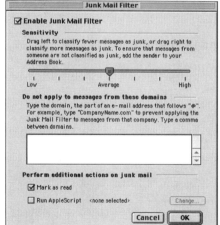

Figure 9-2:
Fighting
spam with
the Junk
Mail Filter.

2. **Make sure that the Enable Junk Mail Filter check box is on.**

3. **The Sensitivity slider will work fine for most people at the Average setting, which is the default.**

   Over time, if too much junk is getting through, nudge the Sensitivity up a notch until you're pleased with the result.

The Junk Mail Filter works pretty well, but it isn't perfect. Sometimes it errs on the side of junkiness, classifying mail as junk that's really just mail from unfamiliar correspondents. To make sure that the filter doesn't mistakenly flag mail as junk that you want, just add the sender of that message to your Address Book.

Once the Junk Mail Filter has identified spam for you, you can act upon it with a mail Rule. That's an important point to remember: Incoming mail passes through the Junk Mail Filter before any of the user-specified Rules, so you can manipulate messages that Entourage has decided are junk.

Using a Rule to add people to your Address Book

Suppose that you work regularly with people at a particular company. While writing this book, for example, I got a great deal of e-mail from some of the people at IDG Books. Because I wanted to make sure that all those people are in my Address Book, I set up a Rule to do the job automatically.

To create a Rule to add people to your Address Book, follow these steps:

1. **Choose Tools⇨Rules.**

   The Rules window appears.

2. **Click the New button, and then select Mail (POP).**

   The Edit Rule dialog box appears, as shown in Figure 9-3.

Criteria (If section)   Actions (Then section)

| Edit Rule |

Rule name: untitled

If
⊹ Add Criterion ✖ Remove Criterion Execute actions [if any criteria are met ⬍]

[All messages ⬍]

Then
⊹ Add Action ✖ Remove Action

[Change status ⬍] [Not junk mail ⬍]

[Set category ⬍] [None ⬍]

☑ Do not apply other rules to messages that meet these criteria

☑ Enabled   [Cancel] [**OK**]

Figure 9-3:
Creating a
mail Rule.

3. **In the first text box, type the name you want to use for the Rule.**

4. **In the If section, make sure that From and Contains are selected in the pop-up menus for the first criterion.**

   Note that if you want to add another factor for the Rule to match, you can click the Add Criterion button.

5. **Type in the box to the right of the two pop-up menus the domain name used by the people you want to add to your Address Book.**

   When I set up this rule, I used the domain name idgbooks.com, although you'll probably want to use something else. Notice that you put in everything to the right of the @ symbol in an e-mail address.

6. **Leave the Execute actions pop-up menu set to if any criteria are met.**

7. **In the Then section, choose Add sender to Address Book from the first Action's pop-up menu.**

8. **From the second Action's pop-up menu, choose Change priority, and when the priority pop-up menu appears, choose High.**

   This step is mainly here as an example of multiple Actions in one Rule; there's no requirement for it. It would make sense that you would want to make messages from important people a High priority, however. If you want to add another Action, click the Add Action button.

9. **Leave the Do not apply other rules to messages that meet these criteria check box checked.**

10. **Make sure that the Enabled check box is checked.**

    The completed Rule should look something like the one shown in Figure 9-4.

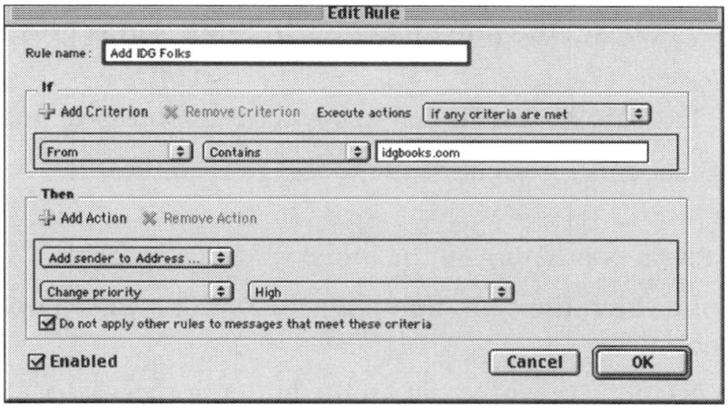

Figure 9-4:
The
completed
mail Rule.

```
┌──────────────────────── Edit Rule ────────────────────────┐
│  Rule name : [ Add IDG Folks                            ]  │
│  ┌─ If ─────────────────────────────────────────────────┐ │
│  │ ⊹ Add Criterion  ✖ Remove Criterion   Execute actions [ if any criteria are met  ▼] │ │
│  │ [ From        ▼] [ Contains    ▼] [ idgbooks.com            ] │ │
│  └──────────────────────────────────────────────────────┘ │
│  ┌─ Then ───────────────────────────────────────────────┐ │
│  │ ⊹ Add Action  ✖ Remove Action                         │ │
│  │ [ Add sender to Address ... ▼]                        │ │
│  │ [ Change priority      ▼] [ High                    ▼] │ │
│  │ ☑ Do not apply other rules to messages that meet these criteria │ │
│  └──────────────────────────────────────────────────────┘ │
│  ☑ Enabled                        [ Cancel ] [  OK  ]     │
└────────────────────────────────────────────────────────────┘
```

11. **Click the OK button to save the new Rule.**

12. **Top off your efforts by switching to your Inbox and clicking the Priority button (the one that looks like an exclamation point) to sort the Inbox by Priority.**

    Clicking the button toggles between sorting in ascending or decending order; to make the Highest priority messages appear at the top of your Inbox, sort in decending order.

Subsequently, whenever you get mail from someone at the domain you put in the Rule, that person's address is automatically added to your Address Book, and they show up at the top of your Inbox. Cool, huh?

Sorting your mail to folders

Because the people in your Address Book generally are people with whom you've already exchanged mail, it makes sense that mail from these folks is a higher priority than mail from people you don't know. You can create a Rule that sorts mail from people in your Address Book into a particular mail folder. To create this filter, follow these steps:

1. **Choose File⇨New⇨Folder to create a new folder, and name it.**

   I named my folder People I Know, but you can name yours whatever you want.

2. **Choose Tools⇨Rules.**

   The Rules window appears.

3. **Click the New button.**

   The Edit Rule dialog box appears.

4. **In the first text box, type the name you want to use for the Rule.**

5. **In the If section, set the pop-up menus to From and Is in Address Book.**

6. **Leave the Execute actions if any criteria are met pop-up menu as it is.**

7. **In the Then section, choose Move message from the first Action pop-up menu.**

   A pop-up menu containing all the folder names appears.

8. **Choose from the folder pop-up menu the folder you created and named in Step 1.**

   If the pop-up menu doesn't contain the folder you created, choose Choose folder from the pop-up menu. The Choose Folder dialog box appears, as shown in Figure 9-5. Select the folder, and then click the Choose button.

9. **Click the OK button to save the new Rule.**

Filtering messages out with Rules

You can use mail Rules to manipulate junk mail so that it goes straight into Entourage's Deleted Items folder, or you can do what I do: Because the Junk Mail Filter isn't perfect, I have a folder called Possible Junk that serves as a

junk mail purgatory. I use other Rules to make sure that mail from people I
know goes to my Inbox or my custom folders, and mail caught by the Junk
Mail Filter goes to Possible Junk so I can decide if it needs to be deleted or
has been unfairly maligned.

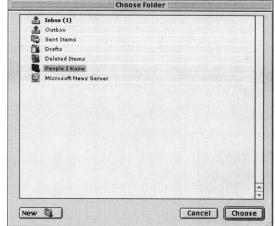

Figure 9-5:
Selecting a
folder for
moved
messages.

To create a mail Rule to send junk to the folder of your choice, follow these
steps:

1. **Choose Tools⇨Rules.**

2. **Click New.**

3. **In the Edit Rule dialog box, give the Rule you're making a name.**

4. **In the If section, choose Is junk mail from the pop-up menu.**

5. **In the Then section, choose Move message from the pop-up menu.**

6. **From the new pop-up menu that appears to the right, choose the
   folder that you want to move the junk mail to.**

7. **Select the second Action by clicking it, and then click the Remove
   Action button.**

8. **Click OK to save the Rule.**

Mail Rules are applied in order, beginning at the top of the Rules list. If it
appears that a Rule you create isn't working, it might be because another,
higher Rule is dealing with the mail before it gets to the Rule you're working
on. If a Rule catches a message, the message stops being processed. For that
reason, you want the mail that is least important to you to be caught by Rules
at the top of the stack, and you want your most important mail to make it
down toward the bottom of the Rules. To reorder the Rules in the Rules
window, select a Rule and drag it up or down in the list.

Using the Mailing List Manager

A special type of e-mail that many people get is from mailing lists. Mailing lists are bulk mail, but good bulk mail; there are mailing lists on virtually every subject you can name, from auto racing to your favorite musical artist. Entourage's Mailing List Manager helps you deal efficiently with the special needs of mailing lists. You'll usually want one Mailing List Rule for each list.

To set up the Mailing List Manager to handle list mail, follow these steps:

1. **Select a mail message that you've received from the mailing list.**

2. **Choose Tools⇨Mailing List Manager.**

   The main Mailing List Manager window appears, as shown in Figure 9-6.

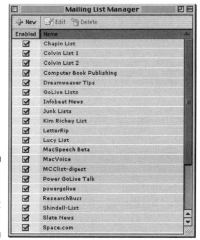

Figure 9-6:
The Mailing
List
Manager.

3. **Click New.**

   The Edit Mailing List Rule window appears.

4. **Entourage has given the new Mailing List Rule a name (it uses the list's address), but you'll probably want to change it to something a bit more descriptive.**

5. **The program also fills in the list address (that's why you highlighted a list message before you began). Don't change this.**

6. **Choose the destination folder for the list mail from the File messages in folder pop-up menu.**

   You might want to apply the regular Rules to list messages, but most people won't need to do anything other than file list messages in a folder where they're easily read. If you agree, leave the Do not apply rules to list messages check box active, as shown in Figure 9-7.

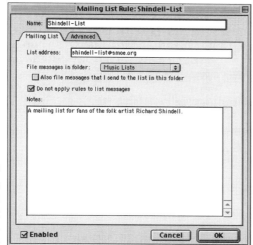

Figure 9-7:
The finished
Mailing List
Rule.

7. **You can optionally add a note about the mailing list.**

   This note area is a good place to copy and paste the "How to get off this mailing list" message that virtually every mailing list sends you when you first join.

8. **Click OK.**

On the Advanced tab of the Mailing List Rule window, there are other useful actions you can take with mailing list messages, including changing message color and specifying whether your replies to the list go to the sender of the message privately, or to the list as a whole.

Searching for E-Mail (Or Anything Else)

Information does you no good if you can't find it. And not being able to find an e-mail message when you need it is practically the same as not having it at all. When you consider that people who get only a moderate amount of e-mail can receive and file more than 10,000 messages per year, an e-mail program needs some serious search tools. Luckily, Entourage is up to the task with its Advanced Find feature. This feature not only allows you to search through e-mail messages, but also through contacts, calendar events, tasks, and notes.

Since a key to efficient searching is often figuring out what you don't want to search through (in other words, narrowing your search), Entourage allows you to limit your search to a particular folder (and its subfolders, if you want). Or if you prefer, you can search all your folders at once, if you don't mind the search taking a while.

You can also set any number of search criteria, based on any of Entourage's usual criteria (you became familiar with those while setting up mail Rules). You can also specify that the search is only valid if any criteria are met, if all criteria are met, unless any criteria are met, or unless all criteria are met.

To perform a search in Entourage, follow these steps:

1. **Choose Edit➪Advanced Find, or press ⌘+Shift+F.**

   The Advanced Find window appears, as shown in Figure 9-8 (though oddly, its title is only Find).

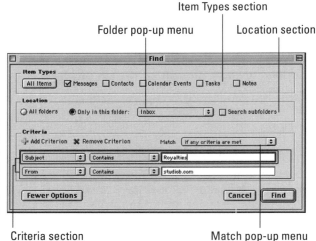

Item Types section

Folder pop-up menu

Location section

Figure 9-8:
The
Advanced
Find
window.

Criteria section

Match pop-up menu

You can certainly choose Find instead of Advanced Find, but the latter is vastly more powerful and probably what you want to be using most of the time. Feel free to experiment with the regular Find, however.

1. **In the Item Types section, click the check boxes next to the kinds of Entourage information in which you wish to search.**

2. **In the Location section, click the button next to All folders or the one next to Only in this folder. If you choose the latter, pick a folder in which you wish to search from the Folder pop-up menu. Click the Search subfolders button if that's what you also want to do.**

3. **In the first criterion, make your choices from the pop-up menus, and if necessary enter text for which you wish to search.**

4. **Click the Add Criterion button (optional).**

5. **Repeat Steps 4 and 5 as needed (optional).**

6. **Click Find.**

   The Search Results window appears, as shown in Figure 9-9. Found items will appear in the top pane; clicking one of the items will display it in the bottom pane.

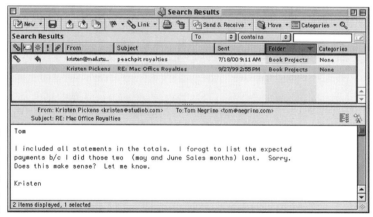

Figure 9-9:
The Search
Results
window.

Chapter 10

Managing Your Contacts, Calendar, and Tasks

*E*ntourage 2001 isn't just an excellent e-mail program. It's also a full-featured Personal Information Manager (PIM) that can handle your schedule, manage your tasks, and organize your notes. Best of all, you can take Entourage's information with you when you're away from your computer, thanks to the program's synchronization with Palm handheld computers.

Besides its capabilities as a stand-alone PIM, Entourage has an important role to play in the Office 2001 suite. Entourage's Address Book is available to the rest of the Office programs as a source for addresses, phone numbers, and e-mail addresses. The Entourage Tasks list is the destination for reminders you create using the other program's Flag for Follow-up feature. And, of course, any of the other Office programs can call upon Entourage to share their documents with colleagues via e-mail.

Managing Contacts with the Address Book

No person is an island, so the heart of any PIM is its contact manager. Entourage keeps all of the information about the people and companies you know and deal with in its Address Book. Greatly upgraded from the anemic address book in the free Outlook Express, Entourage has the horsepower you need to properly manage your Contacts. As you work with your schedule, you can invite people to events in your Calendar, and link notes and tasks.

To access the Entourage Address Book, click the Address Book icon in the Folder list. The list of addresses will appear in the top pane on the right side of the Entourage window, and clicking a name in the list will display the Contact's information in the Preview pane, as shown in Figure 10-1.

Folder list   Address list   Preview pane

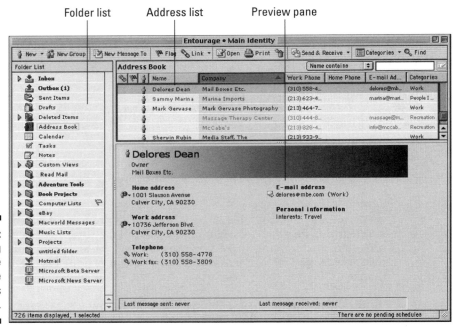

Figure 10-1: Displaying the Entourage Address Book.

Importing Contacts from other programs

If you're new to managing your Contacts on a computer, you'll have the some-what laborious task of typing in all the information in your Address Book into Entourage. In that case, skip directly to the next section. More likely, you used another contact manager before. If so, you may be in luck. Entourage knows how to import data from a variety of other contact managers. If your previous contact manager is on the list, you'll save a lot of time when switching over to Entourage.

To import Contacts from another contact manager, follow these steps:

1. Choose File⊏>Import.

The Begin Import screen appears, as shown in Figure 10-2.

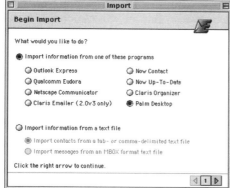

Figure 10-2:
Use this
screen to
begin
importing
your contact
information
from
another
program.

2. **Choose one of the programs listed, and then click the right arrow at the bottom of the window.**

   The Ready to Import screen appears, as shown in Figure 10-3.

   If your previous contact manager isn't listed, don't despair; most contact managers can export their data as a tab or comma-delimited text file, and Entourage will read these text files if you click the Import information from a text file button. You'll then be taken to a dialog box where you can match up the data fields in your old contact manager to fields that appear in Entourage. It's not quite as convenient as when Entourage imports from a program it already knows, but it's a heck of a lot better than retyping a zillion names.

Figure 10-3:
Selecting
the
information
to import.

3. **Entourage knows the capabilities of the other programs it lists, so it provides you with check boxes that let you choose which information to import. Choose what you would like to import, and then click the right arrow.**

Entourage imports the data, presenting a dialog box letting you know it's done.

The import process can take anywhere from a few minutes to a few hours, depending on the amount of information that you are importing. For most people, importing is not a quick process. If you begin the import and it appears that nothing is happening, be patient; it can sometimes take several minutes for the import process to begin in earnest. The good thing about importing, of course, is that it generally only needs to be done once.

Creating a new Contact

When entering a new Contact, you can enter as much or as little information about the Contact as you wish. Entourage has fields in its Address Book for all sorts of things, including pictures and children's names, but you shouldn't feel compelled to fill out all the information.

To create a new Contact, follow these steps:

1. **In the Folder list, click Address Book to select it.**

2. **Click the New button in the toolbar, choose File⇨New⇨Contact, or press ⌘+N.**

The basic Create Contact window appears, as shown in Figure 10-4.

Figure 10-4:
Add the basic Contact information in this window.

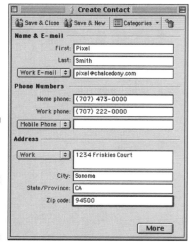

Multiple users, but not multi-user

Entourage 2001 can handle information for more than one user, but that isn't the same thing as it being a multi-user program. That sounds contradictory, but it isn't as confusing as it first appears. For people who share a single computer, Entourage can maintain separate sets of data for each person. Each set of data is known as an *identity,* and each identity contains a complete set of e-mail and PIM information. For example, when my family goes on a trip, we want to be able to bring our e-mail and calendar information along with us. Each of us copies our Entourage identity folder from our desktop machines onto the one laptop that we're bringing with us on the trip. When one of us wants to check his or her e-mail or schedule, he or she fires up Entourage and loads his or her personal identity using File➪Switch Identity. The next person to come along loads his or her own identity and gets a completely different set of e-mail (including different e-mail accounts), Calendar, and Tasks.

A multi-user program, on the other hand, would allow us to share (at least) our Calendar and Contacts, so that one person could add an event to his or her own Calendar and have the event appear on everyone else's Calendar. Multi-user Calendars also typically use the concept of public events (events shared with others) and private events (events that only you can see). In order to share this PIM information, the PIM program's users are typically connected to a network, and the public information is stored on a server elsewhere on the network. That way, each person's computer synchronizes its PIM data with the central copy stored on the server.

3. Enter the name and e-mail information, the phone numbers, and the address for the Contact.

When entering phone numbers, Entourage will format them for you in virtually any format that you like. All you have to do is type the numbers. You can set the phone number format Entourage will use by choosing Edit➪Preferences➪General, and then clicking the Address Book tab. Entourage will also try to enter other information for you; for example, if you enter a Contact's birthdate, Entourage will figure out and enter his or her age and astrological sign.

4. If you want to add more information for this Contact, click the More button.

The Create Contact window expands to its tabbed configuration, as shown in Figure 10-5.

In the expanded view, Entourage provides extra fields that you can customize for your particular needs. By default, these come named as Custom 1, Custom 2, and so on. Click the field name to rename it into something more meaningful.

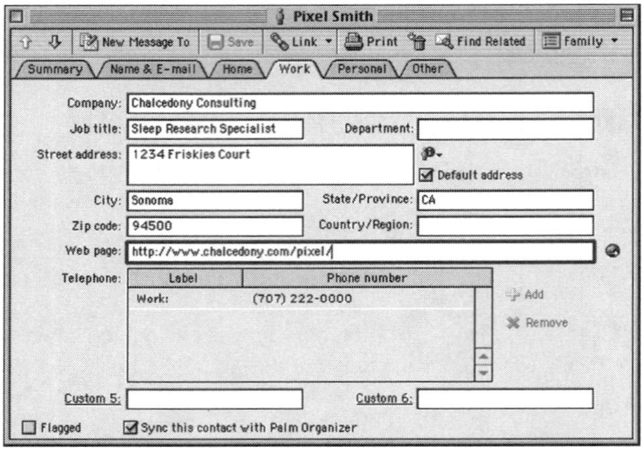

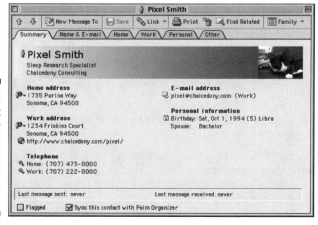

Figure 10-5:
The Work tab of the expanded contact information window. Click each of the tabs to enter more information.

5. **Click the other tabs as needed, and then enter more information in the fields shown.**

6. **Click the Save button, and then close the New Contact window.**

Using Contacts

When using the Address Book, the Contact's Summary tab is a useful way to get an overview of all of that Contact's information. You can view a Contact's summary by selecting the Contact in the Address list, or by double-clicking the Contact in the list to open it. The Contact's window will appear, set to the Summary tab, as shown in Figure 10-6.

Figure 10-6:
The Contact summary tells you most of a Contact's information at a glance.

The Summary page isn't just for display; you can accomplish several useful tasks from it.

Copying contact information

The Contact Summary page makes it easy to copy and paste the name and address information from a Contact into an e-mail or other Macintosh program.

To copy contact information, follow these steps:

1. **Click the Contact's name in the Address list to select it, or double-click the Contact's name to open the Contact window, set to the Summary tab.**

2. **Click the Address Actions icon next to the address that you want to copy.**

   The Address Actions pop-up menu appears, as shown in Figure 10-7.

Figure 10-7:
Copying the
Contact's
name and
address.

3. **Choose Copy Name and Address to Clipboard.**

   Switch to where you want to copy the name and address.

4. **Choose Edit⇨Paste, or press ⌘+P.**

Adding contact dates to the Calendar

One of the nice things about Personal Information Managers is the way that they can integrate contact information with dates. You can use Entourage to remind you of important dates related to your Contacts, such as birthdays and anniversaries.

To add contact dates to Entourage's Calendar, follow these steps:

1. **From a Contact's Summary page, click the Add to Calendar icon next to a date.**

   A Calendar Event window appears, already filled out, as shown in Figure 10-8. The event will be set to recur yearly, and a reminder will be set for five days in advance of the event.

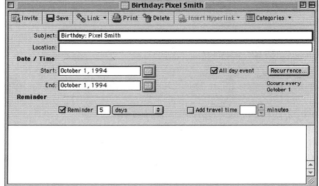

Figure 10-8:
Creating a
Calendar
event from a
contact
date.

2. **Make any changes needed, and then click Save.**

   The event will be added to the Calendar.

Getting maps or driving directions

Entourage can also show you maps of your Contact's address and can even
give you driving directions from your home or office. It does this by calling
on Microsoft's Expedia Web site, so you'll need to have an active Internet
connection.

To get maps or driving directions for Contacts, follow these steps:

1. **From a Contact's Summary page, click the Address Actions icon next
   to one of the Contact's addresses.**

2. **Choose Show on Map, Driving Directions from Home, or Driving
   Directions from Work.**

   Your Web browser will open and display the map or driving directions.

Deleting a Contact

To delete a Contact, follow these steps:

1. **Select the Contact in the Address list.**

2. **Choose Edit⇨Delete Contact, or click the Delete icon in the toolbar.**

   Entourage will ask you to confirm the deletion.

3. **Click Delete.**

Managing Your Calendar

The Calendar is your control center for everything in your life that depends on time. With the Calendar, you can plan events, set reminders for yourself, and follow up on reminders you created with the other Office programs. You can also use the Calendar to send and receive event invitations via e-mail. Like the Address Book, the Calendar takes over the right side of the Entourage screen when you click the Calendar icon in the Folder list, as shown in Figure 10-9.

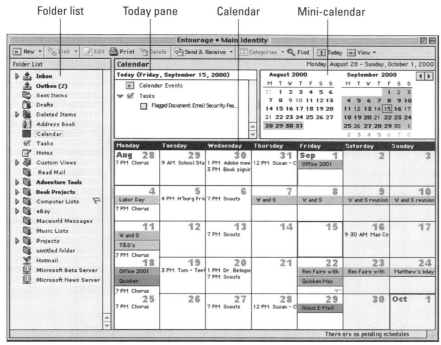

Folder list   Today pane   Calendar   Mini-calendar

Figure 10-9: Entourage's Calendar, set to Month view.

The Calendar is flexible, allowing you to work with your schedule in five views:

- **Day:** Shows the current day, in half-hour time increments. Bars represent events.

- **Week:** Displays the full current week, with bars representing events.

- **Work Week:** This view zooms in on Monday through Friday.

- **Month:** Shows the entire month, with events listed as text in each day.

- **List:** Shows all the events and tasks included in the highlighted area of the mini-calendar.

Displaying calendar views

To change between calendar views, select the Calendar in the Folder list, and then choose which of the five views you wish from the View menu. You can narrow (or expand) the number of days shown in the Calendar by clicking and dragging over days in the mini-calendar. Selecting a single day switches to Day view, of course, but you can select two or more days in the mini-calendar to get as much or as little detail as you need. The maximum selection is six weeks.

Creating an event

To create a new event, follow these steps:

1. **Select Calendar in the Folder list.**

2. **Click the New button in the toolbar, choose File⇨New⇨Calendar Event, or press ⌘+N.**

   A new event window appears, as shown in Figure 10-10.

   You can also create a new event by double-clicking the date and time of the event in the Day, Week, and Work Week views. Double-clicking a day in the Month view creates a new all-day event.

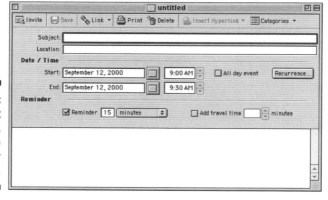

Figure 10-10: A new event window, ready to do your bidding.

3. **In the Subject field, enter the name of the event.**

4. **Enter where the event will occur in the Location box (optional).**

5. **In the Date/Time section, enter the Start and End dates and times.**

   The Start and End dates are set to today by default (or if you selected another day in the Calendar before you created the event, to that date).

If you choose a future day in the End date, you'll naturally be creating an event that spans multiple days.

6. **If the event takes the whole day, click the All day event check box (optional).**

The time fields will disappear from the event.

7. **Use of the Recurrence button will be covered in the next section. Skip it for now.**

8. **If you want Entourage to remind you before the event, make sure the Reminder box is checked, and enter the amount of warning before the event you want.**

You can specify the default reminder time (or have no reminder at all) in Edit➪Preferences➪General, and then click the General tab.

9. **Enter any notes you want for the event (optional).**

10. **Click Save, and then click the close box.**

Working with recurring events

Recurring events are events that repeat on some regular schedule. For example, your wedding anniversary and monthly mortgage payment are both recurring events for which you might want to set up reminders (though they repeat on different schedules: in this case, yearly and monthly). Entourage allows great flexibility in the way it creates such events, and the recurring events are linked. When you change a recurring event, Entourage asks you if you want to change just the current occurrence of the event, or if you want to change the current and all the future occurrences, too.

To create a recurring event, follow these steps:

1. **Follow Steps 1-6 in the "Creating an Event" section.**

2. **Click the Recurrence button.**

The Recurring Event dialog box appears, as shown in Figure 10-11.

Figure 10-11:
Set the frequency of your recurring event in this window.

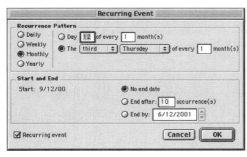

3. **In the Recurrence Pattern section, choose one of the Daily, Weekly, Monthly, or Yearly buttons.**

   Each choice changes the options on the right side of the window. Take a moment to look through the choices presented by each of the four buttons.

4. **Make your choices from the options presented to the right.**

5. **Set the end date, if needed.**

   The default choice is No end date, but you can set the number of occurances, or specify an ending date.

6. **Click OK.**

7. **Complete the event setup.**

Inviting a Contact to an event

When you invite someone to an event, Entourage sends the invitee an e-mail with the invitation and adds a record of the invitation to the event window. After the invitation has been sent, you can track the status of the invitation.

To invite a Contact to an event, follow these steps:

1. **Create an event in the usual fashion.**

2. **Click the Invite button.**

   The familiar From mail pop-up menu appears in the event, allowing you to select from which e-mail account you wish to send the invitation. An Invite field also appears, allowing you to address the e-mail.

3. **Enter an e-mail address as usual.**

   The event with its invitation looks like Figure 10-12.

Figure 10-12:
Attaching an invitation to an event.

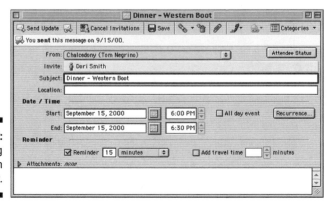

4. Click the Send Now or Send Later button.

To track the invitation status, open the event and click the Attendee Status button. The Attendee Status dialog box will appear. For each invitee, you can choose No Response, Accepted, Tentative, or Declined from their Response pop-up menu.

Dealing with Reminders

When a Reminder comes due, Entourage pops up the Reminders window (see Figure 10-13) and plays a brief sound. To handle a Reminder, select it in the list and then click one of the buttons in the Reminder window's toolbar:

✔ **Open Item:** Opens the Entourage item the reminder is attached to.

✔ **Open Document:** Only available if the reminder is for a flagged document. Clicking the button launches the document.

✔ **Snooze:** Has a pop-up menu that lets you tell Entourage to remind you about this item at a later time, up to a week later.

✔ **Dismiss:** Gets rid of the reminder.

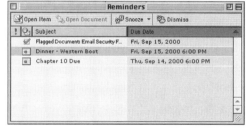

Figure 10-13:
Dealing with
Reminders.

When I was completing this book, Entourage could only display the Reminders window if one of the Office 2001 programs were running. It's more convenient if you don't have to keep Entourage or another Office program open all the time, and most other PIMs solve the problem with a system extension that loads when you start your Mac. Entourage's system extension wasn't ready for the initial release of Office 2001, and didn't make it onto the first pressing of the Office 2001 CD-ROM. The folks at Microsoft assure me that not only will the extension be available on the CD in the future, but also that everyone will be able to download the extension from www.microsoft.com/mac/ by the time this book is published. If it's not there, complain to Microsoft, not to me!

Deleting events

To delete an event, follow these steps:

1. **Select the event in the Calendar.**

2. **Choose Edit⇨Delete, or click the Delete icon in the toolbar.**

   Entourage will ask you to confirm the deletion.

3. **If you are deleting a recurring event, you'll be asked to choose to delete all future occurrences or just the single occurrence you've selected.**

4. **Click Delete.**

Tracking Your Tasks

Who needs those paper to-do lists? You've got Entourage now, buddy! You can use it to keep track of all of your to-do's, which Entourage calls Tasks. You can create Tasks manually, but you'll often create Tasks through follow-ups from the other Office programs.

Creating Tasks

To create a Task, follow these steps:

1. **Click on Tasks in the Folder list.**

2. **Click the New button in the toolbar, Choose File⇨New⇨New Task, or press ⌘+N.**

   A Task window appears; it should look something like Figure 10-14.

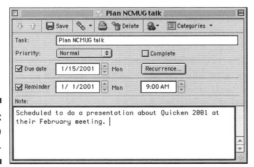

Figure 10-14:
Setting up
a Task.

3. **Give the Task a title.**

4. **Set the Task's priority level (optional).**

   You have five priorities from which to choose: Highest, High, Normal, Low, and Lowest.

5. **If the task needs to be done by a particular date, click the Due date button and set the date (optional).**

6. **If the task will be a recurring one, click the Recurrence button and set the recurrence options, which are very similar to recurring event options (optional).**

7. **Set a Reminder for the Task (optional).**

8. **Enter a Note about the Task (optional).**

9. **Set the Category for the Task (optional).**

10. **Click Save, and then click the close box.**

Setting task progress

There isn't really that much to keeping track of Tasks in Entourage. A Task is either pending or completed, depending on the state of the Status check box. You can sort the Task list by clicking one of the column headers in the list. Clicking on the header a second time reverses the sort direction.

To mark a Task as completed, click its Status check box.

Changing and deleting Tasks

To edit or delete a Task, follow these steps:

1. **Select the Task in the Tasks list.**

2. **Double-click the Task to open it for editing, or to delete it, choose Edit⇨Delete Task, or click the Delete icon in the toolbar.**

3. **If you chose to delete the Task, Entourage will ask you to confirm the deletion.**

4. **Click Delete.**

Creating Notes

Notes are the most free-form of the things you can create in Entourage. Think of them like the sticky notes you probably have stuck to your monitor, or like the notes you create with the Mac OS Stickies application. The benefit to creating Notes in Entourage, however, is that you can use Entourage's Find tools to search for elusive notes on a particular subject.

Working with Notes

To create a Note, follow these steps:

1. **Click on Notes in the Folder list.**
2. **Click the New button in the toolbar, Choose File⇨New⇨Note, or press ⌘+N.**

   A new note window appears.
3. **Enter the Note's title.**
4. **Enter the body of the Note.**
5. **Click Save, and then click the close box.**

Changing or deleting Notes

To edit or delete a Note, follow these steps:

1. **Select the Note in the Notes list.**
2. **Double-click the Note to open it for editing, or to delete it, choose Edit⇨Delete Note, or click the Delete icon in the toolbar.**
3. **If you chose to delete the Note, Entourage will ask you to confirm the deletion.**
4. **Click Delete.**

Data to Go

With the appearance and widespread popularity of handheld computers, such as the ones from Palm Computing and Handspring, it's not enough for a modern PIM to just do a good job on your desktop. People want to take their information with them, and it can't be a one-way trip; when you're away from your main computer, you want to be able to make changes in Contacts and schedules, then come back and update the desktop with those changes. Entourage supports two-way data synchronization with almost all PalmOS compatible devices, including most models from Palm Computing, and all of the Handspring Visor line; the only caveat is that the handheld must be running PalmOS version 2.0 or later.

Entourage copies Calendar events, contact information from the Address Book, the Tasks list, and Notes to and from your handheld. In order to perform the synchronization, you must have the Palm Desktop software, version 2.6.1 or later, already installed on your desktop computer. This software doesn't come with Office 2001; it is provided with your handheld, or may be downloaded from the handheld manufacturer's Web site.

Appropriately for a Macintosh program, Entourage synchronizes data with PalmOS-based handhelds, but not with the other main handheld platform, Microsoft's own PocketPC (formerly known as Windows CE). I say it's appropriate because Microsoft hasn't done the work to make the PocketPC platform compatible with the MacOS. Palm Computing, in contrast, has provided full support (called *conduits*) for two-way data synchronization for Macs, and Microsoft has taken advantage of Palm's work in creating its own conduit for Entourage. Incidentally, Entourage also doesn't support synchronization with palmtop devices from Psion.

Installing the Entourage conduit

The Entourage conduit isn't installed automatically with the rest of Office 2001. Instead, it's part of the Value Pack on the Office 2001 CD-ROM.

To install the Entourage handheld data conduit, follow these steps:

1. **Insert the Office 2001 CD-ROM into your computer.**

   The Office 2001 window appears.

2. **Double-click the Value Pack folder to open it.**

3. **Double-click the Value Pack Installer to launch it.**

   The Installer opens, displaying the scrolling list of Value Pack choices.

4. **Click the check box next to Handheld Synchronization.**

5. **Click Continue.**

   The Installer will inform you that the Palm Desktop conduits must be disabled, and they will be moved to a folder called Disabled Conduits.

6. **Click OK.**

   The Installer does its thing.

7. **Click Quit.**

Synchronizing your handheld with Entourage

In order to synchronize successfully with your Palm device, your Entourage identity's name must be exactly the same as the user name on the handheld. The easiest way to ensure that the names are the same is to rename your Entourage identity to match the handheld. To do this, Choose File⇨Switch Identity, and then click the Rename button.

Before you perform your first synchronization with Entourage, you should check the synchronization settings in the Palm HotSync Manager.

To check synchronization settings, follow these steps:

1. **Double-click the HotSync Manager application in your Palm folder.**

2. **Choose HotSync⇨Conduit Settings.**

   The Conduit Settings window appears.

3. **Double-click Entourage Conduit.**

   The Entourage Conduit Settings window appears, as shown in Figure 10-15.

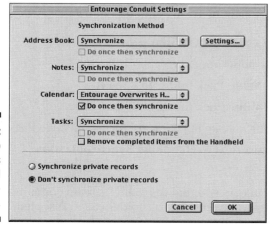

Figure 10-15: Setting up Entourage's handheld synchron- ization.

You can set the synchronization method separately for the Address Book, Notes, Calendar, and Tasks. The choice of method is Synchronize, Entourage Overwrites Handheld, Handheld Overwrites Entourage, or Do Nothing. You'll want to consider which set of data is the most important (the set in Entourage or on your handheld), and pick a method accordingly.

4. **Set the synchronization method for each of the four types of data.**

5. **Click OK.**

6. **Quit the HotSync Manager.**

The actual synchronization is simplicity itself; just place your Palm handheld in its cradle, and press the HotSync button on the cradle. The synchronization occurs, and you're ready to hit the road with all of your Entourage data!

Part IV

Crunching Your Numbers with Excel 2001

The 5th Wave · By Rich Tennant

"OH YEAH, AND TRY NOT TO ENTER THE WRONG PASSWORD."

In this part . . .

Whether it's filling in your expense report or finding
out that your long-lost Uncle Sydney has left you a
seven-figure gift in his will, you need to deal with numbers. Microsoft Excel 2001 is just the ticket. You can use
Excel to track your budget, follow the stock market, project financial results, figure out baseball averages, or do
just about anything else you can imagine doing with
numbers.

New to Excel 2001 is its List Wizard, which lets you use
Excel to create, sort, and manage just about any kind of
list you'll ever need.

After you have made your lists, checked them twice, and
crunched the numbers, Excel 2001 helps you turn your
spreadsheets into cool-looking pie, bar, column, and line
charts, which can tell you at a glance what your numbers
really mean.

Chapter 11

Spreadsheets 101: Behind the Rows and Columns

- -

In This Chapter

▶ Introducing spreadsheets

▶ Navigating a worksheet

▶ Entering information in a worksheet

▶ Improving the look of your worksheet

- -

*T*his chapter explains what spreadsheets are and how to use them in a basic sense. Read Chapter 12 to learn how to make Excel 2001 do the math in spreadsheets for you.

What the Heck Is a Spreadsheet?

This question is a good one to start with. It shows that you're paying attention.

Spreadsheets (also known in Excel as *worksheets*) are pages from an electronic ledger pad — rows and columns of little boxes just waiting to be filled in, as shown in Figure 11-1. The Office 2001 program that creates spreadsheets is Excel 2001.

You can put anything you want in the boxes: words, numbers, pictures, whatever. As you see in this chapter, spreadsheets are most handy for working with numbers because (unlike "real" ledger pads) *spreadsheets can do the math for you.* Imagine typing a bunch of numbers and having them automatically totaled at the bottom of the page or typing a bunch of numbers and having them automatically averaged. Or think of what it would be like to type a bunch of numbers and have the largest one automatically highlighted in green or picture how a spreadsheet may keep you from ever needing to haul out your calculator again.

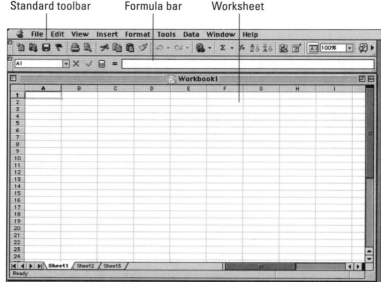

Standard toolbar   Formula bar   Worksheet

Figure 11-1:
An empty
spreadsheet.

Parts of the spreadsheet

Excel 2001 spreadsheets have lots of parts, and, taken all together, those parts can be intimidating. Fortunately, you can ignore many things for now and concentrate on the basics. This section makes you familiar with cells, rows and columns, and the formula bar. That information is enough to get you started.

Cells

Cells are the basic building blocks of a spreadsheet. Every cell in a spreadsheet starts out the same way: blank. You get to put things (such as numbers, formulas, and words) into cells and control the way they appear. Figure 11-2 shows some cells with different types of information in them.

Notice that because Excel 2001 cells can be sized to fit the stuff you enter into them, you don't have to worry about staying within the lines. Cells can be widened and deepened (and de-widened and de-deepened) at your command.

Rows and columns

Look down the left side of an Excel 2001 spreadsheet, and you see a bunch of numbers. These *row labels* help you tell Excel 2001 which row you're interested in. Look across the top of an Excel 2001 spreadsheet, and you see letters rather than numbers. These letters — the labels of the columns — help you tell Excel 2001 which column you're interested in. Figure 11-3 shows the rows and columns in a spreadsheet.

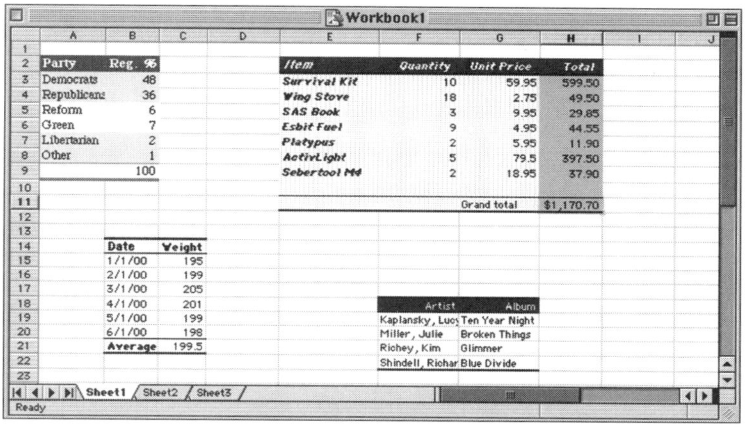

Figure 11-2:
Some cells
and their
varied
contents.

Excel 2001 limits you to 65,536 rows and 256 columns. Naturally, most spreadsheets never get anywhere near that big. When Excel 2001 runs out of letters for columns, it doubles up and the lettering goes X, Y, Z, AA, AB, AC, and so on.

Row labels   Column labels

Figure 11-3:
The row
and column
labels in
an Excel
spreadsheet.

Notice that each cell is the intersection of a row and a column. Thus, you can (and do) refer to the cell in the top-left corner of the spreadsheet as A1. Likewise, the cell at the intersection of Row 2 and Column B is B2, and the cell at the intersection of Row 6 and Column C is C6. Figure 11-4 shows some representative cells.

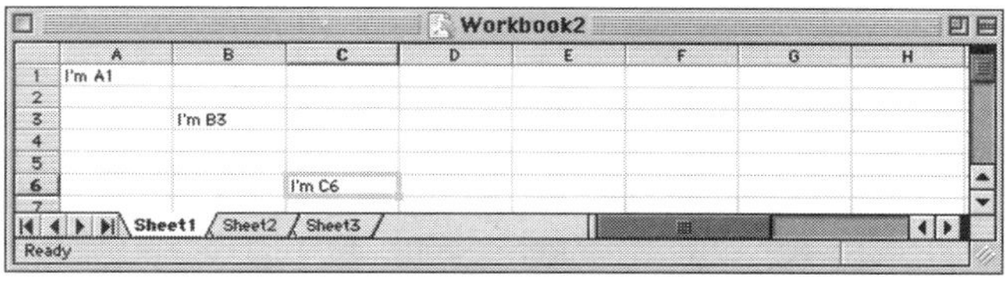

Figure 11-4:
Cells and
the notation
Excel uses
to describe
them.

For some obscure reason, the Excel 2001 cell references are column first, even though most people prefer row first. Thus, although you may expect the cell at the intersection of Row 2 and Column B to be 2B, it's B2.

The formula bar

The term *formula bar* is rather misleading because it is used for much more than just formulas. In fact, you use the formula bar every time you enter something into a cell, whether that something is a formula, a number, or a word. Figure 11-5 shows the formula bar.

Figure 11-5:
The
formula bar.

When you click a cell, the formula bar displays the cell's contents. When you type something inside a cell, the formula bar displays what you type. You find out how to create formulas in Chapter 12; for now, however, it's worth knowing that when you want to create a formula (something that means, for example, "This cell equals that cell minus that other cell"), you do it on the formula bar.

What spreadsheets are good for

Spreadsheets excel (pardon the pun) at handling numbers. Spreadsheets are good, therefore, for doing math-type things you may always have done on paper, such as tracking your checks, stocks, and net income. But with a spreadsheet, the math is done by Excel 2001, not by you. All you do is enter the words and numbers and set up the formulas. Excel 2001 gives you the answers.

Things that spreadsheets don't do well

Back home, they have a saying: "When all you know is a hammer, everything looks like a nail." Roughly translated, that saying means, "Use the right tool for the job." Spreadsheets are the right tools for many jobs, but not for all jobs. Spreadsheets are terrible word processors, for example. (Here's some advice: Use Word 2001.) Spreadsheets are also terrible *food* processors. (More advice: Use a Cuisinart.) Do you want to make presentations, draw a floor plan, or maintain an address book? Although you can use Excel 2001 for all three tasks, using it would be a great deal of trouble, and you would really have to work. Why bother, when other programs are better suited to these tasks? Take it from me (I ruined a number of wood screws when I was ten years old) — easier ways exist.

Cruising through a Worksheet

Before you go any further in this book, getting some terms straight is important. The discussion earlier in this chapter describes spreadsheets in general terms. This section, however, focuses on Excel 2001, which has a few terms of its own:

- The basic Excel 2001 document is called a *workbook*.

- A workbook can have multiple pages, which are called *worksheets*.

- Each worksheet is really just a *spreadsheet,* and you already know what a spreadsheet is.

Now you're ready to move ahead.

Right out of the box, Excel 2001 assumes that you want to have three worksheets per workbook. Three pages may not be enough for you, but don't worry — the number of worksheets you can have in a workbook is unlimited. (You find out how to add worksheets in Chapter 13, so stay tuned.)

Excel 2001 is literal: It does exactly what you tell it to do and, just as important, does so exactly *where* you say to do it. In this section, you find out how to move around in a worksheet so that you have an easier time of telling Excel 2001 what tasks to perform and where to perform them.

Selecting cells with the mouse

You select cells to show Excel 2001 which cells you're talking about. If you click a cell, Excel 2001 highlights it with a little border and displays the name of the cell to the left of the formula bar, as shown in Figure 11-6.

Cell reference in formula bar

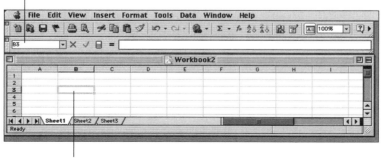

Figure 11-6: Someone clicked Cell B3, and Excel 2001 put a border around it.

Selected cell

If you click a cell, hold down the mouse button, and drag the mouse pointer toward some other cell, you select all the cells between those two cells. This technique is handy for quickly selecting a chunk, or a *range,* of the spreadsheet.

Figure 11-7 shows a range of selected cells. Notice that if you drag past the edge of the worksheet, Excel 2001 scrolls automatically, so even if you can't see all the cells you want to select, you can do so by dragging. Just click where you want to start the selection and drag in the direction of the final cell.

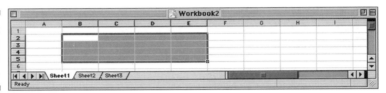

Figure 11-7:
Selecting
a range
of cells.

If you're selecting a range and go too far, don't panic. Just keep holding down the mouse button and move back the other way. Everything's cool as long as you hold down the mouse button.

Variations on this theme exist, of course. If you select a cell, hold down the Shift key, and then click another cell, for example, Excel 2001 selects everything between the two cells. This technique is one of the fastest ways to select a large group of cells, especially if they are widely separated. If you keep holding down the Shift key and continue to click cells, Excel 2001 continues to adjust the highlighted range accordingly. The key to the technique, really, is choosing a good cell to start in and a good cell to stop in.

If you select a range of cells, hold down the Shift key, and click another cell, Excel 2001 selects everything between where you originally clicked and where you Shift+clicked. In effect, Excel ignores the dragging you did.

If you select a range of cells and hold down the ⌘ key while selecting a different range of cells in another part of the spreadsheet, Excel 2001 does *not* select everything between the first and second selections; rather, it highlights just what you dragged through the cells you selected, leaving the cells between unselected. This method of making a selection, called *discontiguous selection,* is extremely handy because it enables you to skip cells you want to leave alone.

If you click a cell, you select the cell. You knew that. If you click the name of a column or a row (the number or letter label), however, you select the entire column or row, all the way to the end! If you click the name of a column or a row and drag to another column's or row's label, you select all the columns or rows between them. If you click one column or row label, hold down the Shift key, and click another column or row label, you select everything between them; if you substitute the ⌘ key for the Shift key, you select just the columns or rows you clicked. This technique is definitely worth trying.

Using the keyboard

Using the mouse to select cells is easy and more or less intuitive. The technique isn't all that fast, however, and you can easily make mistakes by clicking the wrong places. You're much better off using the keyboard to select cells.

The arrow keys do the same thing you can do with the mouse, but in one-cell increments. If you want to select the cell one cell above the selected cell, press the up-arrow key one time. Want to move up two cells? Press the up-arrow key twice. Want to zoom around the worksheet? Press an arrow key and hold it down. Pretty elementary. But wait — there's more!

When you hold down the Shift key while you press an arrow key, something nice happens: You select cells, just like you do when you drag the mouse. If you hold down the Shift key, press the right-arrow key three times, and then (still holding down the Shift key) press the down-arrow key four times, you select a range of cells three cells wide and four cells deep.

If you go too far, don't worry. Keep holding down the Shift key and then press the arrow key that goes back the other way. If you accidentally select an extra row because of pressing the down-arrow key one too many times, just press the Shift key and then the up-arrow key. Voilà!

Hold down the ⌘ key while you press an arrow key, and you zip to an edge of an empty spreadsheet. Which edge depends on which arrow key you press. If you're way over in Column Z and want to get back to Column A, therefore, just hold down the ⌘ key and press the left-arrow key. If you're way down in Row 200 and want to get back to Row 1, hold down the ⌘ key and press the up-arrow key. Easy. When you have entries in the spreadsheet, Excel changes this behavior and tries to bring you to the next useful cell. That's the first cell with something in it, or the last cell before a blank cell.

While you're at it, give the Home, End, Page Up, and Page Down keys a try too. Pressing Home zips you back to the first cell in the row you're in. Pressing Control+Home takes you back to Cell A1 — the first cell in the spreadsheet. Pressing Control+End takes you to the last cell in your spreadsheet (the last cell you used, not the geographic last cell). Pressing Page Up scrolls up a screen's worth of data, and pressing Page Down scrolls down a screen.

Naming cells and ranges

If you read the section "Parts of the spreadsheet," earlier in this chapter, you know that Excel 2001 refers to its cells with row and column identifiers. You can go straight to a cell by telling Excel 2001, "I want to go to Cell B4:"

1. **Choose Edit⇨Go To.**

   The Go To dialog box appears.

2. In the Reference box, type B4.

3. Click OK.

B4 becomes the active cell.

When you use this technique, you have one big problem, and you've probably already guessed what it is: Remembering the row and column descriptions for more than a couple of cells is close to impossible. If you're trying to zip to a section of a worksheet and you can't remember whether it starts at Z99 or Y78, the Edit➪Go To command doesn't do you much good. Enter the concept of naming cells and ranges.

Naming a cell or a range means giving it a name that makes sense to you. Suppose that your spreadsheet looks like the one shown in Figure 11-8.

Figure 11-8:
Baseball standings.

	A	B	C	D	E	F	G	H	I	J
1										
2	2000 American League Standings					2000 National League Standings				
3										
4	EAST	Won	Lost	Pct		EAST	Won	Lost	Pct	
5	NY Yankees	64	50	0.561		Atlanta	73	46	0.613	
6	Boston	60	55	0.522		NY Mets	70	48	0.593	
7	Toronto	61	60	0.504		Florida	60	59	0.504	
8	Baltimore	52	66	0.441		Montreal	51	64	0.443	
9	Tampa Bay	52	66	0.441		Philadelphia	50	68	0.424	
10										
11	CENTRAL	Won	Lost	Pct		CENTRAL	Won	Lost	Pct	
12	Chicago	71	48	0.597		St. Louis	65	54	0.546	
13	Cleveland	61	54	0.53		Cincinnati	59	59	0.5	
14	Detroit	57	61	0.483		Chicago	54	64	0.458	
15	Kansas City	54	64	0.458		Milwaukee	50	69	0.42	
16	Minnesota	55	66	0.455		Pittsburgh	49	69	0.415	
17						Houston	47	73	0.392	
18	WEST	Won	Lost	Pct						
19	Seattle	69	51	0.575		WEST	Won	Lost	Pct	
20	Oakland	63	54	0.538		San Francisco	66	51	0.564	
21	Anaheim	62	57	0.521		Arizona	66	53	0.555	
22	Texas	54	62	0.466		Los Angeles	60	58	0.508	
23						Colorado	59	59	0.5	
24						San Diego	57	63	0.475	
25										

Being able to quickly jump to the National League West section, for example, and selecting the cells you want may be handy. Follow these steps:

1. Select the cell or range you want to name.

2. Choose Insert➪Name➪Define.

The Define Name dialog box appears.

3. In the Names in Workbook box, type a name that describes the selected cell or range.

4. Click OK.

You have to follow the Excel 2001 rules for naming things. You can't use spaces in a name, you can't use apostrophes, and you can't use numbers. The name in the preceding example, therefore, could be NationalLeagueWest, but it couldn't be National League West or even Nat'lWest. Stick with one-word names, and you'll be okay. Try to make your names long enough to make sense, but short enough to type easily.

To use a named range, start by selecting something else, away from the range. Choose Edit➪Go To, choose your named range (it ought to be in the Go To dialog box), and click OK. Presto — you're in the right place, and the proper cells are selected. Very slick.

One amazingly cool feature of Excel 2001 is its capability to select all cells of a certain kind. Suppose that you want to select in a spreadsheet all the cells that contain words. (Perhaps you want to make them bold or green or something else along those lines.)

It would be a drag, as it were, if you had to select all these cells by hand. Excel 2001 is up to the task. To select cells of a particular type, follow these steps:

1. **Choose Edit➪Go To.**

   The Go To dialog box appears.

2. **Click the Special button.**

3. **Make your choices. For example, to select text but not numbers, click Constants, and then clear all the check boxes except Text, as shown in Figure 11-9.**

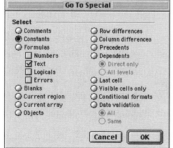

Figure 11-9:
You want to select the words, but not the numbers.

4. **Click OK.**

   All the words are selected.

Remember this technique; you're sure to use it sooner or later.

Entering Information into a Worksheet

Even though you may know how to move around in a worksheet, you may not know how to put stuff into one. That situation will change — and fast. Master this section, and you're on your way to Spreadsheet 101 graduation ceremonies, with honors.

Putting information in a cell

As usual, you have a bunch of ways to put information in a cell. The simplest way is to select a cell, type something, and then press the Return key. This technique works with words and numbers, and you'll use it often.

Rather than press Return to tell Excel 2001 that you're done typing, you can click the green check mark next to the formula bar. Although this method is slower, it has the advantage of being harder, which means that you're less likely to make mistakes when you're just starting. Clicking the red X next to the check mark means, "Never mind; I liked things better the way they were before I started typing."

Again, as usual, variations on the theme exist. If you select a cell, type something, and press the Return key, the information is entered into the selected cell and the next cell down is selected. (When you press the Enter key, on the numeric keypad, the selected cell doesn't change.) If you select a cell, type something, and then press the Tab key, the information is entered in the selected cell and the cell to the right is selected. You can press the right-arrow key rather than Tab. The rest of the arrow keys work as you may expect, entering information and selecting the neighboring cell in whichever direction.

When you're working with numbers, the easiest method is to type them from the numeric keypad on the right side of most keyboards. You don't have to type decimal points if the numbers don't have them (if the number is 100.00, for example, you can just type **100**), and you don't have to type dollar signs, even if the numbers do have them. (Excel 2001 has a way of automatically putting them in for you, as you see later in this chapter.)

You can, of course, copy the information in a cell or range and paste it somewhere else. Just select the cell (or cells) you want to copy, choose Edit⇨Copy (or press ⌘+C), click where you want to begin pasting, and choose Edit⇨Paste (or press ⌘+V). This technique puts the information in two places, which may not be what you want. If you simply want to move the information, choose Edit⇨Cut (or press ⌘+X), rather than Edit⇨Copy.

If you're really looking to cut down on keystrokes or mouse clicks, you don't even need to choose Edit➪Paste; all you need to do after a Cut or Copy is to select the destination cell and press Enter.

In the olden days (only a few years ago), cutting and pasting was about as good as it got. Nowadays, the drag-and-drop technique enables you to cut your steps in half.

Suppose that your spreadsheet looks like the one shown in Figure 11-10.

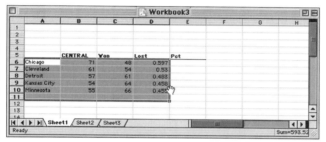

Figure 11-10:
A spread-sheet with stuff in the wrong places.

Now suppose that you want to move the selected stuff one cell to the right. You can cut and paste, of course, although the drag-and-drop method enables you to simply plop the selection into a new home:

1. **Click and hold the mouse button on any edge of the selection.**

   You know that the mouse pointer is in the right place when it changes from the standard Excel 2001 cross to a grabber hand.

2. **Drag the selection anywhere you want.**

3. **When the selected cells are in the right place, release the mouse button.**

When you drop cells over cells that already contain data, Excel 2001 assumes that you want to replace the old contents with the ones you are about to drop. Excel 2001 displays a warning message every time this replacement is about to happen.

You see special effects when you hold down certain keys. If you hold down the Option key while dragging a range of cells to a new location, for example, you don't move them; you copy them.

How do you like that? You just finish reading that Excel 2001 warns you when you are about to replace the contents of cells by dropping something on them, and now you find an exception — namely, if you use the Option-key technique to drag a copy of the cells, you do *not* see the warning. You simply replace whatever you drop on the cell. Be careful.

If you hold down the Control key while dragging, you get a slew of options, as shown in Figure 11-11. The figure shows an example of the Excel 2001 contextual menus, which you see again later.

Figure 11-11:
The
contextual
menu gives
you many
more
options
when you
Control+
drag a
selection.

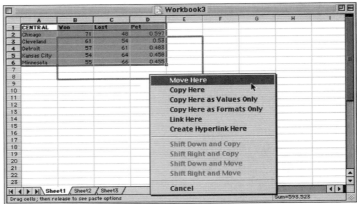

If you drag from a special place (the bottom-right corner, which is also known as the *fill handle*), Excel 2001 doesn't move the cells. What it *does* do depends on the contents of the selected cells. If a cell contains the word *Monday,* for example, and you drag its bottom-right corner to the right, you fill the cells to the right with the days of the week as far as you like. Just drag to the right and release the mouse button, and you see how it works. Dragging down works as well.

When you fill cells in this way, you are creating a *series.* Excel 2001 recognizes a bunch of series, including

- **Days of the week:** Full and abbreviated (Mon–Tues–Wed)

- **Months of the year:** Full and abbreviated (Jan–Feb–Mar)

- **Hours:** 10:00, 11:00, 12:00, and so on

- **Quarters of the year:** Full and abbreviated (1st Qtr–2nd Qtr–3rd Qtr)

- **Positional numbers:** 1st–2nd–3rd

Excel 2001 can also figure out numeric series based on what you select. If you select two cells — one containing 10 and the other containing 20, for example — and then drag the fill handle further, Excel 2001 guesses that the next number ought to be 30; the next number after that, 40; and so on. For this technique to work, select at least two cells; otherwise, Excel 2001 can't figure out what you're trying to do.

Editing or deleting the contents of a cell

Unless you're always perfect, you may want to change the contents of a cell. Maybe you weren't looking when you typed things; maybe someone else did the typing; maybe you really were right the first time, and now you want to change something. No problem. Excel 2001 enables you to make changes whenever you want.

Editing a cell's contents is as easy as selecting the cell and typing. The stuff you type replaces the stuff that used to be in the cell. Press Return (or click the green check next to the formula bar), and you're done.

Don't care for this method? Do you think that typing on the formula bar is awkward, especially when the cell you're editing is a long way from the formula bar? You're not alone, and Excel 2001 knows that, so it gives you the option of editing cell contents *directly in the cell!* Simply double-click a cell, and you can type all over it, in much the same way as you would in a word processor. Feel free to use both the formula bar and the edit-in-cell methods in the same worksheet; Excel 2001 doesn't care one whit.

Deleting the contents of a cell isn't rocket science: Click a cell and press the Delete key. Alternatively, click a cell, choose Edit⇨Clear, and then choose Contents from the hierarchical menu. You can also click a cell and then choose Edit⇨Cut. Whichever method you use — poof! — the cell contents are gone.

Deleting the contents of a cell is not the same as deleting the cell itself. You may want to read that sentence again. *Deleting the contents of a cell clears it out but leaves the cell itself alone.* Deleting a cell creates a hole in your spreadsheet, and Excel 2001 doesn't like holes, so it immediately asks how you want to close the hole — slide cells over from the right or up from the bottom. Make sure that you know what you're doing when you start deleting cells, because deleting is one of the easiest ways to louse up a good spreadsheet.

Managing Lists with Excel 2001

Remember a few pages back when I was talking about the things that Excel is good for, and the things that it isn't so great for? One of those things that it really hasn't been that well suited for is as a list manager. When people put lists in a computer program, they usually want to sort the information or make reports out of it. For that sort of thing, a database program is usually the ticket. But Microsoft noticed an odd thing when it was trying to figure out what to put in Excel 2001: One of the top things that people were doing with Excel 98 was using it to keep lists. Seems that those rows and columns just beg for bits of information, and people were just determined to use worksheets as lists.

Rather than fight its customers, Microsoft has wisely decided to help them out by adding the new List Wizard and the List Manager, and by introducing the idea of *list frames.* The List Wizard helps you make lists; the List Manager allows you to sort lists on any of their columns and filter the data to show the information you want. A list frame surrounds the list data in a worksheet and lets you know the data are being managed by the List Manager. When the list is active, the list frame looks like a window overlaid on the worksheet. When the list isn't active, the list frame is a blue border around the list.

Creating a list

When you go to make a list, you can make it from scratch, or you can use some existing information in a worksheet. In the example below, I've used an existing worksheet, but either way, you'll want to use the List Wizard to get you started.

To create a list, follow these steps:

1. **Select the information you want to turn into a list.**

2. **Choose Insert⇨List.**

   The first screen of the List Wizard appears, as shown in Figure 11-12.

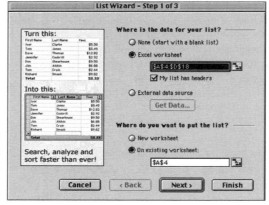

Figure 11-12:
The List
Wizard.

3. **Tell the Wizard where the data is (if you selected the data in Step 1, this is already filled in for you), and decide if you want the list to appear on the worksheet or as a new worksheet, then click Next.**

   The second screen of the List Wizard appears, as shown in Figure 11-13. In this screen, you get the chance to tell Excel about the kinds of data in your list by classifying the kind of data in each column. Why is it a good idea to let Excel know this? Glad you asked; it's because different kinds of data sort in different ways. Text has different sorting rules than whole numbers, and time sorts differently from both of them.

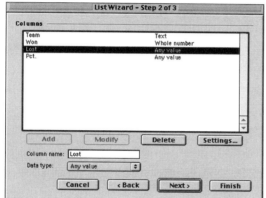

Figure 11-13:
Classifying
your list
data.

4. **Click one of the column names to select it.**

5. **Make a choice from the Data type pop-up menu.**

6. **Click the Modify button.**

7. **Repeat Steps 4 through 6 for the rest of the columns.**

8. **Click Next.**

   The last screen of the List Wizard appears. It allows you to name the list and specify its appearance.

9. **Make your choices, and then click Finish.**

   The new list appears, along with the List toolbar, as shown in Figure 11-14.

Sorting and filtering lists

After you've created a list, you'll probably want to work with the data in the list. Sorting is the most common way to manipulate lists. Excel 2001 can sort lists in *ascending order* (for example, from 0 to 9) or *descending order* (for example, from Z to A).

To sort a list, follow these steps:

1. **Click into a list to select it.**

Header row   Sort and Filter buttons

Figure 11-14:
The new list
in your
worksheet.

List toolbar

List

2. **Choose which column you wish to sort, and click its Sort and Filter button.**

   The column's Sort and Filter pop-up menu appears, as shown in Figure 11-15.

3. **Choose Sort Ascending or Sort Descending.**

   The list rows rearrange according to the sort option you chose.

List tips

When you're making a list, it's a good idea to keep a few rules in mind:

✔ Don't have any blank rows or columns in your list. When you sort the list later, you'll end up with gaps in your list.

✔ Make sure the first row of the data contains headings for each column. Excel will be able to use these headers when you sort or filter the column.

✔ Set the list off from the rest of your worksheet by leaving a blank column and a blank row between the list and other information on the worksheet. It makes it easier for the List Wizard to decide what's in the list and what shouldn't be.

Sort criteria

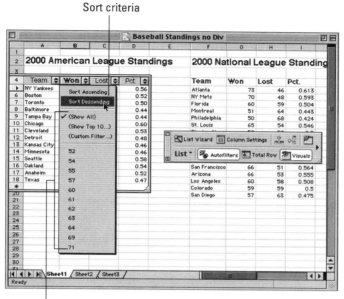

Figure 11-15:
Choosing a
sort order.

Filter criteria

To filter a list, follow these steps:

1. **Click into a list to select it.**

2. **Choose which column you wish to sort, and click its Sort and Filter button.**

   The column's Sort and Filter pop-up menu appears (refer to Figure 11-15).

3. **Choose one of the Filter Criteria. For example, choose the Top 10 filter to see just the top ten choices on the list.**

   The number of list items shown shrinks to just the top ten.

To get all of the list items back, choose Show All from the Sort and Filter pop-up menu.

Making Your Worksheet Look Good

Nothing says "raise" to the boss louder than a smartly formatted spreadsheet. Excel 2001 enables you to dress up your otherwise plain spreadsheet with colors, fonts, sizes, and even pictures. This section shows you how to format text and numbers — first, the easy AutoFormat way and then the harder, but more controllable, manual way. (You find out how to add pictures in the following section.)

Using AutoFormat

As its name suggests, AutoFormat performs automatic formatting. Excel 2001 looks at the cells you selected, guesses which have headings and which have numeric data, and presents a bunch of ready-made formatting choices. In a jiffy, you can turn a general-issue spreadsheet like the one shown in Figure 11-16 into a snappy, income-adjusting masterpiece like the one shown in Figure 11-17:

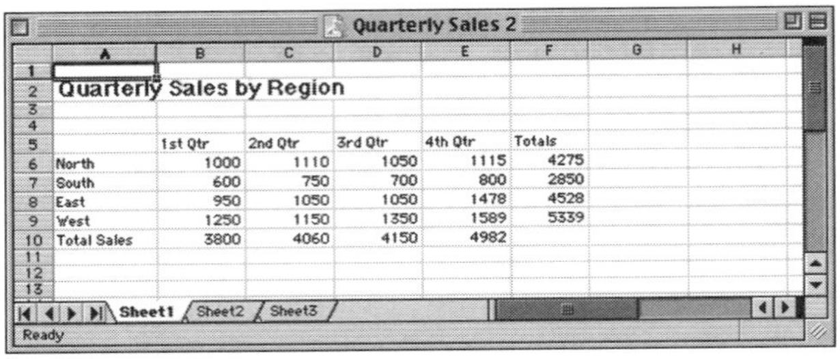

Figure 11-16:
A dull, general-issue spreadsheet.

1. **Select the cells you want to format.**

2. **Choose Format⇨AutoFormat.**

   The AutoFormat dialog box appears.

3. **Choose a format from the list.**

   When you click the name of a format, representative samples appear to the right of the dialog box. You can click the Options button and refine your choice (though I don't recommend doing that until you've tried doing things the Excel 2001 way first because you can easily ruin a good formatting scheme).

4. **Click the OK button.**

   Excel automatically formats your spreadsheet.

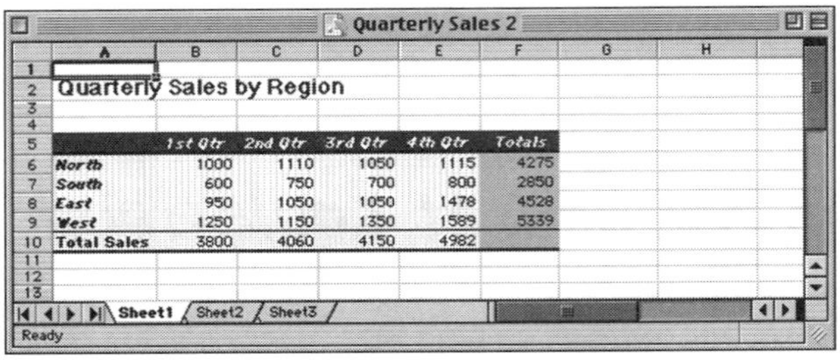

Figure 11-17:
A snappy, income-adjusting spreadsheet.

If you don't like the way things turn out, don't worry; you can go straight back to the AutoFormat dialog box and choose another format. You can also modify the formatting that was applied automatically. Finally, remember that the Undo command is available until you do something else.

Information in your spreadsheet can look a little weird when you use AutoFormat. That's just the way things are when your cells are still selected. Click outside the cells you just formatted, and they'll probably look better.

Formatting numbers and text

AutoFormatting is great as long as you like the Excel 2001 choices. For most people, AutoFormatting is a start, not a finished product. You have to do the rest of the formatting by hand if you're after a gorgeous spreadsheet. Fortunately, formatting is not hard, and you have options galore. This section starts by explaining number formatting and then moves on to text formatting.

Number formatting in Excel 2001 is unbelievably powerful and, with this version of the program, is fairly easy to control. You can tell Excel 2001 how many decimal places to use, whether to format numbers as dollars and cents, whether to use commas in long numbers, whether to display negative numbers in red or in parentheses, whether to format numbers as percentages, and on and on and on. Best of all, after you decide exactly what you want your numbers to look like, you can save the complete formatting instructions in a *style* and apply that style to numeric cells anywhere in your spreadsheet.

Applying formatting via a style is much faster than choosing countless options from the Excel 2001 menus. Take a little extra time to set up some styles: Your work goes faster in the long run, and your spreadsheets have a consistent, professional look. Also, because number formatting is done on a cell-by-cell basis, some cells can be formatted one way and others can be formatted another. It's all up to you, although formatting is easiest when you use styles. But for really quick formatting, there's an even better tool than styles. The Format Painter tool makes it quick and easy to copy the formatting of one cell to one or more other cells.

The spreadsheet shown back in Figure 11-17 isn't a bad-looking spreadsheet, but you may want to display dollar signs before every number. Follow these steps:

1. **Select the cells you want to format.**

2. **On the Number section of the Formatting palette, choose Accounting from the Format pop-up menu.**

   Accounting format shows dollars and cents, with parentheses around negative numbers. You have options here too: Rather than parentheses, negative numbers can be colored red, just have a minus sign in front of them, or anything else you want.

Uh-oh — disaster! Your beautiful spreadsheet is full of number signs, as shown in Figure 11-18. Where are your numbers?

Figure 11-18:
A spread-
sheet with
number
signs, rather
than
numbers.

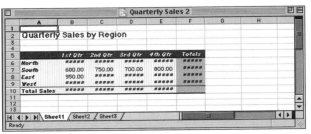

Although the numbers are in the cells, with this new-and-improved format, Excel 2001 doesn't have room to display them. It fills a cell with number signs to tell you that the real information doesn't fit. You can make the cells wider so that the information does fit, however.

3. **With the problem cells selected, choose Format⇨Column⇨ AutoFit Selection.**

   Congratulate yourself for not panicking. You're back on track for that raise. Figure 11-19 shows the spreadsheet so far.

Figure 11-19:
A good-
looking
spreadsheet.

You can also format text — make it bold or italic or display text in 24-point type, for example. You can make the bottom row of a spreadsheet bold, for example. You've already seen how to use the Formatting Palette to do the job, and chances are that's what you'll use most of the time. But Excel 2001 has another way to format text that you should know about.

To format text, follow these steps:

1. **Select the cells you want to format.**

2. **Choose Format⇨Cells.**

   The Format Cells dialog box appears, as shown in Figure 11-20.

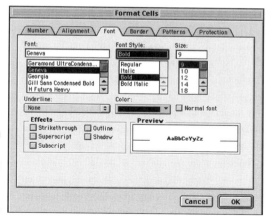

Figure 11-20:
The Format
Cells dialog
box.

3. **Click the Font tab.**

4. **Choose your options.**

5. **Click OK.**

If your changes mean that the text doesn't fit in the cells anymore, choose Format⇨Column⇨AutoFit Selection.

Although you can format text in other ways (gee, what a surprise!), the preceding method is the most powerful because it enables you to change everything in one swoop. In this case, though, you just made something bold. You can choose an easier way:

1. **Select the cells you want to format.**

2. **Click the Bold button (it looks like a capital *B*) on the Formatting Palette.**

The Formatting Palette has a plethora of options, which include font, size, alignment, and color. Play around with the Formatting Palette; it's time well spent.

Chapter 12

Formulas Work — So That You Don't Have To!

This chapter shows you how to make Excel 2001 do the math for you. The program does this chore by manipulating the numbers in spreadsheet cells with formulas. A *formula* is just an instruction that tells Excel 2001 what to do with the number in one or more cells. For example, a formula could tell Excel 2001 to add the number in one cell to the number in another cell and put the result in a third cell. Because the biggest part of Excel 2001 is its capability to use formulas for calculations, you may want to be especially careful as you work through some of the examples.

Introducing Formulas

Excel 2001 can do all sorts of math for you, from the simplest addition to stuff you probably learned about and promptly forgot after the exam in high school or college. In this section, you start with the easy stuff and work your way up.

Starting with formulas

You begin with something interesting: figuring out how much money you have left after paying the bills. Here's how you do it with Excel 2001:

1. **Create a new spreadsheet, and enter data to make it look like Figure 12-1.**

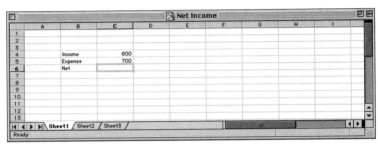

Figure 12-1:
A
spreadsheet
showing
income and
expenses.

Refer to Chapter 11 if you need to know how to create a spreadsheet.

2. **Click the cell to the right of the word *Net*.**

   This cell is where you want to have Excel 2001 put the difference between your income and your expenses.

3. **Press the equal (=) key.**

4. **Click the cell that contains your income (the number, not the word).**

5. **Press the minus (–) key on your keyboard.**

6. **Click the cell that contains your expenses (the number).**

   Notice that the cell contains the formula you've created so far. (So does the formula bar, but looking way up there for your formula right now isn't convenient.)

7. **If you like the formula, press the Enter key on the numeric keypad (or click the check mark next to your formula on the formula bar).**

   Your answer appears. Hey, you're making money.

Every Excel 2001 formula starts with an equal sign. Every one.

Look at the formula on the formula bar. This formula is pretty understandable: *This* cell equals *that* cell minus some *other* cell. (If those cell references don't make sense to you, reviewing the beginning of Chapter 11 may do you good. Don't worry; I'll be here when you come back.)

Using names in formulas

Formulas would be easier to understand if you could type them the way you say them. In fact, you can. Follow these steps:

1. **Start by undoing the formula you just made in cell C6. Choose Edit⇨Undo Typing.**

   You're back where you started.

2. **Press the equal (=) key to begin the formula.**

3. **Type Income - Expense in the cell (or on the formula bar).**

4. **Press Enter.**

   You get the same answer as before, except that this formula is in English. Pretty nice.

You've made a simple formula. So far, no big deal. You could have made this calculation faster on a calculator or on paper or even on your fingers. Ah, but Excel 2001 does more than calculate the difference between the numbers as they are entered — it enables you to plug in *different* numbers, and the formula keeps on working!

Suppose that you get a raise, from $800 monthly to $900 monthly. To change the spreadsheet's values, follow these steps:

1. **Type 900 in the cell next to the word *income*.**

2. **Press Enter (or click the check mark on the formula bar).**

   Now you're doing even better. This step leaves more money to buy black-and-yellow how-to books for all that software you've acquired.

Try typing other numbers in both the monthly-income and monthly-expense cells. Remember to press the Enter key (or click the check mark on the formula bar) to tell Excel 2001 that you're done typing.

You can improve this little spreadsheet by making it something you can use for a couple of months. To do so, you need more cells for future income and expense data. Follow these steps:

1. **Click the cell on top of the column of numbers (C3).**

2. **Type January.**

3. **Click the green check mark in the formula bar.**

4. **Click the fill handle in the bottom-right corner of the cell that contains the word *January,* and hold down the mouse button.**

   The mouse pointer looks like a small box with little arrows when you're close enough to the fill handle to click it.

5. **Drag the fill handle to the right. As you drag, a yellow ScreenTip box shows the value of the cells you're filling. Drag until the ScreenTip shows that you've gone all the way to June.**

6. **Release the mouse button.**

   Your spreadsheet should look like the one shown in Figure 12-2.

Figure 12-2:
A spread-
sheet with
month
headings.

	A	B	C	D	E	F	G	H	I
				January	February	March	April	May	June
		Income	900						
		Expense	700						
		Net	200						

Net Income

To add some data for those other months, click a cell and type. Leave the "Net" alone for now because you're going to calculate it for each month.

If you highlight, before you start typing, the cells in which you're going to enter data, you can get the entering done in a hurry. Try highlighting the Income and Expense cells (just drag through them). Then press the Enter key repeatedly, and notice how the selected cell moves around. When you type numbers and then press Enter, Excel 2001 automatically selects the next cell for you. After you enter data this way a few times, you develop a rhythm: type numbers, press Enter, type numbers, press Enter.

If you've filled your spreadsheet with data for the months other than January, you're ready to figure out the amount of money left over for each month, all in one shot. Follow these steps:

1. **Select the one cell that already has the net figured out (the cell that contains a formula).**

2. **Click the fill handle.**

3. **Drag the fill handle to the right.**

   If all has gone well, the difference between income and expenses is displayed for every month. Figure 12-3 shows how your screen looks if you typed the same numbers I typed.

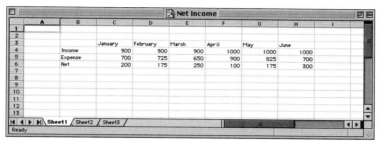

Figure 12-3:
A spread-
sheet with
the net
values
calculated
for every
month.

Formatting the spreadsheet with AutoFormat

If you're feeling cocky (and why wouldn't you, with a net income like yours?), try applying the AutoFormat feature to your work so that it looks a little nicer. You can see in Chapter 11 how to use AutoFormat, but here's a quick refresher:

1. **Select all the cells in the spreadsheet that have something in them.**

2. **Choose Format⇨AutoFormat.**

   The AutoFormat dialog box appears.

3. **Pick a formatting scheme from the list on the left.**

4. **Click OK.**

Figure 12-4 shows how the spreadsheet may look, depending on which AutoFormat scheme you choose.

Figure 12-4:
The
spreadsheet
after
applying
Auto
Formatting.

The hardest part about doing what you just did wasn't the formatting; it was the selecting. As usual, you have a choice of the ordinary way to do things and the unbelievably cool way to do things. Here's how to select cells the unbelievably cool way:

1. **Click *one* of the cells you want to select.**

2. **Choose Edit⇨Go To.**

3. **Click Special.**

   The Go To Special dialog box appears.

4. **Click the Current Region radio button.**

5. **Click OK.**

   The active area of the spreadsheet gets selected.

Is this method exceptionally cool? You bet it is. Remember it, and dazzle your friends.

 Want to *really* impress people? Put the Select Current Region button on a toolbar so that it's literally a click away. Not sure how to add a button to a toolbar? Have no fear — the Microsoft Excel 2001 Assistant is here. Follow these steps:

1. **Choose Help⇨Microsoft Excel Help.**

   The Office Assistant appears.

2. **Type the question,** How do I add a button to a toolbar?

3. **Click the Search button.**

   The Assistant shows you the rest of what you need to know.

This method is even more cool than unbelievably cool. Cosmically cool, perhaps.

Adding another formula

Now you're ready to create another formula. You use the same spreadsheet to figure out how much you ought to be saving each month, based on the assumption that 25 percent of your net income is the amount you ought to save. Follow these steps:

1. **Click the cell below the word *Net* and type** Savings.

2. **Move one cell to the right and type** = **(an equal sign).**

3. **Click the cell that contains the Net amount.**

4. **Type * (an asterisk).**

   The asterisk tells Excel to multiply. The easiest way to enter an asterisk is to press the asterisk key on the numeric keypad.

5. **Type** 25%.

Typing **0.25** also works.

6. **Press Enter on the keyboard or click the check mark next to the formula bar.**

Your answer appears in the cell.

You can drag the cell's fill handle to the right to fill in the formula for the other months. If you change the income or expense data, your savings numbers change as well. The formula is live — not a one-time deal.

Editing a formula

You have to know how to edit formulas because people sometimes make mistakes or simply change their minds. Yes, it could even happen to you.

Suppose that you look at the spreadsheet you've been working on and think, "Gee, 25 percent seems like a lot to put away each month. I'll make it 10 percent." Okay, Mr. or Ms. Spendthrift — no problem. Just follow these steps:

1. **Click the cell that contains the savings calculation.**

The formula bar should display something like C6*25%, as shown in Figure 12-5.

Figure 12-5:
A formula in
the formula
bar.

2. **Click the formula bar and change** 25% **to** 10%.

3. **Press Enter on the keyboard or click the check mark next to the formula bar.**

Excel 2001 computes a new savings target.

You can drag the cell's fill handle to the right, wiping out the old 25 percent formulas and replacing them with your new 10 percent ones. See how easy?

Deleting a formula

Think that editing a formula is easy? Wait until you try deleting one. This process is so easy that getting paid to write about it is embarrassing (but I'll get over it).

First, think about why you want to delete a formula. Maybe setting your savings goal as a percentage of net income is the wrong way to do things. Maybe simply having a dollar amount in mind each month — $50, for example — makes more sense. Follow these steps to make the change:

1. **Click the January savings cell.**

2. **Type 50 (assuming that you want to save $50 in January).**

3. **Press the Enter key on the keyboard or click the check mark to the left of the formula bar.**

   The number you typed replaces the formula.

If you want the formula to come back, you can choose Edit⇨Undo Typing 50 in C7 (or whichever cell you typed in) — but only if you choose the command right away. Otherwise, you have to enter the formula the same way you did the first time.

Incidentally, you don't have to *replace* the formula with anything. You can just as easily (and just as properly) press the Delete key. In that case, your cell would be blank — which, perhaps, is exactly what you're looking for.

May I See Your References?

Excel 2001 uses *references* to describe cells and ranges. References are important because they keep Excel 2001 from using the wrong numbers in your formulas. References come in two flavors — relative and absolute — as you see in this section.

Creating cell and range references

Excel 2001 uses notations such as C1 to describe a cell in a spreadsheet. The first part of the notation — in this case, the C — specifies the column the cell is in. The second part of the notation — in this case, the 1 — specifies the row. You use the net income spreadsheet you've been working on in this chapter to illustrate the use of cell references in formulas.

Suppose that you want to see how much money you would save if you saved 15 percent of your net income each month. You could redo the formula easily enough. But what if you then want to see how much money you would save if you saved 16 percent? Or 17 percent? Or whatever? You would soon grow tired of redoing formulas. Wouldn't it be helpful if you could simply type the percentage number in a cell somewhere and have Excel 2001 use it in the formula? Well, guess what — it's not only helpful but also easy to do, and you're going to do it now. Follow these steps:

1. **Click Cell C10.**

2. **Type** Savings Rate.

3. **Press Enter.**

4. **Select the cell below Savings Rate (C11).**

5. **Type** 15%.

6. **Press Enter.**

Did your savings numbers change? Of course not. You haven't worked the savings rate into the formula. All you've done so far is create a box in which to type a rate you want. Here's how you make Excel 2001 use your number in the calculation:

1. **Select the cell containing the savings number for January.**

2. **Press the = (equal sign) key on the keyboard.**

3. **Click the cell containing the Savings Rate number (15%).**

4. **Press the * (asterisk) key.**

5. **Click the cell containing the net figure for January.**

6. **Press Enter.**

   Excel 2001 figures out the target savings number, using your 15 percent rate.

If you type another rate (try it!), the number for January changes as soon as you press Enter.

Uh-oh — you forgot about the rest of the months. You haven't pulled the formula over from January to the rest of the months. Solving this problem is easy. Just click the savings figure for January, and grab the cell's fill handle; then drag the fill handle over to the column for June. Now you're done.

Or are you? Except for January, all the savings numbers are zero! What's going on here?

An examination of the formulas in the cells provides the answer. Start by clicking the savings cell for January. Look at the formula bar; the formula refers to the savings-rate number you typed earlier. If your spreadsheet looks just like mine at this point, the reference is to Cell C11.

Now click the savings cell for February. Notice that the formula doesn't refer to C11 anymore — it refers to *D*11 instead. Because Cell D11 is empty, the formula computes a big zero. The story is the same for the rest of the months. The formulas don't refer to C11; rather, the column references increase by 1 as you move across the months. For February, the reference is D11; for March, E11; for April, F11; and so on.

In many cases, this method of *relative referencing* is just what you needed. But not this time. You have to tell Excel 2001 to use the value in Cell C11 all the time, no matter what, *absolutely.* Follow these steps:

1. **Click the savings cell for January and look at the formula bar.**

   You should see a formula like the one shown in Figure 12-6.

Figure 12-6:
This formula contains a relative reference.

C7   × ✓ 📖 = =C11*C6

2. **On the formula bar, change the formula to look like the one shown in Figure 12-7.**

   (Just click into the formula bar and type the dollar signs in the appropriate places.)

3. **Press Enter.**

Figure 12-7:
This formula uses an absolute reference.

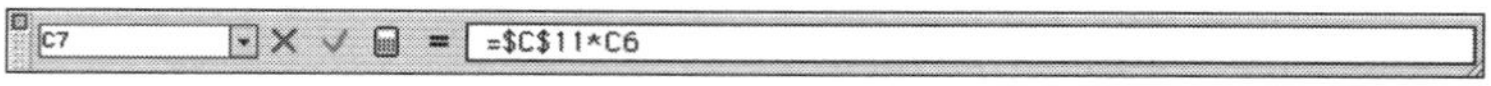

C7   × ✓ 📖 = =C11*C6

No difference yet, right? But what happens when you drag the January cell's fill handle to the right? Ah — you get some savings numbers! If you click those numbers, you see that the formulas for each of them use the value in C11. This process is called using *absolute* references (as opposed to relative ones), and in cases like this one, it's exactly what is called for.

When you put a dollar sign before a column reference, you tell Excel 2001 to refrain from changing the column. When you put a dollar sign before a row reference, you tell Excel 2001 to refrain from changing the row. It is entirely possible, and in many cases entirely handy, to lock down only the row or only the column, rather than both. You can toggle through the three types of absolute reference (row, column, or row and column), by selecting the cell reference in the formula bar and pressing ⌘+T. Each time you press ⌘+T, the reference type changes.

That's about all there is where individual cell references are concerned. Sometimes, it's convenient to refer to a group, or *range,* of cells rather than to each one individually. Because Excel 2001 uses range references often, you may as well find out how to do them yourself.

If you were to talk about the income numbers for all the months in your spreadsheet, you would talk about C4, D4, E4, F4, G4, and H4, using cell references. If you had a spreadsheet that covered several years, you would have to type a large number of cell references to describe the lot of them.

Range references are simply notations describing the starting and ending cells in question. Because your income numbers start at C4 and end at H4, the range reference becomes C4:H4.

Range references really just describe the beginning cell through the ending of a group of cells you have selected. Put a colon between the cell references, and there you are.

Grouping references with parentheses

I hate to do this to you, but I have to show you some math. Just a little, though.

Suppose that you want to make a formula that subtracts one number from another and multiplies the answer by another number. (This is what you're doing in the savings row, except that you first figure out the net income in a separate formula.) Suppose that you want to do all these things in one shot. Here's one way the formula may look:

```
C7 = C4 - C5 * C11
```

If you plug in the numbers from your worksheet, you get this result:

```
C7 = 900 - 700 * 15%
```

And the answer is . . . $795. That can't be right, can it? No, it can't be. In this scenario, you save more than your net income for the month. Something must be wrong.

Something *is* wrong, and it's the formula. Because Excel 2001 is not very good at figuring out what you mean, you have to be explicit. In this case, Excel 2001 multiplied C5 and C11 and then subtracted their product from C4, which is not what you intended. You wanted *first* to figure out what C4 minus C5 is and then multiply the result by 15 percent. Here's how the formula has to look for Excel 2001 to get the answer right:

```
C7 = (C4 - C5) * C11
```

And the answer is . . . $30, which makes more sense.

Technically, what you're doing is the same thing you did in high-school algebra class — namely, using the *distributive property*. In case you were sick that day, the distributive property states that for any real numbers A, B, and C:

```
(A + B) * C = A*C + B*C
```

(This question will not be on the final exam.)

The parentheses tell Excel 2001 "do this first." All you have to do is get the parentheses into the formula, which is a snap. Just follow these steps:

1. **Click the January savings cell.**

2. **Press the = (equal-sign) key.**

3. **Click Cell C4.**

   Watch the formula bar as your formula takes shape.

4. **Press the minus (–) key.**

5. **Click Cell C5.**

   Again, notice how your formula is being recorded on the formula bar.

6. **Press the asterisk (multiply) key.**

7. **Click Cell C11.**

8. **Press Enter.**

   If all goes according to plan, your answer is $795.

I had to trick you into making a mistake to give you something to correct, and you've done the first part. Here's how to correct the mistake:

1. **Click the January savings cell.**

2. **Insert right and left parentheses into the appropriate places in the formula bar's formula.**

   You need an opening parenthesis before C4 and a closing one after C5.

3. **Press Enter.**

   Your answer should be $30.

Does this process seem to be complicated? It isn't, really. Just remember that Excel 2001 evaluates the stuff inside parentheses before it performs any other calculations.

Excel 2001 is smart enough to catch — and offer to fix — common mistakes and typos you may make in a formula. If you leave off a parenthesis and press the Enter key, for example, the Office Assistant complains and asks to fix the problem, as shown in Figure 12-8.

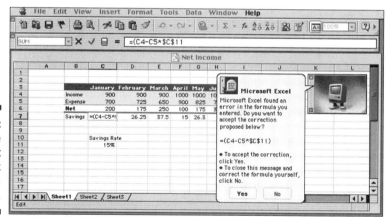

Figure 12-8: The Office Assistant offers to fix your formula typo.

Sometimes, the Assistant's suggestion isn't the right one, so you should click No to its offer and fix it yourself. That persistent Assistant still tries to be helpful by telling you what the problem was in the formula, as seen in Figure 12-9.

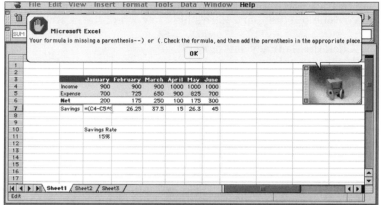

Figure 12-9:
Even if you refuse its help, the Assistant still tells you what's wrong with the formula.

Using Functions

Remember sines and cosines? How about square roots? No? Excel 2001 does. In fact, Excel 2001 remembers these and 326 other *functions.* With functions, you plug in the numbers, and Excel 2001 computes the answer. In this section, you get your feet wet with functions by computing an average monthly income, using the same spreadsheet you've been using in this chapter.

Suppose that you want your average monthly income to show up in the cell just to the right of June's income figure. Follow these steps:

1. **Click the desired cell.**

2. **Press the equal key on the keyboard.**

3. **Choose Insert⇨Function.**

   The Paste Function dialog box appears, as shown in Figure 12-10. Notice that the Excel 2001 functions are divided into categories.

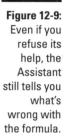

Figure 12-10:
The Paste Function window lets you insert functions into your formulas.

4. **If you want to see all the functions, click the All category; otherwise, choose a category to see only that category's functions.**

   Because Average is a statistical function, you should click Statistical.

5. **Choose Average from the list on the right side of the dialog box.**

   Excel 2001 displays a description of the Average function at the bottom of the dialog box.

6. **Click OK.**

   Excel displays the Formula Palette to help you finish the formula, as shown in Figure 12-11. Excel's first guess — that you want to average all the cells in the income row — is correct.

7. **Click OK in the Formula Palette.**

Notice that Excel 2001 uses a range reference (C4:H4) in the formula rather than list each cell in the computation individually.

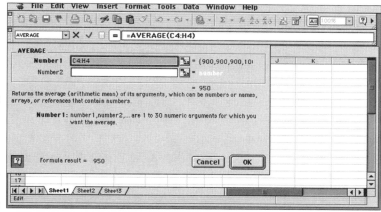

Figure 12-11:
The Formula
Palette
helps you
build your
formula.

This news probably won't come as a shock to you: You can use another method to put a function into a formula, and it's faster. Use this other method to compute the average for the expenses by following these steps:

1. **Click the cell at the end of the expenses row (just below where you figured out the average for income).**

2. **Press the equal key on the keyboard.**

3. **Open the pop-up menu that appears to the left of the formula bar (see Figure 12-12).**

   This list contains recently used functions, including AVERAGE.

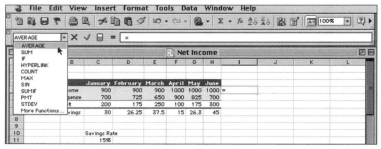

Figure 12-12:
The list of functions appropriate to the selected cell range.

4. Choose AVERAGE.

You're back in a familiar place.

Excel 2001 should have displayed C5:H5 in the Formula Palette. If not, you need to show Excel 2001 which numbers you're averaging. Follow these steps:

1. Click the Expand/Contract button in the Formula Palette (see Figure 12-13).

The Formula Palette shrinks to enable you to select the cells you want to use in the function. Select Cells C5 through H5.

Expand/Contract Formula Palette

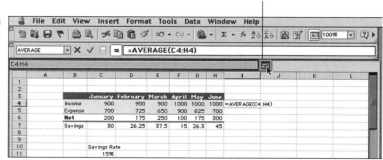

Figure 12-13:
The contracted Formula Palette. Click again to expand the palette.

2. Click the Expand/Contract button again.

The palette expands, showing the range of cells you want to average.

3. Click OK.

Using AutoSum

You can do one more thing: Figure out how much money you will save if you manage to meet your savings goal each month. To do it in the easiest way possible, follow these steps:

1. **Click the cell at the end of the savings row.**

2. **Click the AutoSum button on the toolbar.**

   The symbol on the button is a capital sigma — something that symbolizes summation to math majors.

   Excel 2001 guesses that you want to add everything to the left of the current cell, which is why it put SUM(C7:H7) in the formula.

3. **Press Enter.**

Nine times out of ten, Excel 2001 guesses correctly when you click the AutoSum button. If it doesn't guess correctly, you can fix things by editing the formula on the formula bar.

Clicking just to the right of the AutoSum button makes a pop-up menu appear with other common formula choices. Besides Sum, there's also:

- ✔ **Average:** Calculates the average of the selected range of cells.
- ✔ **Count:** Enters the number of cells in the range.
- ✔ **Max:** Your cousin from Schenectady. No, it really enters the maximum value in the range.
- ✔ **Min:** Enters the minimum value in the range.
- ✔ **More Functions:** Opens the Past Function window.

Using the Calculator

Excel 2001 gives you a new tool to help build formulas. It's the Calculator, which lets you use a familiar metaphor — a hand calculator — to create formulas. As you click the buttons on the Calculator, Excel builds the formula. When you're done, Excel inserts the formula into the cell you've been working in.

To use the Calculator to create a formula, follow these steps:

1. **Click on the cell into which you want to place the formula.**

2. **On the formula bar, click the Calculator icon.**

   The Calculator appears.

3. **Click cells on the worksheet to insert cell references into the Calculator. Click and drag cells to insert references to a range of cells.**

4. **Use the Calculator's buttons to enter numbers, arithmetic operators, or parenthesis into your formulas.**

   As the formula takes shape, the result of the formula will appear in the Calculator's Answer box, as shown in Figure 12-14. Clicking the Sum button will expand the Calculator to let you type in (or select with the mouse) the range of cells you need summed. If you need to use some other function, click the More button, which opens the Paste Function window.

Figure 12-14:
A completed formula, ready to insert into the worksheet.

5. **To accept the formula and insert it into the cell shown in the Place in cell box, click OK.**

Everyday Excel 2001 functions

Even though Excel 2001 has hundreds of available functions, most of them are specialized functions for people who do statistics, hardcore financial forecasting, or scientific calculations. The following list gives you a rundown of what commonly used Excel 2001 functions do, followed by an example of their formats:

- ✔ **AVERAGE:** Finds the average of a range of cells

  AVERAGE(number1,number2)

- ✔ **CONCATENATE:** Joins several text strings into one text string

  CONCATENATE (text1,text2)

- ✔ **COUNT:** Counts how many cells in a range contain numbers rather than text

  COUNT(value1,value2)

- ✔ **IF:** Applies a logical test in a formula, such as performing a calculation only if the value of a particular cell is zero

  IF(logical_test,value_if_true, value_if_false)

- ✔ **MAX:** Finds the largest number in a range of cells

  MAX(number1,number2)

- ✔ **MIN:** Finds the smallest number in a range of cells

  MIN(number1,number2)

- ✔ **ROUND:** Rounds a decimal number to a specified number of places

  ROUND(number,num_digits)

- ✔ **SQRT:** Finds the square root of a number

  SQRT(number)

- ✔ **SUM:** Adds the values in two or more cells

  SUM(number1,number2)

Chapter 13

Working with Worksheets and Workbooks

*E*xcel 2001 calls the documents you make *workbooks* and the pages in the workbooks *worksheets*. Pages, you say? Yessiree, Bob! Excel 2001 workbooks can have as many pages as you want them to have, and this chapter tells you all about them.

Naming Worksheets

Before you start naming worksheets, you have to be clear about the worksheet concept. Here goes.

When you create a new Excel 2001 document, it's an empty grid of cells. The cells go to the right for 256 columns, and they go down for 65,536 rows. Although it sounds like a great deal of room to work in, it isn't always enough. Sometimes, you need a second page.

Or you don't *need* a second page, but you want one anyway. Suppose that you're keeping track of the students in a small school and you want to keep the first grade, second grade, and third grade on separate spreadsheets. One way, of course, is to make separate Excel 2001 documents for each grade. A better way, however, is to make separate pages — or *worksheets* — in a single Excel 2001 document, called a *workbook*. This way, you have only one document to keep track of, one document to back up, and one document taking up room on your screen.

Figure 13-1 shows how you can set up the first grade's worksheet. (Granted, the class is small.)

	A	B	C	D	E	F	G	H	I
				🗋 Class Records					
1	First Grade								
2									
3									
4	Student Name	Age		Breakfast?	Scholarship				
5									
6	Sean	12		5	$650				
7	Rachel	11			$1,000				
8	Aaron	9		5	$400				
9	Brandy	15		5	$400				
10	Sierra	8			$650				
11									
12	Avg age:	11							
13	Breakfasts/week:			15					
14	Total scholarship $$				$3,100.00				
15									

Figure 13-1:
A worksheet for the first grade.

Naming the sheets makes it easier for you and for Excel 2001 to keep track of which sheet you're working on. Name the sheet before you go any further:

1. **Double-click the tab that says Sheet1 at the bottom of the window.**

   The current title (the generic, default Sheet1) is highlighted.

2. **Type the title you want for the sheet.**

   For example, you could type First Grade.

3. **Press Enter.**

If you ever feel like changing the name again, just repeat these steps. Excel 2001 enables you to change the name of a worksheet whenever you want.

You can use one of a couple of ways to make a second sheet just like the first — this time, with information for the second grade. Here's one of the easiest methods:

1. **Select all the cells that have something in them.**

   You can select all the cells (whether they contain something or not) if you want. The fastest way is to press ⌘+A, which is the shortcut for Select All.

2. **Choose Edit➪Copy.**

   Although nothing seems to happen, a copy of the First Grade page has been placed on the Clipboard, ready for pasting.

3. **Double-click the Sheet2 tab.**

   This step has the dual effect of switching to the second worksheet in the workbook and of selecting the name of the sheet so that you can give it a new name.

4. Rename the sheet by typing Second Grade **and pressing Enter.**

Now you're ready to paste.

5. Choose Edit⇨Paste.

Your new Second Grade worksheet looks just like the first!

You can change the data for the Second Grade sheet by just typing over it. One of the nice things about this copy-and-paste technique is that it brings along the formatting, so make sure that you like the formatting of the First Grade page before you start copying and pasting it all over the place. There's no sense in doing the formatting more than once.

At this point, creating a Third Grade worksheet should be a snap for you. Go ahead and do it, following the same steps you used to make the Second Grade sheet.

Now try moving between the worksheets. Just click the correct tab — the one with the correct name at the bottom of the window. Notice that the worksheet in the front has a white tab, whereas the other worksheets have gray tabs, as shown in Figure 13-2. That color difference is the only clue you have to which worksheet you're in, so watch for it!

Figure 13-2: The white tab shows you the active, frontmost worksheet in the workbook.

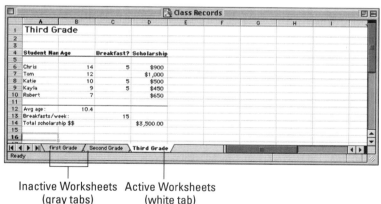

Inactive Worksheets (gray tabs)   Active Worksheets (white tab)

Creating and Deleting Worksheets

You're probably wondering what happens if you want another sheet — for the fourth grade, maybe? You don't have any more worksheet tabs to click, so it looks as though you're out of luck. As you may suspect, however, you aren't really out of luck because you aren't really out of sheets.

By default (which means "unless you explicitly take steps to make a change"), Excel 2001 puts three worksheets in a workbook. You can change this default action by choosing Edit⇨Preferences. The rest you can figure out on your own.

No matter how many worksheets your workbook has, you can always add another. (Excel 2001 places no limits on the number of sheets in a workbook, though your computer may poop out after a couple of hundred.) Adding a sheet is as easy as choosing Insert⇨Worksheet.

Excel 2001 doesn't necessarily put the new sheet where you want it, however. Excel 2001 doesn't even ask. Instead, the new sheet is placed *before* the sheet you're now using. What a drag.

Actually, "a drag" is exactly what's called for here. Want to move a sheet to a new location? All you do is drag it:

1. **Click the tab for the sheet you're trying to move, and hold down the mouse button.**

2. **Drag the tab to the location you want.**

   A small, black triangle points to the place where the sheet will land if you drop it.

3. **When the triangle points just after the Third Grade tab, release the mouse button.**

How about that!

Deleting worksheets is just as easy. Activate the sheet you want to delete and then choose Edit⇨Delete Sheet. Excel 2001 gives you one chance to change your mind, although that's all you get. When that chance is gone, it's gone. Undo doesn't work.

The one way to get the sheet back is to close the document without saving it. Excel 2001 asks whether you want to save an unsaved workbook, and if you've made a big mistake, the answer is No. The next time you open that workbook, it reverts to the way that it looked the last time you saved it. Saving your workbook just before you do something extreme, such as delete sheets, makes this technique more useful; otherwise, you could lose too much work.

Linking Worksheets with Formulas

Although it's useful to have different worksheets within a workbook, one of the real strengths of Excel is its capability to make all the worksheets cooperate. In the grade example used in the preceding section, it would be a good idea to have a single summary page with results from each of the individual grade pages.

If you don't have four worksheets in your workbook, add one and name it Summary. Drag the Summary sheet to a place *in front* of the First Grade sheet. (The idea is to make this page an executive summary, with the supporting data behind it. This kind of thing makes the boss very happy.)

Listing just the total amount of scholarship money on the Summary page, by grade, may be interesting:

1. **On your Summary page, create some labels for the data, as shown in Figure 13-3.**

Figure 13-3:
Labels on the Summary worksheet.

2. **To get the numbers from the individual sheets to show up on the Summary sheet, start by clicking the cell next to the First Grade label.**

   For this example, click Cell B5.

3. **Type = (an equal sign), which is how every formula in Excel 2001 begins.**

4. **Click the First Grade tab to switch to the First Grade worksheet.**

5. **Click the cell of the First Grade sheet that contains the Total Scholarship figure.**

6. **Press Enter.**

   Excel 2001 takes you back to the Summary sheet, where the formula was created, and you see the total scholarship number from the First Grade sheet.

To see whether the Summary sheet is updated if you change something on the First Grade sheet, follow these steps:

1. **Switch to the First Grade sheet by clicking its tab.**

2. **Change the scholarship amount for Sean from 650 to 750.**

   Notice that the total scholarship money for First Grade changes, as it should, to $3,200.

3. **Switch back to the Summary sheet by clicking its tab.**

   Hey — the sheet has been updated! The Summary sheet's number really is linked to the corresponding number on the First Grade sheet.

Using AutoSum

Repeating this process with the Second Grade and Third Grade sheets is a snap, so go ahead and do it. That Total cell on the Summary sheet is just waiting for you to fill it in. If you click it and then click the AutoSum button on the toolbar, Excel 2001 creates the formula for you.

If you click the AutoSum button, you get a chance to review what Excel 2001 thinks you want to add. If Excel guesses right, all you have to do is press Enter. If Excel doesn't guess right, you can change the formula and *then* press Enter. On the other hand, when you have a hunch that Excel 2001 will get it right on the first try, you can *double-click* the AutoSum button. When you do, Excel not only figures out the formula but also, in effect, presses the Enter key for you. Pretty swell.

Analyzing your data

After the data has been brought into the Summary sheet, you can do some analysis on it. You may want to know, percentagewise, how much of the total scholarship money is going to the first, second, and third grades, for example. To figure that out, follow these steps:

1. **Give Column C the heading** Percentages.

2. **Click Cell C5, which is next to the First Grade scholarship-money cell.**

3. **Press the = (equal) key to begin a formula.**

4. **Click the cell that contains the First Grade total.**

5. **Press the / (slash, or division) key.**

6. **Click the Total number (B8).**

7. **Press Enter.**

The number doesn't look like a percentage, but ignore that fact for now. Repeat Steps 2 through 7 for the second- and third-grade figures, and you end up with something that looks like Figure 13-4.

Figure 13-4:
A Summary
sheet with
poorly
formatted
percentages.

	A	B	C	D	E	F	G	H
3			Percentages					
4	Scholarship Money							
5	First Grade	$3,200.00	0.33					
6	Second Grade	$2,975.00	0.31					
7	Third Grade	$3,400.00	0.36					
8	Total	$9,575.00						

Class Records

Summary / First Grade / Second Grade / Third Grade

Ready

To change the appearance of those percentage figures, follow these steps:

1. **Select the cells that contain the percentages (Cells C5 through C7).**

2. **Choose View⇨Toolbars⇨Formatting.**

3. **Click the Percent button on the Formatting toolbar.**

Your numbers look a little more like percentages.

Using worksheet references

You probably understand the concept of cell references, and you may even have a feeling for what range references are. Now you take another step in the same direction, a step that takes you to *worksheet references,* which define relationships between two or more worksheets.

Worksheet references are important because Excel 2001 needs to know which sheet you're talking about when you say, "Use Cell D11." The worksheet references are inserted automatically when you make your formulas the way you do in the preceding sections. If you wonder what the formulas look like, click the cell that contains the first-grade scholarship total (B5) on the Summary sheet; then look at the formula bar, which should look like this line:

```
='First Grade'!D14
```

The first part of the formula tells you the name of the worksheet. Excel requires that the name be enclosed in single quotes. You can't use double quotes because Excel uses double quotes to store text in formulas. The exclamation point just says, "The stuff up to now was a worksheet reference." D14 is just D14, but not any old D14 — it's the D14 on the First Grade sheet.

Although you can type this formula (don't forget the single quotes, and don't use double quotes), having Excel 2001 do it for you is much easier.

Adding Worksheets to Workbooks

Combining individual spreadsheets into workbooks makes a great deal of sense, and it's easy to do if you're thinking about it at the beginning. The problem is that you might still have some old Excel 4 or 5 single-sheet documents lying around, in a one-sheet-per-document format, and you don't want to re-create them in a multiple-sheet format just because I say that that format is cool. What you might do, though, is *combine* the existing sheets into multiple-sheet workbooks, as long as it's easy enough to do. You can decide for yourself whether the steps are easy enough:

1. **Create a new Excel 2001 document and save it.**

   (You bring the other documents into this one.)

2. **Open one of your old documents, and make sure that the page you want to move or copy is in front.**

   Click the tabs at the bottom of the window to switch to the proper sheet, if necessary.

3. **Choose Edit⇨Move or Copy Sheet.**

   A poorly designed dialog box appears, as shown in Figure 13-5. This dialog box is so unintuitive that it feels like the first time every time you see it, which shows that Excel 2001 still has room for improvement.

   You use the Move or Copy dialog box to tell Excel 2001 to which workbook you want to move or copy the current worksheet and where (in front of which current worksheet page) you want to put it.

Figure 13-5:
The Move or
Copy dialog
box.

4. **Choose a target workbook from the To book drop-down list (where the sheet will go).**

5. **In the Before sheet scrollbox, select the worksheet (page) that the moved or copied sheet will be placed in front of.**

6. **Decide whether to move or copy the sheet.**

   (Copying is safer and usually the better choice.)

7. **Click OK.**

Excel 2001 does what you ask it to, and if you check, you see that you have indeed added a worksheet to your new Excel 2001 document. Half the time, you will have the wrong sheet in the wrong place, but you'll get better with practice. It's not your fault; the dialog box really isn't very intuitive. Remember to save your documents just *before* making major moves such as this one, just to be safe.

Chapter 14

Turning Numbers into Pictures with Charts

*I*f a picture's worth a thousand words, then a chart is worth a million and twelve cells in a spreadsheet. Excel 2001 lets you turn humdrum rows and columns of numbers into eye-grabbing, message-sending, wallop-packing charts — all without breaking a sweat.

The Right Kind of Chart

As far as Excel 2001 is concerned, charts come in 12 basic types. Choosing the right chart type for the type of data you're representing is important because the wrong chart type may either mislead viewers or hopelessly confuse them. The figures in this section display each chart type and explain how each one is used.

A *column chart,* as shown in Figure 14-1, is perfect for showing how something changes over time, such as sales or expenses per quarter.

Figure 14-1:
A column chart.

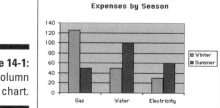

A *bar chart* is much like a column chart turned on its side, as shown in Figure 14-2. Most bar charts could have been column charts, but bar charts are useful when you are not trying to emphasize the passage of time.

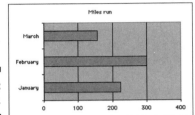

Figure 14-2:
A bar chart.

A *line chart* displays the same kind of data as a column chart, with the addition of *trend lines,* which show you how the data is changing, as shown in Figure 14-3. With a line chart, you convey an idea of *how* something changed, not just what the changes were.

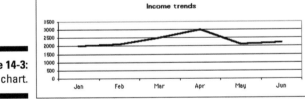

Figure 14-3:
A line chart.

Seemingly everybody's favorite, a *pie chart* is excellent for showing percentages of something, as shown in Figure 14-4. The pie wedges always add up to 100 percent.

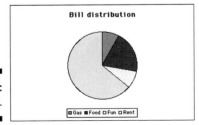

Figure 14-4:
A pie chart.

Figure 14-5 shows an *XY chart* (or *scatter chart*), which plots data points against two axes (X and Y). This chart type is commonly used for scientific data.

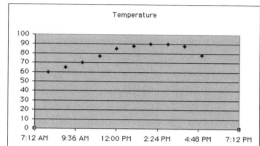

Figure 14-5:
An XY
(scatter)
chart.

An *area chart* is a cross between a column chart and a pie chart. As you can see in Figure 14-6, this type of chart displays, in essence, pie-chart data changing over time.

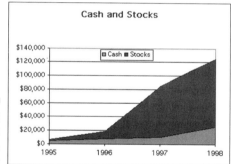

Figure 14-6:
An area
chart.

I'm tempted to tell you that doughnut charts are for charting doughnuts, but I'll refrain. A *doughnut chart* is much like a pie chart, in fact, with one pie placed atop another, as shown in Figure 14-7. Multiple pie charts can convey the same information, but not as neatly as a single doughnut chart.

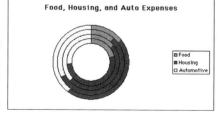

Figure 14-7:
A doughnut
chart.

A *radar chart* looks like a line chart with multiple-value axes. This chart type shows how the shape of the connected lines can show how two things are similar or different (see Figure 14-8).

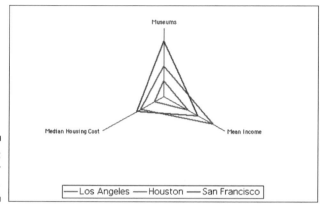

Figure 14-8:
A radar
chart.

A *surface chart* is similar to a topographic map, showing areas that fall into the same range of values, as shown in Figure 14-9. This type of chart is easy to make incorrectly!

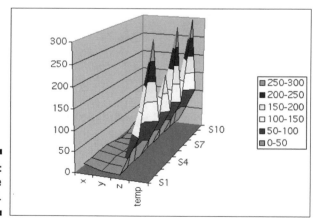

Figure 14-9:
A surface
chart.

A *bubble chart* is a variation of an XY chart. Figure 14-10 shows how the sizes of the bubbles represent the value of a third variable.

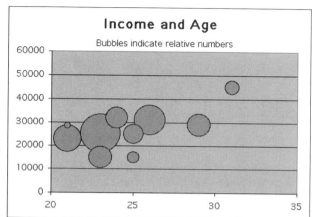

Figure 14-10:
A bubble
chart.

A *stock chart* can be used to display any changing data (including stock high–low–close prices). This type of chart, as shown in Figure 14-11, is similar to an XY chart with multiple Ys per X.

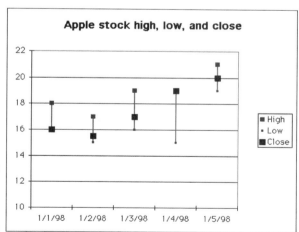

Figure 14-11:
A stock
chart.

Cone, cylinder, and *pyramid charts* are nothing more than gussied-up column and bar charts, as shown in Figure 14-12.

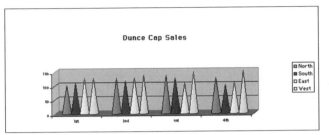

Figure 14-12:
Cone,
cylinder, and
pyramid
charts.

Enough about what charts are and when to use them! In the following section, you get on with the business of making them.

Creating a Chart with the Chart Wizard

You can use Excel 2001 to make a chart in at least a couple of ways. The Chart Wizard is by far the easiest way, especially for beginners. In this section, you use the Chart Wizard to make a simple chart, and when you're done, you'll know enough to make almost any type of chart you want. To turn those boring numbers into a thrilling column chart, follow these steps:

1. **For starters, you need a spreadsheet with some data in it. Create a new Excel 2001 document and put data in it, as shown in Figure 14-13.**

Figure 14-13:
A
spreadsheet
with data in
it for
charting.

	A	B	C	D	E	F	G	H	I
1									
2	Quarterly Sales by Region								
3									
4									
5		1st Qtr	2nd Qtr	3rd Qtr	4th Qtr				
6	North	100	110	105	115				
7	South	60	75	70	80				
8	East	95	105	105	100				
9	West	125	115	135	140				
10									

2. **Select the portion of the spreadsheet that contains the data you want to chart.**

Figure 14-14 shows you the right stuff to select.

Figure 14-14:
Selecting
the data you
want to
chart.

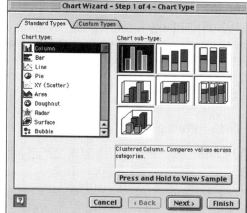

3. Click the Chart Wizard button on the Standard toolbar.

The Chart Wizard dialog box appears.

4. Choose Column as the chart type.

5. Choose the first chart subtype, as shown in Figure 14-15.

Figure 14-15:
The Chart
Wizard, with
the column
chart type
and the first
subtype
selected.

6. Click the Next button.

The next page in the Chart Wizard dialog box shows a miniature version of your chart-to-be.

7. If the miniature version of the chart is what you had in mind, click Next. Otherwise, click Cancel and select your data again.

Page 3 of the Chart Wizard gives you the opportunity to pretty things up, as shown in Figure 14-16.

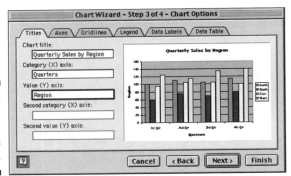

Figure 14-16:
Adding a
chart title
and axis
labels.

8. **Click the Titles tab.**

9. **Enter a title for the chart in the Chart Title box, and then enter labels for the X (horizontal) and Y (vertical) axes.**

   The tabs across the top of the dialog box allow you to modify the look of the chart and the way the data are presented. You should experiment with these the next time you build a chart.

10. **Click Next.**

   The last page of the Chart Wizard gives you a choice between putting your chart in a new worksheet (in the same workbook) or in the same worksheet that contains your data.

11. **Choose As Object In to place the chart in the worksheet you're working on.**

12. **Click Finish.**

Wow! You have a chart, and it's much nicer to look at than the numbers. Notice that the chart itself is selected, and so are parts of the data. A special Chart toolbar has also appeared. Figure 14-17 shows the changes.

Excel 2001 outlines with a thin, blue border the data (numbers) it plotted. The program outlines the *series labels* (the words in the legend) with a thin, green border and outlines the *category labels* (the words across the category axis) in purple.

The chart is *live,* which means that if you click one of the cells containing the information you charted and then change that data, the chart changes too. Because of this arrangement, you can make the chart once and forget about it because the chart is always connected to the data in the spreadsheet. This is known as A Very Good Feature.

Series labels Category labels Data Chart toolbar

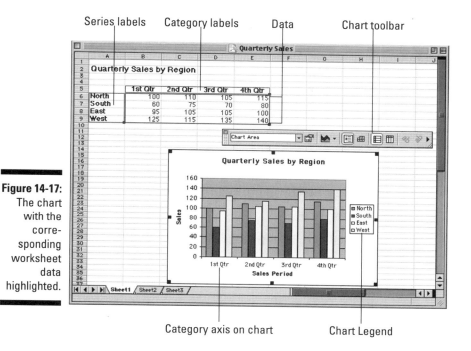

Figure 14-17:
The chart with the corresponding worksheet data highlighted.

Category axis on chart Chart Legend

Modifying a Chart

Excel 2001 does a good job of guessing what you want in a chart, but sometimes you have another chart in mind. Or maybe after seeing the chart Excel 2001 created, you come up with another idea. Or maybe you just want to experiment with different options to see how things turn out. No problem — Excel 2001 charts are flexible, and you can easily change just about anything. The Chart toolbar, as shown in Figure 14-18, comes in handy for this purpose.

DataTable

Chart type By Column

Chart Objects Angle Text Upward

Figure 14-18:
The Chart toolbar.

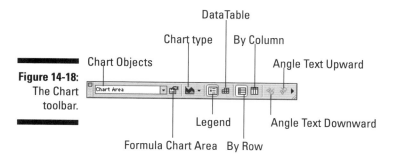

Formula Chart Area By Row

Legend Angle Text Downward

Changing the chart size

Start by changing the size of the chart. The Chart toolbar has a pop-up menu, which you use to select parts of the chart for later modification. Follow these steps:

1. **Open the Chart Objects pop-up menu.**

2. **If it's not already selected, choose Chart Area (refer to Figure 14-18).**

   The entire chart area (not just the chart but also the area around it, including the legend and the title) is selected.

3. **Click and drag a handle at the edge of the chart to resize the chart.**

4. **Release the mouse button.**

You can use other choices from the Chart Objects pop-up menu to select different parts of the chart, and then you can resize or modify those parts with any of Excel's formatting tools, such as the Formatting Palette.

Changing the chart orientation

Now you can change the nature of the chart. Right now, you have a chart with different-colored columns for North, South, East, and West. Maybe it would be more interesting if the chart had North, South, East, and West across the bottom as category labels and 1st Qtr, 2nd Qtr, 3rd Qtr, and 4th Qtr in the legend.

To make these changes, click the By Column button on the Chart toolbar. The chart changes as you want it to. If you click the By Rows button, you change it back.

If you forget which toolbar button is which, just place the mouse pointer on a button and wait a moment. Excel 2001 displays the button's name on a small, yellow label, called a *ScreenTip.*

When you click the By Column button, you're telling Excel 2001 that you want to look at *columns* of data rather than rows. For the example in this section, the *columns* (1st Qtr, 2nd Qtr, 3rd Qtr, and 4th Qtr) are the data series — not the rows. When you click the By Row button, you're telling Excel 2001 just the opposite. A *data series* is a group of numbers in a particular category. Data series are a big deal because Excel 2001 creates entirely different charts for different data series. The most important thing is to remember that you can flip things around by clicking the By Column and By Row buttons.

Changing the chart type

You can change the chart type, if you want. (Choosing a chart type is the first step in the Chart Wizard process.) Naturally, you can wipe out what you have and run through the Chart Wizard again, but you don't have to do that. Instead, you can use the Chart toolbar and change the type instantly, without doing any other work:

1. **Open the Chart Type pop-up menu on the Chart toolbar.**

   A list of chart types appears; each type is represented by a small icon of what the chart looks like.

2. **Slide down to the button labeled Bar Chart.**

   If you don't see the label, wait a moment for it to appear.

   You can tear off the list of chart types and make them a separate toolbar. Your clue that this act is possible is the double-dotted lines across the top of the Chart Type list. To tear off the list, just click the down arrow next to the Chart Type button, drag to the edge of the menu that appears, and then *keep going*. The menu sticks to your mouse pointer, and when you release the mouse button, you see a separate Chart Type toolbar, giving you a choice of places from which to choose a chart type.

3. **Release the mouse button.**

   The result is shown in Figure 14-19.

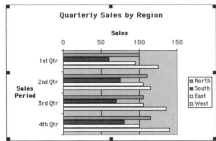

Figure 14-19: A finished bar chart.

You can easily spin things around by clicking the By Column and By Row buttons. Give them a try! Notice that if you click By Row, the chart may appear to be upside down (with 4th Qtr at the top and 1st Qtr at the bottom). You'll see how to fix that in the next section.

Changing the axis of a bar chart

You shouldn't be surprised to know that you can change the axis of a bar chart, which will solve the problem, where the 4th quarter data was showing up above the other three quarters. All you need are your friend the Chart toolbar and a little instruction. You want to change the category axis (the value axis is the one that displays numbers, and you do *not* want to change that one). Follow these steps:

1. **Choose Category Axis from the Chart Objects pop-up menu on the Chart toolbar.**

 2. **Click the Format Axis button.**

    This button changes names, depending on what is selected in the Chart Objects list.

    The Format Axis dialog box appears, displaying a gaggle of options. Because you want to reverse the order of things in the category axis, and nothing in the Patterns section can help you in this regard, you're in the wrong place and should move on.

3. **Click the Scale tab at the top of the dialog box.**

    (Check out the other tabs in this dialog box on your own someday.)

4. **Click the Categories in Reverse Order check box.**

5. **Click OK.**

You now know the general routine for changing part of a chart: Choose a part from the Chart Objects drop-down list, click the Format button, and then choose some options. As usual, you can do these tasks in other ways, although they're harder and slower. What's the point?

Part V

Putting on a Show with PowerPoint 2001

The 5th Wave   By Rich Tennant

NETWORK JONES AND THE *LOST FILE* OF WENDY

Oh Nety—
be careful!

In this part . . .

Unfair as it may seem, people don't always immediately agree with every idea you have. Unless, of
course, you're the Dictator for Life in your particular
country. However, the crack IDG Books Worldwide
Marketing Research Department has assured me that very
few Dictators for Life have been known to read books in
the ...*For Dummies* series. They're probably reading *World
Domination For Dummies,* anyway. It's a good bet that, like
most people, sooner or later you'll have to persuade your
co-workers with a presentation. That's where PowerPoint
2001 comes in.

In this part, you discover the basics of creating slide
shows and sprucing up a plain presentation with sizzling
images, exciting video, and flashy effects. One section
even helps you battle the dread specter of stage fright.

Chapter 15

Creating PowerPoint Slide Shows

In This Chapter

▶ Creating your first presentation

▶ Working with slides

▶ Reviewing the show

▶ Printing your presentation

*F*or many people, giving presentations is the part of their jobs they like the least. Standing up in front of co-workers and speaking makes their hearts pound, their palms sweat, and their knees knock.

Although Microsoft Office 2001 can't do much about stage fright, it can help you be prepared and confident in the quality of your presentation. You create your presentation by using PowerPoint 2001 to outline your thoughts, turn those thoughts into slides, and then add interesting visuals to amuse and distract your audience. You can use PowerPoint 2001 to show presentations on your computer, print them as handouts, or even produce 35mm slides. (You remember slides, don't you? That old analog film technology? See, before computers . . . oh, never mind.)

Creating Your First Presentation

To create a presentation in PowerPoint 2001, you have three choices:

- ✔ **Have the PowerPoint 2001 AutoContent Wizard walk you through the steps of creating the presentation.** The Wizard helps you with what to say and with the appearance of the presentation. This method is the best choice when you're new to PowerPoint.

- ✔ **Build your show based on one of the dozens of templates that come with PowerPoint 2001.** The templates take care of the attractive graphics; you take care of the interesting text.

- ✔ **Start with a blank canvas and create your presentation from scratch.**

It may seem that building a presentation from scratch gives you the most creative flexibility, and it does — if you're a talented graphic artist. If that were the case, though, chances are that you wouldn't be reading this chapter. Creating a good-looking presentation takes a special kind of talent, and Microsoft has already paid for that talent and put the results on the Office 2001 CD-ROM. Why not take advantage of this Microsoft largess? Use the AutoContent Wizard or one of the templates to get started on your presentation. There's nothing to stop you from modifying it later.

Using the AutoContent Wizard

The AutoContent Wizard steps you through the process of creating a presentation, based on any of 24 preset presentation types. The Wizard asks you some basic questions about your presentation and then drops you into the PowerPoint Outline composition window to add the text to your presentation.

To use the AutoContent Wizard to create a presentation, follow these steps:

1. **Launch PowerPoint 2001.**

   The Project Gallery appears, as shown in Figure 15-1.

   If the Project Gallery doesn't show up, it may have been turned off in the PowerPoint Preferences dialog box. You can still get to the AutoContent Wizard by choosing File➪Project Gallery, clicking the General tab, selecting the AutoContent Wizard, and clicking the OK button.

2. **Click the AutoContent Wizard icon.**

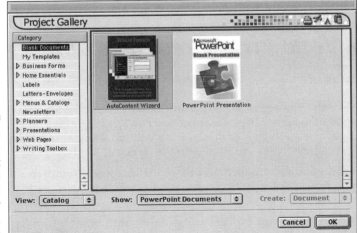

Figure 15-1:
Select the AutoContent Wizard to get started with your presentation.

3. Click the OK button.

The Presentation Type window appears, as shown in Figure 15-2.

The presentation choices in the Presentation Type window come from PowerPoint templates that were installed on your hard disk with the rest of Office 2001. Specifically, those templates live in the folder at the end of this path: Microsoft Office 2001:Templates:Presentations:Content. There's nothing magical about these templates; you can add your own to the list. If you create a presentation that you want to use as the basis for future presentations, you can save it as a template, use the Add button in the Presentation Type window, and it will thereafter be available to you in the AutoContent Wizard.

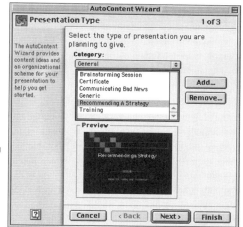

Figure 15-2:
Choosing a
presentation
type.

4. Using the Category pop-up menu and the scrollbox, select a presentation type, and then click the Next button.

The Presentation Media window appears.

5. Choose the output option you want to use — On-screen presentations, Black and white overheads, Color overheads, or 35mm slides — and then click the Next button.

The Presentation Title and Footers window appears, as shown in Figure 15-3.

6. Type the presentation title, your name, and any additional information you want to include on the first slide. If you want text to appear at the bottom of each slide, enter the text in the Footer box. Click the check boxes if you want to have the slide number or the date the presentation was last updated appear on each slide.

Stop me before I present again!

There's nothing quite like a brilliant presentation, one suffused with humor, wit, and solid information and presented with style and panache. Unfortunately, there's also nothing quite like a dull presentation. Okay, maybe a root canal (with apologies to our dentist friends).

Although PowerPoint 2001 can add a great deal of visual flash to your presentation, there's no substitute for interesting content. All the clever slide transitions, animated text and charts, and whizzy graphics in the world can't punch up information that is dull, dull, dull.

Luckily, the solution is simple. When you create a slide show, spend most of your time working on your words in Outline mode. Share your outline with co-workers, and make changes based on their feedback. When the words are right, spice them up with visuals. Get the words right first, however.

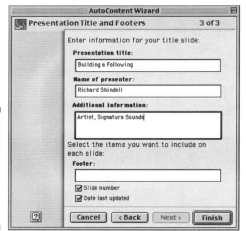

Figure 15-3:
Adding the information for the title slide and slide footers.

7. **Click the Finish button.**

   PowerPoint 2001 displays in Normal view the presentation you built, as shown in Figure 15-4.

8. **Replace the text provided by the AutoContent Wizard with your own text in the rest of the outline.**

9. **Click the Slide View button to get a full-size look at your slides, or click the Slide Show button to view the presentation.**

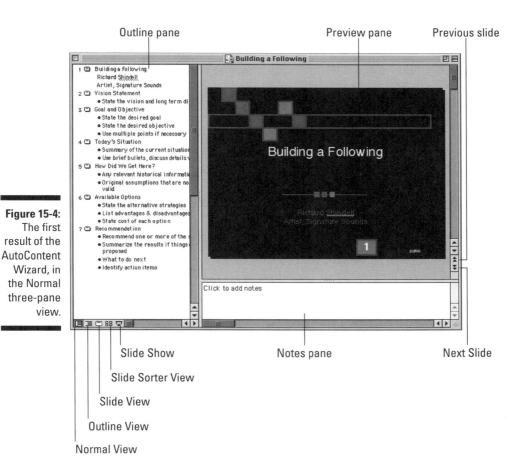

Outline pane   Preview pane   Previous slide

Figure 15-4: The first result of the AutoContent Wizard, in the Normal three-pane view.

Slide Show

Slide Sorter View

Slide View

Outline View

Normal View

Notes pane   Next Slide

Using a PowerPoint template

PowerPoint 2001 comes with dozens of templates that contain predefined formats and graphics, just waiting for you to fill them with text. The difference between using the templates and using the AutoContent Wizard is that with a template, you have to add all the text from scratch. Microsoft has done the tough work for you, however, by creating the template. Follow these steps to use a PowerPoint template:

1. **Choose File⇨Project Gallery.**

   The Project Gallery appears.

2. **Click the Presentations category to see the Presentations subcategories.**

3. **Click the Designs subcategory.**

4. **Click the icon for the template you want to use.**

5. **Click the OK button.**

   PowerPoint 2001 loads the template and shows you the New Slide window, set to the layout for a title slide.

6. **Click the OK button.**

   A blank title slide appears, with text boxes for a title and a subtitle.

7. **Click a text box in the slide and type in text.**

8. **Click the Next Slide button on the Standard toolbar and type the text in the new slide as necessary.**

9. **Repeat the editing process until you're done with the presentation.**

You might find it to be easier to enter text in the Outline pane, rather than directly into the slide. Working in the Outline gives you the ability to easily look at text in previous slides, allowing you to write tighter presentations.

Working with Your Slides

After you start a presentation with the AutoContent Wizard or a template, you'll want to change the presentation to your liking. PowerPoint gives you many tools to add features to your slides. In this chapter, I stick with the basics of adding text to slides; in Chapter 16, I show you how to add graphics, QuickTime movies, sounds, and animation to your presentation.

Creating a new slide

To create a new slide, follow these steps:

1. **Choose Insert⊏>New Slide, press ⌘+M, or click the New Slide button in the Standard toolbar.**

   The New Slide dialog box appears, as shown in Figure 15-5.

2. **Choose one of the slide layouts.**

   A *slide layout* is a predefined arrangement of graphical elements and text boxes in a slide. PowerPoint suggests the layout it thinks is most appropriate for this point in your presentation.

3. **Click the OK button.**

4. **Enter text into the text boxes in the new slide.**

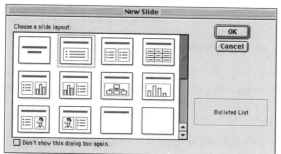

Figure 15-5:
The New
Slide dialog
box.

Deleting a slide

To delete a slide, click the Previous Slide or Next Slide buttons to display the slide you want to get rid of; then choose Edit⇨Delete Slide. You can also select a slide in the Outline pane before choosing Delete Slide.

One annoying feature of PowerPoint 2001 is that you don't see an "Are you sure?" dialog box when you delete a slide. *Be certain before you delete.* If you accidentally delete the wrong slide, you can choose Edit⇨Undo Delete Slide; you don't get an unlimited number of Undo chances, so be careful.

Working with text boxes

You can edit and add text to a text box you get from a slide layout. In addition to adding text, you can also modify the font, style, and size of the text in the text box. But most of the time you won't need to. One of the new features in PowerPoint 2001 is AutoFit Text. This feature watches as you type, and automatically changes the line spacing, then the font size, and then both (if necessary) so that the text fits into the text box. It works pretty well, though you have to be reasonable; there's only so much text that can fit in a text box and still be readable, so keep your text short and sweet.

To edit text in a text box, follow these steps:

1. **Display the slide you want to change.**
2. **Click the text box you want to modify.**

   A patterned border and white handles appear at the edges of the text box.

3. **Make your changes.**

   You can select the text in the usual way and then choose the font, font size, font color, or other options on the Formatting Palette.

   To resize a text box, drag one of the white handles.

   To move a text box, click in the box to select it. The cursor turns into a grabber hand when you move it over the box's patterned border. Grab the border and drag the box.

   To delete a text box, click the border of the text box and then press the Delete key.

 Most of the time, the slide layouts give you a slide that has all the text boxes you need. If you want to add a text box to a slide, however, choose Insert⇨ Text Box.

Reviewing Your Presentation

After you create a presentation, you should preview it to make sure that it looks right and that the content is the way you want it. PowerPoint 2001 has five viewing modes; you switch among them by choosing them from the View menu or by clicking the View buttons at the bottom of the document window.

Using Normal view

The Normal view, new to PowerPoint 2001, combines the Outline, Slide, and Notes views into a window with three panes. Microsoft found that in previous versions of PowerPoint, many people worked exclusively in Slide view, and never knew the other views existed. By providing panes for Outline and Notes, it makes it easier to take advantage of those features.

You can resize any pane by grabbing the border between it and another pane and dragging with the mouse.

Using Outline view

Outline view is the PowerPoint secret weapon for making better presentations (well, maybe it's not so secret anymore). The key to the Outline is that it enables you to edit the content of your presentation without focusing on the presentation's appearance. Although you still see a miniature color preview pane of the slide you're working on, the focus is on the text, as in Figure 15-6.

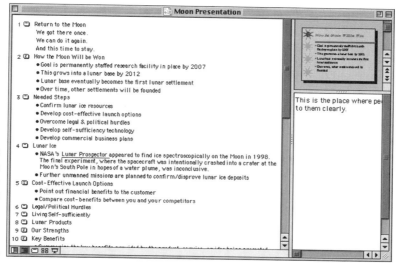

Figure 15-6:
It's easy to
add and edit
text in the
Outline
view.

To switch to Outline view, click the Outline View button at the bottom of the PowerPoint window. You can see that what really happens is that the panes of the Normal view rearrange themselves, resizing so that the Outline is the largest and dominant pane, with the Slide and Notes panes moving or shrinking. All three panes still allow editing, however, though with the slide miniaturized, you probably won't want to change it much, if at all.

Outline view is the best view to use if you want to move a bunch of text from one slide to another. You can do this task in Slide view, although it's not nearly as easy as it is in Outline view, which enables you to simply drag and drop text.

In Outline view, each heading represents a slide (and is also the title of the slide). A numbered slide icon appears to the left of each heading. Outline view works much like outlines in Microsoft Word: You can expand and collapse headings, move headings up and down in the outline, and promote and demote the levels of headings.

Creating a heading

When you create a heading in PowerPoint's Outline, you're creating a new slide. To make a new heading, move the insertion point to the beginning of an existing heading and then press the Return key. You can also create a new heading by choosing Insert⇨New Slide or pressing ⌘+M.

Deleting a heading

Sometimes, slides just fall out of favor — the honeymoon is over, and they need to go away. To delete a heading, click the slide icon for the heading you want to delete, and then press the Delete key.

Moving a heading

To reorganize your presentation, you can drag headings in the outline, thereby rearranging the order of the slides. To move a heading to a different place in your presentation, click the slide icon of the heading you want to move and drag the heading to its new home.

Using Slide view

Slide view, which displays one slide at a time, is a good view to work with when you're changing the appearance of a slide. Again, it's a resizing of the Normal view's panes, with the borders for the Outline and Notes panes dragged to the edge of the window, as shown in Figure 15-7. Click the Slide View button at the bottom of the PowerPoint window to switch to Slide view.

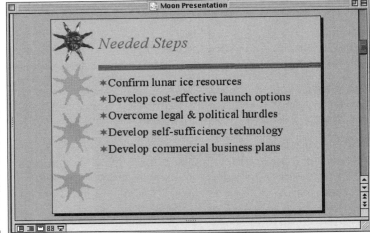

Figure 15-7: You can really focus on looks over content in the Slide view.

Using Slide Sorter view

Slide Sorter view shrinks your slides so that thumbnails of many slides fit on your screen. This "big picture" gives you an overview of your presentation, allowing you to rearrange and drag and drop slides from one place in the presentation to another. You can change the number of slides that are visible at any time by choosing a different figure from the Zoom pop-up menu on the Standard toolbar. To switch to Slide Sorter view, click the Slide Sorter View button at the bottom of the PowerPoint window, or choose View⇨Slide Sorter.

The selected slide has a thick, black border, as shown in Figure 15-8. To move a slide, drag it to a new position. PowerPoint 2001 displays a vertical line where the slide will move when you release the mouse button.

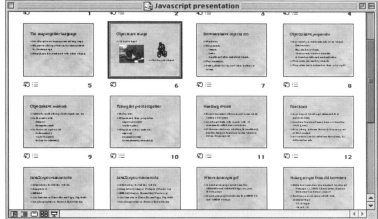

Figure 15-8:
Slide Sorter view lets you rearrange slides quickly.

Using Notes Page view

Notes Page view enables you to add speaker notes that go along with each slide. You can add these notes in the Notes pane of the Normal view, of course, but the Notes Page view shows you what these notes will look like when printed as handouts.

To add notes to your presentation in Notes Page view, follow these steps:

1. **Choose View⇨Notes Page.**

   Notes Page view appears, displaying the current slide with a text box below it, where you can enter your notes.

2. **Click the text box and add your notes for this slide.**

Playing a slide show

Now you're ready for the real preview. Slide Show view takes over your screen and shows you exactly how your presentation will look. You also use this view to check out slide transitions, examine slide timings, and ensure that you haven't made any mistakes.

To play a slide show, follow these steps:

1. **Choose View⇨Slide Show.**

   The first slide in the presentation appears full screen.

   To start the slide show with the current slide rather than the first slide, click the Slide Show button at the bottom of the document window.

2. **To get to the next slide, click the mouse or press the right-arrow key; to back up a slide, press the left-arrow key or ⌘+click the mouse.**

3. **To end the slide show, press ⌘+. (⌘+period) or press the Escape key.**

Printing Your Presentation

When you're done with your presentation, you can print it as slides, handouts with 2, 3, or 6 slides per page, or notes (which feature a slide and speaker notes), or you can print the outline. To print your presentation, follow these steps:

1. **Choose File⇨Print.**

   The Print dialog box appears.

2. **From the pop-up menu, choose Microsoft PowerPoint 2001.**

3. **From the Print What pop-up menu, choose the kind of printout you want.**

4. **Click the Print button.**

Chapter 16

Spiffing Up Your Presentations

. . . .

In This Chapter

▶ Adding pictures and media to your slides

▶ Using the drawing tools

▶ Changing the appearance of your slides

▶ Adding slide transitions

▶ Adding interactivity to your show

. . . .

*I*n any good presentation, the text is the most important part. What you say, not the flash of your slides or graphics, will make or break your show. Still, the good use of graphic elements will engage your audience's interest and help to highlight your key points. This chapter focuses on the numerous PowerPoint 2001 tools that let you add visual flash to your presentations.

Adding Graphics and Media

Unless you're a skilled artist, you probably won't be drawing much in your slides other than basic shapes, such as lines, arrows, and boxes. (Later in this chapter, you find out how to do that.) You have a practical alternative to drawing pictures that look like bad cave paintings — you can use some of the nearly 100MB worth of clip art that Microsoft thoughtfully included on the Office 2001 CD-ROM. *Clip art* consists of graphics files, created by an artist, that you can reuse with the artist's permission. Office 2001 has a shared Clip Gallery that includes clip art; you can also insert a picture that's on your hard disk. You can freely reuse in your documents any of the art in the Clip Gallery. If you find some artwork you want to use on the Internet, be sure to get permission from the person who owns the art before you use it, or else you could be the unfortunate target of a lawsuit. In addition, PowerPoint 2001 can use *clip media,* which are QuickTime movies and sound files.

Putting in pictures

To add a picture from the PowerPoint 2001 Clip Gallery, follow these steps:

1. **Choose View➪Normal to switch to the Normal view (if you're not already there).**

2. **Select the slide to which you want to add the picture.**

3. **Choose Insert➪Picture➪Clip Art.**

   After a short delay, the Microsoft Clip Gallery opens, as shown in Figure 16-1.

Figure 16-1: Selecting an image from the Clip Gallery.

4. **Click the image you want to use.**

   The scrollbox of categories on the left side of the Clip Gallery window helps you narrow your choices and find your clip art faster. You can also search through the clip art index by typing words into the Search field, then clicking the Search button.

5. **Click the Insert button.**

   PowerPoint 2001 puts the image into the slide — where it almost certainly will be too large, in the wrong place, or both.

6. **To resize the graphic, click the graphic once to select it; then click one of the white handles and drag.**

   You can resize the graphic proportionally if you drag one of the corner handles.

7. **If you need to move the graphic, click anywhere within the graphic and drag it to where you want it.**

If you created your own artwork (or picked up some good-looking art from an artist friend), you can add that art to your presentation without needing to add it to the Clip Gallery. Follow these steps:

1. **Choose Insert⇨Picture⇨From File.**

   The standard Open dialog box appears.

2. **Select the file that contains the artwork.**

3. **Click the Insert button.**

Again, you'll probably want to resize or move the image.

You can use two main types of graphics files in your presentations. *Bitmaps* are detailed pictures, such as photographs, that can be modified inside PowerPoint 2001 using the Picture tools, including changes such as cropping and resizing, and color and contrast adjustments. You can even add special effects. *Vector graphics,* like most of the clip art that comes with Office 2001, can be ungrouped and then edited with the PowerPoint drawing tools. There are different formats of vector graphics, but the clip art that come with Office 2001 are done in PICT format, which is a standard Mac graphics format. You can edit PICT files in most other Mac graphics programs, including Adobe Photoshop, Macromedia Fireworks, or even with the shareware GraphicConverter, by LemkeSoft.

Besides PICT, PowerPoint 2001 can use still images in any format that QuickTime understands, including these popular image formats:

- ✔ JPEG
- ✔ GIF (and also animated GIF)
- ✔ Adobe Photoshop
- ✔ PNG
- ✔ TIFF

Adding movies and sounds

Adding QuickTime movies or sound files is almost the same as adding pictures that don't move. You can pick if you want a movie or a sound file, and you can further pick from the Clip Gallery or a file on your hard disk. In the case of sounds, you can also choose to play an audio track from a CD, or you can even record your own sound and use it in your presentation. Follow these steps (this example assumes that you're inserting a QuickTime movie):

1. **Choose View⇨Normal to switch to the Normal view.**

2. **Select the slide to which you want to add the picture.**

3. **Choose Insert➪Movies and Sounds➪Movie from File.**

   The standard Open dialog box appears.

4. **Select the movie or sound file you want to use.**

5. **Click the Insert button.**

Another, even easier, way to insert a movie or sound file is to simply drag and drop it from the Finder onto a slide in your presentation.

If you inserted a QuickTime movie, the Movie toolbar also appears, as shown in Figure 16-2. You can use this toolbar to control playback. The Movie toolbar has several buttons:

- ✔ **Insert Movie:** Inserts a QuickTime movie or other video clip into the presentation.

- ✔ **Play:** Allows you to play the movie to preview it.

- ✔ **Show Controller:** Displays the standard QuickTime controller bar below the movie, with the Volume slider, Play/Pause button, and Position slider.

- ✔ **Loop:** Tells PowerPoint to continuously play the movie for as long as you're on that slide.

- ✔ **Set as Poster Frame:** Lets you choose what frame of the movie is displayed before the movie begins to play.

- ✔ **Format Picture:** Gives you control over the movie's size, position, colors, and other image details.

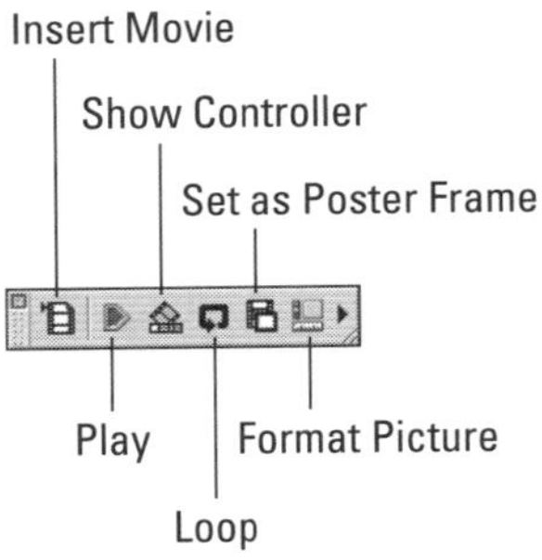

Figure 16-2:
The Movie toolbar lets you set how a QuickTime movie will be displayed in your presentation.

Insert Movie

Show Controller

Set as Poster Frame

Play Format Picture

Loop

Because movies are large files, they aren't saved inside PowerPoint presentation files. Instead, movie files are linked to the presentation files. If you show your presentation on another computer, you must remember to also copy the movie file when you copy the presentation file. If you don't, all you get is a single still frame — the poster frame — of the movie. It's a good idea to put a presentation and all of the media files you have linked to it in the same folder, so you don't lose part of your show.

PowerPoint 2001 can use video and animation clips in any format that QuickTime understands, including these formats:

- ✔ QuickTime movies

- ✔ Flash animations

- ✔ QuickTime VR movies (movies that enable you to tilt, pan, and zoom your viewpoint)

- ✔ DV format (used by many digital camcorders)

- ✔ MPEG videos

- ✔ Video for Windows (also known as AVI movies)

PowerPoint 2001 can use audio clips in any format that QuickTime understands, including these formats:

- ✔ AIFF

- ✔ AU

- ✔ MPEG audio, including Layer 1, Layer 2, and the popular Layer 3, more commonly known as MP3

- ✔ WAV (Pronounced "wave;" Windows sound format)

- ✔ MIDI

- ✔ Audio CD

Boosting PowerPoint's Memory

Active media, such as video and sound, ask a great deal from your computer and from PowerPoint 2001. To handle the load, you may have to increase the PowerPoint 2001 memory allocation. To do that, follow these steps:

1. **Make sure that PowerPoint 2001 is *not* open.**

2. **On the desktop, click the PowerPoint 2001 icon *once* to select it.**

3. **Choose File⇨Get Info, or press ⌘+I.**

   The PowerPoint 2001 Info window appears.

4. **From the pop-up menu next to Show, choose Memory.**

5. **Click into the Preferred Size box and increase the figure, taking into account the amount of RAM in your Mac.**

   If your Mac has tons of RAM, give PowerPoint a hefty increase. A good general rule is to try adding about 4,000K first and then adding more later if PowerPoint ever complains that it's running out of memory.

6. **Click the close box to dismiss the Info window.**

Drawing in PowerPoint

You use the Drawing toolbar in PowerPoint 2001 to create shapes, align objects, and add lines, connectors, and arrows. If you like, you can even draw free-form in your slides. By default, the Drawing toolbar appears as a floating palette to the left of your presentation document window, but like any toolbar in Office, you can move it around the screen as you wish. Also like the Formatting Palette, the Drawing toolbar is automatically hidden when PowerPoint 2001 isn't the frontmost application. Figure 16-3 gives you a close-up view of the Drawing toolbar.

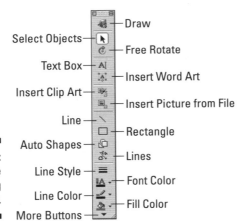

Figure 16-3: The Drawing toolbar.

Select Objects, Text Box, Insert Clip Art, Line, Auto Shapes, Line Style, Line Color, More Buttons

Draw, Free Rotate, Insert Word Art, Insert Picture from File, Rectangle, Lines, Font Color, Fill Color

The More Buttons button at the bottom of the Drawing toolbar is a pop-up menu that gives you access to lesser-used features like Arrows, Ovals, Dash Style, and 3-D Shapes. Check it out if you need additional drawing options.

Drawing lines and boxes

Maybe you can't draw a straight line, but PowerPoint 2001 certainly can. Lines are most often used in slides to set off one part of a slide from another; boxes are usually used as graphic highlights. To draw a line or a box in a slide, follow these steps:

1. **Select the slide to which you want to add the line or box.**

2. **Click either the Line or Rectangle button on the Drawing toolbar.**

3. **Put the mouse pointer where you want your line or box to begin on the slide, hold down the mouse button, drag the mouse, and release the mouse button where you want the line or box to stop.**

   PowerPoint 2001 draws the line or box.

Holding down the Shift key while drawing constrains the tool that you're using; if it's a line, it will constrain the angle of the line; if you're using the Rectangle tool, the box you are drawing will be a perfect square.

Now you can format the line or box. To change the object's style, follow these steps:

1. **Click the object you want to modify.**

   PowerPoint 2001 displays a handle at each end of the line or arrow.

2. **Click the Line Style button on the Drawing toolbar.**

   The button is actually a pop-up menu with various styles.

3. **Choose the style you want to use.**

4. **Repeat this process as necessary until the line or box is formatted as you like it.**

Using AutoShapes

AutoShapes are objects you can add to your slides. The shapes can be resized, rotated, colored, and modified in other ways. You can add text to AutoShapes, for example, and the text becomes part of the shape, so if you stretch, rotate, or flip the shape, the text follows suit.

The AutoShapes menu on the Drawing toolbar has eight categories of objects, each offering from 6 to 24 items.

You can tear off any of the submenus of the AutoShapes menu, turning them into floating palettes. Just keep holding down the mouse button as you choose one of these submenus, and drag to the right. An outline follows your mouse pointer as you drag. Release the mouse button, and the floating palette appears, as shown in Figure 16-4.

Figure 16-4:
A floating
palette
from the
AutoShapes
menu.

To add an AutoShape to a slide, follow these steps:

1. **From the AutoShapes pop-up menu, choose a submenu and then, finally, an object.**

   The mouse pointer changes to a crosshair pointer.

2. **Click and drag the mouse to draw the shape.**

3. **Release the mouse button.**

   The shape appears, with selection handles around it.

4. **Modify the shape by dragging its handles to resize it or by clicking any of the style buttons on the Drawing toolbar.**

For some cool effects, try using AutoShapes in conjunction with the Shadow or 3-D button that you'll find under the More Buttons pop-up menu at the bottom of the Drawing toolbar. Depending on what you do, this experiment can also be the fast track to tastelessness.

Adding connectors

Connectors are smart lines. Each end of the line sticks to a different object, and moving that object causes the connector to follow along. Connectors are terrific for organizational charts, flowcharts, and any other chart you're using to denote a relationship between two things.

To add a connector, follow these steps:

1. **Using any of the drawing tools, draw a shape in a slide.**

   I suggest that you draw a rectangle or a box.

2. **Draw a second shape of the same type next to the first object.**

3. **From the Drawing toolbar, choose AutoShapes, and then choose one of the connectors from the Connectors box, as shown in Figure 16-5.**

   The mouse pointer turns into a combination of a crosshair and a small box.

Figure 16-5:
Choosing a
connector.

4. **Click the first shape you want to connect.**

5. **Click the second shape.**

Now, whenever you move either of the shapes to which the connector is connected, the ends of the connector's line are stuck to both objects. When you move one object, the connector moves along.

Taking notes with callouts

Another special type of AutoShape is the callout. Callouts are like cartoon thought balloons, and you add them the way you add any other AutoShape. Clicking inside a callout displays a blinking vertical text cursor and enables you to add text to the callout balloon.

Moving or deleting drawn objects

Easy come, easy go. If you want to move or get rid of an object you drew, follow these steps:

1. **Click the object you want to move or delete.**

   PowerPoint 2001 shows that the object is selected by displaying white handles around it.

2. **Move the object by dragging it, or bid it a fond farewell by pressing the Delete key.**

Changing Slide Backgrounds and Styles

The longer you use PowerPoint 2001, the better you become at judging which elements work in a presentation and which don't. If you've been using one of the templates or the AutoContent Wizard, you may get tired of the canned backgrounds and styles those features give you. No problem: You can freshen the appearance of your slides by switching backgrounds.

When you choose a slide background or style, remember that sooner or later you may print the presentation. To get an idea of what a slide will look like when you print it (on a noncolor printer, that is), choose View⇨Grayscale. The color information will leave the slide in the presentation window, but a Slide Miniature window will open up so you can compare the two versions.

Swapping backgrounds

To change the color of the background, follow these steps:

1. **Select the slide you want to modify.**

2. **Choose Format⇨Background.**

   The Background dialog box appears, as shown in Figure 16-6.

Figure 16-6:
The Background dialog box, where you can change the background's color scheme.

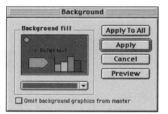

3. **Choose a new color from the Background Fill pop-up menu.**

   If you don't like any of the choices that PowerPoint 2001 offers, click More Colors. The Mac OS Color Picker appears, as shown in Figure 16-7. When you're done picking a color, click the OK button to return to the Background dialog box.

4. **If you want your color changes to apply to all the slides in this presentation, click the Apply to All button; if you want to make changes only in the current slide, click the Apply button.**

To change the style of the background, follow these steps:

1. **Choose Format⇨Apply Design Template.**

   An Open dialog box appears, including a preview area that enables you to inspect the slide styles.

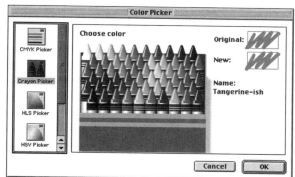

Figure 16-7:
Choosing a
new color
from the
Color
Picker.

> 2. **Select a style.**
>
> 3. **Click the Apply button.**

Unlike background colors, which can vary from slide to slide, this new style is applied to all slides in your presentation. Be careful when you apply this style so that you don't inadvertently mess up all the slides.

Changing slide layouts

The *slide layout* specifies the location of text and pictures in a slide. Slide layouts should be taken as a starting point; you can always move things around. To pick a new slide layout for a particular slide, follow these steps:

1. **Select the slide you want to change.**

2. **Choose Format⇨Slide Layout.**

   The Slide Layout dialog box appears.

3. **Select the new layout you want to use for the current slide.**

4. **Click the Apply button.**

   PowerPoint 2001 changes the current slide's layout.

Creating Transitions

PowerPoint 2001 enables you to create animated transitions between slides, and it can animate the way text or pictures appear in slides. You usually use animated transitions to reveal your bullet points one at a time, as you talk about each one, thereby keeping audience members interested (because they can't read ahead of you).

Slide transitions determine how your slide arrives on your screen. Think about the effects you see between scenes in a movie. Slides can dissolve from one to another, wipe across the screen, reveal like an opening door, or zip up like a window shade to show the slide below. PowerPoint 2001 also enables you to associate a sound with each of the 42 preset transitions (although if you do that, you may be cited by the Presentation Taste Police). Besides the built-in transitions, PowerPoint 2001 has gained the ability to use transitions from QuickTime, which add additional attractive options.

Text transitions affect how the bullet points on your slide reveal themselves. It's nice to have one bullet point appear and then have that point's text dim as the next point comes in. This type of transition keeps the attention of your audience on what you're saying now. PowerPoint 2001 includes 56 types of text transitions.

Making slide transitions

To set the transition between slides in your presentation, follow these steps:

1. **Choose Slide Show⊅Slide Transition.**

   The Slide Transition dialog box appears, as shown in Figure 16-8.

2. **Choose an effect from the Effect pop-up menu.**

   You see a preview of the effect in the preview box.

3. **Choose the transition speed by clicking one of the radio buttons below the Effect pop-up menu.**

   As you make changes, you again see a preview in the preview box.

4. **In the Advance section, choose how one slide will advance to the next.**

   Click the On Mouse Click button if you'll be advancing the slides manually by clicking the mouse (or using the keyboard). If your presentation will be running by itself (if it will run in an informational kiosk, for example), click the Automatically after check box and then, in the text box, enter the number of seconds' delay you want to occur between slides.

   Did you notice that both the check boxes in the Advance section can be checked? This arrangement means that you can have an automatically running presentation but override the time settings between slides by clicking the mouse.

5. **If you want PowerPoint 2001 to play a sound file every time it changes slides, choose a sound from the Sound pop-up menu.**

Effect Pop-up menu

Preview box

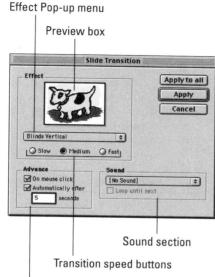

Figure 16-8:
Changing
slide
transitions.

Sound section

Transition speed buttons

Advance section

6. **To apply the settings to only the current slide, click the Apply button; to apply them to all the slides in your presentation in one fell swoop, click the Apply to All button.**

7. **Repeat the preceding steps if you want to apply different transitions between some slides.**

Using QuickTime transitions

If you want to take advantage of PowerPoint 2001's new ability to use QuickTime transitions, choose "QuickTime Transition" in step 2, above. The Select Effect dialog box will open, as shown in Figure 16-9. Choose a transition, and then click OK.

Creating text transitions

One of the best ways to make a presentation is to use transitions from one slide to the next so that when the second slide appears, all the audience sees is the title of the slide. You introduce the slide's topic, and as you begin to talk about the slide's bullet points, they appear one by one.

To create a text transition, follow these steps:

1. **Click a text box in a slide.**

   PowerPoint 2001 shows that the text box is selected by displaying a border and white handles around it.

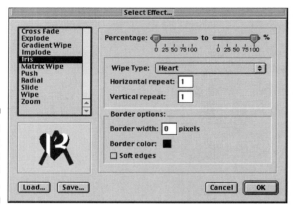

Figure 16-9:
Choosing a
QuickTime
slide
transition.

2. **Choose Slide Show⇨Animations, and then choose an effect from the hierarchical menu (as shown in Figure 16-10).**

3. **Choose Slide Show⇨Animation Preview to see what your text transition looks like in the small preview window; for a full-size view of the slide, choose View⇨Slide Show.**

Once the preview window is open, it's easy to choose a new animation. Then click the preview window to see how the new effect will look.

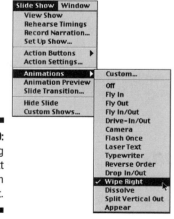

Figure 16-10:
Choosing
a text
animation
effect.

Keeping your eye on the (nonbouncing) ball

When you're using flashy transitions and animated effects, you can easily slide right over the line between attracting attention and annoying your audience. The key to using effects is to use them sparingly. You want to persuade the members of your audience, not pummel them into submission via motion sickness. Here are a few points to keep in mind:

✔ Try to use the same transition effect for all the slides in your presentation. Audiences get disoriented if you change things after every slide.

✔ In the same fashion, be consistent with your text transitions within each slide. Having one line of text fly in and having the next one do a rumba before it settles on the screen is a great way to get your audience running for the exits.

✔ The Preset Animation effects that use sounds (such as Typewriter and Laser Text) get old fast. If you use these effects at all, limit them to just the title of a slide.

✔ If you have any doubt about whether you should use an animated effect, don't use it.

Chapter 17

Doing the Presentation

. . . .

In This Chapter

▶ Making your presentation interactive

▶ Creating Custom Shows

▶ Rehearsing the presentation

▶ Winning the stage-fright battle

▶ Presentation tips

. . . .

I do not object to people looking at their watches when I am speaking. But I strongly object when they start shaking them to make certain they are still going.

— Lord Birkett (1883–1962), British lawyer and politician

This quote neatly pinpoints many people's fear of doing presentations. It's natural to be worried that you will make a mistake, bore your audience, be publicly humiliated, and be banished from society for the rest of your natural life. The ghost of Dale Carnegie will haunt you forever, tormenting you with a hollow laugh that only you can hear.

Relax — those things won't happen. In this chapter, you see how you can add interactivity to your presentations, customize your presentation for specific audiences, and rehearse your show so that it runs smoothly. By the time you're done, you'll have the tools you need to have your presentation go swimmingly.

Adding Interactivity to Your Show

You can have a presentation with a fixed order and format ready to go, and often, that's the best way to set up a presentation, especially if the presentation has to run automatically. Sometimes, however, you want to add more flexibility to your show so that you can either change it on the fly or allow other people to control it if they are running it for themselves.

Adding Action Buttons

Action Buttons are AutoShapes you can drop into your slides to enable a user to control the pace of your presentation. Action Buttons are just hyperlinks a user clicks to jump elsewhere — to another place in the same presentation, to another presentation on your hard disk, or to any Internet site.

To add an Action Button to a slide, follow these steps:

1. **On the Drawing toolbar, choose AutoShapes⇨Action Buttons.**

   If you leave the mouse cursor over an Action Button, a Tool Tip will pop up, describing that button's function.

2. **Click the button that has the design you want to put in the slide.**

   The mouse pointer turns into a small cross.

   Another way to insert an Action Button is to choose Slide Show⇨Action Buttons and then pick one of the 12 choices.

3. **Click the place in the slide where you want the button to appear.**

   You don't have to be too precise, because you can always move the button later.

   The Action Settings dialog box appears, as shown in Figure 17-1.

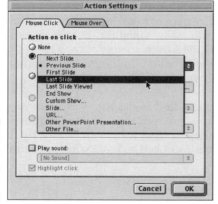

Figure 17-1: The Action Settings dialog box.

4. **From the Hyperlink To pop-up menu, choose the value you want to use for this button.**

   You're not limited to the choices in the Hyperlink To list. You can choose any of the slides in your presentation by choosing Slide from the pop-up menu. Pick a slide in the Hyperlink To Slide dialog box, as shown in Figure 17-2; then click the OK button.

Figure 17-2:
Enable
users to
jump to a
specific
slide with
appropriate
settings in
this dialog
box.

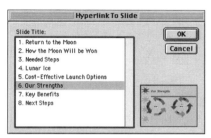

5. **Click the OK button.**

The pop-up menu in the Action Settings dialog box also enables you to link to another PowerPoint presentation on your hard disk, to a URL on the World Wide Web (useful if the presentation will be given on a computer with a connection to the Internet), or to any other document on your hard disk. The latter feature enables you to create buttons that link to items such as Word 2001 and Excel 2001 documents.

Inserting hyperlinks to Web sites

Because all the Office 2001 programs are Web-enabled, you can turn almost any text into a hyperlink. To turn text in a slide into a hyperlink, follow these steps:

1. **If you're not already in Normal view, choose View⇨Normal.**

2. **Select the slide into which you want to insert a hyperlink.**

3. **Select the text you want to turn into a hyperlink.**

4. **Choose Insert⇨Hyperlink or press ⌘+K.**

   The Insert Hyperlink dialog box appears, as shown in Figure 17-3.

5. **In the Link to: box, type the URL that will be the destination of the hyperlink.**

6. **The Display: box will be the text on the slide that is hyperlinked. PowerPoint fills this box in with the text you selected in Step 3, but you can change it here if you want.**

   Clicking the ScreenTip button lets you add a brief comment to the hyperlink, which will appear like a Tool Tip when the user places his or her mouse cursor over the hyperlink. ScreenTips only appear when you export the presentation as Web pages, and then only in Internet Explorer 4.0 or later. Still, they can be useful for some presentations.

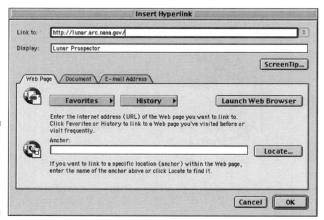

Figure 17-3:
Turning
some text in
a slide into a
hyperlink.

7. **Depending on the kind of hyperlink you want to create, click one of the Web Page, Document, or E-mail Address tabs at the bottom of the Insert Hyperlink dialog box.**

   Each tab shows you options to help you select the target of the hyperlink. On the Web page and Document tabs, if you're using Internet Explorer 5 as your Web browser, you can click the Favorites button to get a pop-up menu of Web sites that you've previously added to your Favorites list, or click the History button to get a pop-up menu of sites that you have recently browsed. On the E-mail Address tab, you can click the Recent Addresses button to get a pop-up menu of people you have recently sent mail to using Entourage 2001.

8. **Click the OK button.**

   The text is underlined, indicating that it is now a hyperlink.

   If you want to remove a hyperlink that you've previously created, click the hyperlink, click the arrow next to the Insert Hyperlink icon on the Standard toolbar, and select None from the resulting pop-up menu.

Creating Custom Shows

After you've been doing presentations for a while, you'll find that you're often asked to do a successful presentation more than once. Because the second (or subsequent) time around is for a slightly different audience, however, you change a few slides in your presentation. You can save the new version of your presentation as a new file (and indeed, older versions of PowerPoint made you do just that). If you have many versions of the same presentation, however, remembering which specialized slides are in which version becomes a big pain.

PowerPoint 2001 solves the problem with *Custom Shows,* which are like presentations inside presentations. Suppose that you're the product manager for the amazing new WonderWidget Pro. You're assigned to brief your company's manufacturing and sales departments about the product. Most of your presentation — the part that describes the product — is the same for both groups. The presentation to manufacturing, however, includes three slides detailing the special manufacturing processes required to produce the fabulous WonderWidget Pro. The salespeople don't need to see those slides; instead, they get a set of slides explaining their new commission structure for this product. Creating a Custom Show enables you to use one basic presentation for both audiences.

To create a Custom Show, follow these steps:

1. **Choose Slide Show⇨Custom Shows.**

   The Custom Shows dialog box appears, as shown in Figure 17-4.

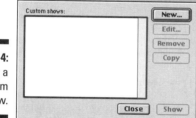

Figure 17-4:
Starting a
Custom
Show.

2. **Click the New button.**

   The Define Custom Show dialog box appears, as shown in Figure 17-5.

3. **In the Slide Show Name box, type the name for your Custom Show.**

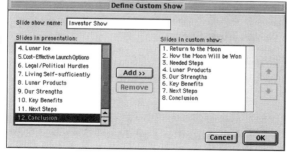

Figure 17-5:
Using the
Define
Custom
Show dialog
box.

4. **Double-click names of slides in the Slides in Presentation box to copy them to the Slides in Custom Show box.**

   You can change the order of items in the Slides in Custom Show box by selecting a slide and then clicking the up- or down-arrow button in the dialog box.

5. **Click the OK button to dismiss the Define Custom Show dialog box and return to the Custom Shows dialog box.**

6. **If you want to jump to Slide Show mode and view your Custom Show, click the Show button; otherwise, click the Close button.**

Practicing Your Presentation

Remember that ancient joke in which a man carrying a violin gets into a taxi-cab in New York City? He asks, "How do I get to Carnegie Hall?" The cabdriver eyes him and then says, "Practice, practice, practice."

That's how you get to be a good presenter, too — attention to detail and plenty of practice.

Running through your slide show

Testing your slide show before you subject it to the criticism of an audience is vitally important. A test run-through helps you find errors in slide transitions; typos in the slides themselves; and other mistakes, large and small.

The old adage about two heads being better than one is never truer than with presentations. If you can, let a friend or co-worker look through your presentation before you give it. You'll be surprised at how often they find a typo that you missed, even though you've looked at that slide a dozen times.

To test your slide show, follow these steps:

1. **Choose Slide Show⇨View Show.**

   PowerPoint 2001 displays the first slide in full-screen view.

2. **Advance through your presentation, noting any problems.**

   You can stop the slide show at any time by pressing ⌘+. (that's ⌘+period). You can also press the Escape (Esc) key.

3. **Go back and fix the presentation's problems, or break out the champagne.**

Rehearsing your timing

Timing your presentation is a good idea, and PowerPoint 2001 has some built-in tools to help with that task. You can rehearse the timings for each slide by choosing Slide Show➪Rehearse Timings. The slide show starts, with a timer appearing in the bottom-right corner of the screen. Clicking the timer advances to the next slide and resets the timer. Rehearse your presentation, and when the presentation is done, PowerPoint 2001 displays a dialog box, telling you how long the presentation is and asking whether you want to apply the amount of time you took for each slide to the slides in the presentation. That helps you if you decide to have the presentation run automatically while you speak instead of advancing slides manually.

In Slide Sorter view, you can manually add the number of seconds, which will then appear below each slide. Just click a slide to select it, and then choose Slide Show➪Slide Transition. In the Slide Transition dialog box, check the Automatically after check box, fill in the number of seconds for the slide duration, and click Apply (to apply the duration to just this slide) or Apply to All (to set a uniform duration for all your slides).

Conquering Stage Fright and Doing the Show

All the preparation is done. Your PowerPoint 2001 file is ready (not to mention brilliant), and suddenly, you're gripped with mind-numbing terror as you remember that you have to get up and give this speech. You're far from alone — the vast majority of people hate to speak in public. At least one study claims that people are more apprehensive about public speaking than they are about dying. Although that may be the case, personally, I'd rather die on stage than in real life. At least I can try to give that speech again and do a better job next time!

Here are some tips for conquering stage fright:

✔ **Unless you're speaking to a convention of your sworn enemies, realize that your audience wants you to succeed.** Think about the last time you saw someone else give a presentation. Were you thinking, "I sure hope this guy freezes up and makes a fool of himself"? Of course, you weren't. Your audience won't be thinking that about you, either.

✔ **Go early to the room where you'll be speaking, and get used to the place.** Stand at the podium, test the microphone, and make sure that you have a spot to place a cup of water. As the audience members come in, take a few minutes to chat with some of them. It's always easier to talk to people you know, even if you don't know them well.

✔ **Before you start to speak, take a moment to visualize yourself speaking — and doing a darned good job.** Picture yourself speaking well. Hear the audience's applause. This technique sounds weird, but it works.

✔ **Never apologize for being nervous.** Usually, you are the only one who knows that you're nervous, so if you don't say anything about it, nobody will notice.

✔ **Concentrate on your message.** By focusing on what you're saying, you don't let your nervousness gain a foothold.

✔ **Hone your message so that your most important information gets through to your audience.** Repeating your most important points is okay — it's common practice, in fact. Presenters have an old saw: "Tell them what you're going to tell them. Then tell them. Then tell them what you told them."

✔ **Be prepared.** The Boy Scouts truly got this one right. Audiences can usually tell when you're on top of a subject and when you're winging it.

✔ **Never read word for word from a script.** Only trained actors and professional speakers can read from a script without putting their audiences into a coma.

✔ **Don't run overtime.** (This rule is the one I struggle with the most.)

✔ **It's always a good idea to end your presentation with a summary slide.** It brings natural closure to your talk, and it cements your main points in the minds of the audience.

✔ **When you're done, you're not done.** After the presentation is over, thank your audience; make yourself available for questions; provide the audience with a method of reaching you (your phone number or e-mail address on the last slide, which you keep displayed afterwards, is always good); and most important, get feedback from your audience so you can improve the next show.

✔ **Do more presentations.** Every time you do a presentation, the next one gets easier.

Presentation Tips

Here's a grab-bag of tips that may help you give better presentations.

✔ Rather than being tied in front of your computer when you give presentations, go wireless; invest in the Keyspan Digital Media Remote. This device ($79 list) plugs into the USB port on late-model Macs and gives you a remote control with preassigned keys for PowerPoint, QuickTime, and other applications. Being able to walk around while presenting brings a remarkable sense of freedom and interactivity. Being mobile keeps you from hiding behind your computer and helps put you where you belong — in front of the group, as presenter, communicator, and moderator.

✔ There are times when you need to pause during a slide show; for example, you may need to answer some unexpected questions. When you pause your slide show, you may prefer to set the screen to black, rather than leave a slide in view. Just press the B or period key, and PowerPoint will blank the screen. To get back to your current slide, press the B or period key again. If you would prefer to set the screen to white, you can use the W or comma key.

✔ If you need to transport your PowerPoint presentation to another computer, consider saving it as a QuickTime movie by choosing File➪Make Movie. You'll get a QuickTime file that can be played on any Mac or Windows machine that has QuickTime installed (that's virtually any Macintosh, and most Windows machines). You can copy the QuickTime movie onto a Zip disk, copy it across a network, or upload it to the Internet.

✔ Invest in a laser pointer. They're inexpensive, and amazingly useful.

✔ Always have a backup of your presentation on disk and a printout of your presentation. Computers have an amazing ability to crash at the most inconvenient times. Be prepared to present, even if your computer isn't.

Part VI
Working Well with Others

The 5th Wave   By Rich Tennant

Testing the G4 Chip

"Think that's fast enough?"

In this part . . .

When you were a kid, did you get a check on your report card in the box that said "Works well with others"? No? That's probably because you didn't have Microsoft Office 2001 to help you out. Using any of the Office programs, you can share information with colleagues around the corner or halfway around the world. You can even share documents with those poor souls who use Microsoft Office on Windows! Yes, it's true. In this part, you discover how to turn your documents into Web pages and how every Office program can nag you through Entourage 2001's calendar.

You also see how you can mix and match information from any of the Office programs, how you can enlist your co-workers' help with your documents, and how new features in Office 2001 make it easy to trade information with other Macintosh programs.

Chapter 18

Using the Office 2001 Collaboration Features

*E*ach Office 2001 program is an individual powerhouse, and you can use them together for even more power. You can bring an Excel chart into a report you create with Word, or you can include a Word table inside a PowerPoint presentation. Any of the programs can use Entourage to e-mail their documents and keep track of upcoming events. Microsoft has made sharing information among the four programs easy, and Office 2001 uses Entourage to orchestrate your effort among the other Office programs to save you time and help you produce better work.

Office 2001 also includes excellent capabilities to share and collaborate with your co-workers. Other people in your workgroup can review your documents, make revisions, and add comments. As you go through the revision process, you can save each revision as a version so that you can see the evolution of your document.

Share and Share Alike

The Office 2001 programs offer a multitude of ways to share information between the programs. Because some of these ways are vestigial remnants of previously hot but now out-of-favor Microsoft or Apple technologies, I mention them here, although I don't fully explain them.

You can share information among programs in the following ways that I cover in detail in this chapter:

- ✔ **Copying:** Use the Clipboard or Office Clipboard to copy data between two programs.

- ✔ **Moving:** Use the Clipboard or Office Clipboard to cut data between two programs.

- ✔ **Dragging and dropping:** Select information in one document, and drag it into an open window in another program. You can also drag and drop information from the Office Clipboard.

- ✔ **Linking:** Insert part of one document into another document. For example, you can insert part of an Excel spreadsheet into a report you create in Word. Changes made in the spreadsheet are automatically reflected in the Word document.

You can also share information with these other, obsolete techniques, which I don't cover in this book:

- ✔ **Embedding:** A technique similar to linking (described previously) that includes an entire document from another application in your current document. It wasn't a beloved approach because it resulted in huge file sizes (and frequent crashes, in my experience).

- ✔ **Publish and Subscribe:** An Apple technology feature that was widely hyped but never widely used.

Of course, you can also share information between two programs by using one program to open a document created by another program — if the first program knows how to read the files created by the second. For example, you can use Word 2001 to open files created in SimpleText, although SimpleText can't understand Word 2001 documents.

In all the techniques I show you in this section, I make the assumption that you have at least two different programs open: Word and Excel, Word and PowerPoint, Excel and PowerPoint, or whatever. In this section, I discuss how to move information between two programs, so I refer to the program from which the data comes as the *source program* and the program where the data is going as the *destination program*. You always start in the source program, and you use one of the techniques described in the following set of steps to end with information in the destination program. Similarly, I refer to a document that contains the information to begin with as a *source document* and the document that receives the data as the *destination document*.

I refer to several of the buttons on the Standard toolbar throughout this chapter, as shown in Figure 18-1.

Figure 18-1:
The buttons used to share information.

Flag for Follow Up   Copy

Cut Paste

More Buttons pop-up menu

Copying and moving information

Copying and moving information between Office 2001 programs is done in much the same way that you copy and move information within a single program, except that in the middle of the process, you switch to a second program. To copy or move information between two programs, follow these steps:

1. **Select in the source program the information you want to copy or move.**

   The source program (remember that it could be any of the Office 2001 applications) highlights the information.

2. **Do one of the following:**

   To copy the information:

   - Choose File➪Copy.
   - Click the Copy button on the Standard toolbar (refer to Figure 18-1).
   - Press ⌘+C.

   To move the information:

   - Choose File➪Cut.
   - Click the Cut button on the Standard toolbar (refer to Figure 18-1).
   - Press ⌘+X.

   The source program copies or moves the highlighted information to the Clipboard, although you don't see any changes if you're copying something.

3. **Switch to the destination program.**

4. **Click the insertion point in the destination document where you want the copied data to appear.**

5. **Do one of the following:**

- Choose File⇔Paste.

- Click the Paste button on the Standard toolbar.

- Press ⌘+V.

The information appears in the destination document.

Moving information using the Office Clipboard

The Office Clipboard is useful for two main reasons. The most important is that it can contain more than one item, unlike the standard Mac OS Clipboard. The other is that you can drag and drop information to and from the Office Clipboard window, and to other Office document windows. To use the Office Clipboard instead of the Mac OS Clipboard in the steps above, choose View⇔Office Clipboard in the source program before you begin, then do the cut or copy procedure. You'll see the item you cut or copied appear in the Office Clipboard window, as shown in Figure 18-2. Then, without switching out of the source application, drag the item out of the Office Clipboard and to the destination document's window. The Office Clipboard appears in all of the Office 2001 programs except for Entourage.

Figure 18-2:
The Office
Clipboard,
containing
four items.

You're not limited to dragging and dropping items from the Office Clipboard just onto other Office documents. Any other Mac application that understands dragging and dropping (and these days, that's the vast majority) can be the target of a drag and drop. Just make sure that the Office Clipboard and the destination document are both visible, and then drag and drop away.

Using Paste Special

After you cut or copy data, you usually choose to paste the data into the destination document. The data flows into the destination document and retains the formatting it had in the source document. Sometimes the original formatting is not what you want, however. For example, if you copy or cut a group of cells in an Excel spreadsheet and then paste them into Word, they show up in the Word document as a table. If you want the contents of the cells to flow in as regular text, choose Paste Special. Follow these steps:

1. **Select in the source program the information you want to cut or copy.**

   The source program highlights the information.

2. **Cut or copy the information.**

3. **Switch to the destination program.**

4. **Choose Edit⇨Paste Special.**

   The Paste Special dialog box appears, as shown in Figure 18-3.

5. **Select from the As box the format for the pasted data.**

   If you want the data to flow in as regular text, select Unformatted Text.

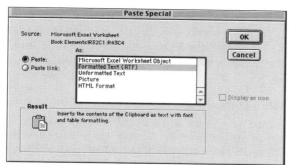

Figure 18-3:
The Paste
Special
dialog box.

Dragging and dropping information

Just as you can drag and drop information within the same document (for more about drag-and-drop editing, see the section in Chapter 5 about dragging and dropping), you can move information between Office programs by dragging and dropping. The support for Macintosh Drag-and-Drop allows you to trade information by dragging and dropping it with any other Macintosh program that is drag-enabled.

If you're not sure whether any particular Macintosh program is drag-enabled, you can easily find out. Just select some text or another object within the program, and try to drag and drop it on your desktop. The Finder is drag-enabled and can accept data from any other drag-enabled program. When you drop an object on the desktop, it becomes a *clipping file*. Clipping files can reside on your desktop or anywhere else on your hard disk, and you can drag them into any program that supports Macintosh Drag-and-Drop. When you drag a clipping file on a document, a copy of the clipping file's contents appears in the document. For example, I often get questions about a particular book that I co-wrote. On my desktop, I keep the clipping file that points people to the FAQ (Frequently Asked Questions) Web page for the book. Whenever I receive e-mail with a question about the book, I drag the clipping file from my desktop into a new e-mail message. The text I have previously written appears in the new message, and all I have to do is click Send. This clipping file saves me a tremendous amount of time.

Dragging information between Office programs

You may expect that because Office 2001 is an integrated suite of programs, you can drag and drop information between any two of the programs in the same way, regardless of which programs you are using. If that was your expectation, then you have forgotten that these programs were written by Microsoft, which loves to throw the user a curve ball. Dragging and dropping between Word and PowerPoint, and dragging and dropping from either of these two programs to Excel, works in a simple, obvious fashion. You select, you drag, you drop, and you're done. Dragging and dropping from Excel to the other programs requires a slightly different technique, as you see in the following sections.

Dragging between Word and PowerPoint

To drag between a Word document and a PowerPoint document, arrange the two document windows on your screen so that you can see the point from which you want to drag and also the place to which you want to drop. Then follow these steps:

1. **Select in the source document the object you want to drag to the destination document.**

2. **Drag the object to the destination document's window.**

   As you move the cursor into the destination window, you see a dashed outline of the object you're moving, which gives you feedback about where you're going to drop the object.

3. **Release the mouse button.**

   The object you dragged appears in the destination document.

Dragging from Excel to Word or PowerPoint

The most useful way of dragging information from Excel to Word or PowerPoint doesn't simply copy the data (though you can do that if you wish). Instead, the spreadsheet data appears in your destination document with a *link* to the original spreadsheet. If you double-click the linked spread-sheet data in Word, Excel starts up and enables you to edit the data in Excel. Changes you make in the Excel document are reflected in the Word document. (Keep in mind that the changes flow only one way; changes you make in the Word copy of the data are not reflected in the Excel document.)

To link cells from Excel to Word or PowerPoint, follow these steps:

1. **Make sure that both the source and destination files are visible on your screen.**

2. **Select in the Excel document the cells you want to copy.**

3. **Move the cursor to one edge of the selection until the mouse pointer turns into a hand.**

4. **Holding down the Option+⌘ keys, click and drag the selection to the destination document.**

5. **In the destination document, you'll see a contextual menu that lets you choose from a few different ways of placing the selection. Choose Link Excel object here.**

   The selection appears in Word or PowerPoint as a linked spreadsheet object.

If you want to move or copy the data from Excel into Word, choose Move Here or Copy Here from the contextual menu in Step 5.

Working with text clippings from the Finder

It's convenient to keep boilerplate text in a clipping file on the desktop and then drag the clipping file into your Office document to insert the text in one step. Although you can do so in Word by using the AutoText feature (see the section in Chapter 5 about inserting text automatically with AutoText), I can tell you two advantages to using clipping files instead. One advantage is that the clipping file works in all the Office programs, not just in Word. The other is that you can drag that same clipping file into any other drag-enabled program, such as an e-mail program like Entourage, or Apple's SimpleText.

To create a text clipping, select some text in one of the Office programs, and then drag the text from the document window and drop it on the desktop. The icon for the new clipping file appears, as in Figure 18-4.

Figure 18-4:
An icon for
a text
clipping on
the desktop.

To use the text clipping in one of your documents, drag the icon of the clipping file into your document window, and then release the mouse button. The text in the clipping file appears in your document.

Dragging graphics from the Scrapbook into Office programs

Because the Scrapbook is also drag-enabled, you can drag graphics from the Scrapbook directly into any Office document. Follow these steps:

1. **From the Apple menu, choose Scrapbook.**

   The Scrapbook appears.

2. **Scroll through the Scrapbook until you find the graphic you want.**

3. **Click and drag the graphic from the Scrapbook into the document window of the Office program you're working with.**

   The graphic appears in your document, as shown in Figure 18-5.

Linking information

Linking is useful when you want to make sure that the data in your document is always up to date. Suppose that you have a quarterly financial report in Word. You crunch the numbers for the report in Excel, and you know that you'll be making changes to the spreadsheet up to the last minute before you have to submit your report. Because you have a linked Excel spreadsheet inside your Word document, whenever you make a change in the Excel spreadsheet, the copy of the spreadsheet in your report is automatically updated. Because all the Office 2001 programs have excellent support for linking, you can put almost any information from any Office program into any other Office document. Once again, the exception is Entourage, which doesn't support the Paste Special command needed for linking.

To link information, follow these steps:

1. **Switch to the program containing the information you want to link.**

   For example, if you are linking an Excel chart into a Word document, switch to Excel.

2. **Select the information you want to link.**

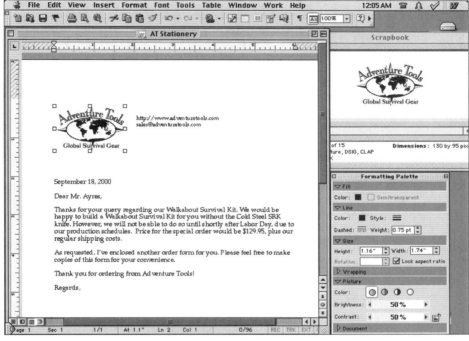

Figure 18-5:
The logo was just dragged in from the Scrapbook, which is on the right.

3. **Copy the information by choosing Edit⇨Copy or by pressing ⌘+C.**

4. **Switch to the destination program.**

5. **Put the cursor where you want the linked information to appear.**

6. **Choose Edit⇨Paste Special.**

   The Paste Special dialog box appears (refer to Figure 18-3).

7. **Click the Paste Link radio button.**

8. **In the As box, select the type of link you want, such as Formatted Text.**

9. **Click OK.**

Sharing Information Using Entourage

Entourage 2001 gives you the ability to schedule tasks on its Calendar from within any of the other Office 2001 programs. Microsoft refers to this capability as scheduling follow-ups. For example, you can be working on a Word 2001 document, e-mail it to a co-worker via Entourage, and then create a reminder in Entourage to check with your co-worker next Tuesday for her comments. Excel and PowerPoint work with Entourage in similar ways.

E-mailing Office documents with Entourage (or other programs)

Microsoft Office 2001 makes it easy to send Word, Excel, or PowerPoint documents as attachments to e-mail messages. Although it's likely that you'll be using Microsoft Entourage as your e-mail program (after all, it's part of Office 2001), you're not required to do so. The choice of an e-mail program is a very personal one, and there are people out there who won't give up their favorite e-mail program until you pry it out of their cold, dead hands. Happily avoiding wholesale slaughter, Office 2001 allows you to use the following e-mail programs to send documents as attachments:

- ✔ Microsoft Entourage
- ✔ Microsoft Outlook Express
- ✔ Qualcomm Eudora Pro
- ✔ Qualcomm Eudora Light
- ✔ Claris Emailer
- ✔ Microsoft Outlook for Macintosh, Microsoft Exchange Server Edition

This is the official list of programs that will work to send attachments from Office 2001, but it isn't necessarily complete. Other Macintosh e-mail programs may also work, and if you use a different e-mail program, you should try it and see.

To send an Office document as an e-mail attachment, follow these steps:

1. **Create or open a document in Word, Excel, or PowerPoint.**

2. **Choose File➪Send To➪Mail Recipient.**

   In Word, the choice is Mail Recipient (as Attachment); in the other two programs, it's just Mail Recipient. Roll your eyes at the inconsistency and forge onward. In any case, your e-mail program will launch (if it isn't already open) and will create a new mail message with the Office document attached.

3. **Address the e-mail (see Chapter 8 if you need help).**

4. **In the Subject field, enter a descriptive subject for the e-mail message.**

5. **Enter any text you wish in the message body (optional).**

   The result should look something like Figure 18-6.

6. **Click the Send button (or if your e-mail program has it and you wish to delay sending, the Send Later button).**

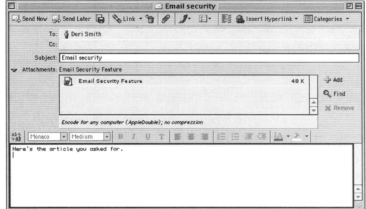

Figure 18-6:
The e-mail message with attachment, ready to be sent.

If another e-mail program opens up instead of Entourage when you choose Send To from Word, Excel, or PowerPoint, it's probably because the Mac OS has the other program registered as its default e-mail program. To select Entourage as your default e-mail program, open the Internet control panel, click the E-mail tab, and choose Microsoft Entourage from the Default E-mail Application pop-up menu at the bottom of the window. If Entourage isn't among the choices, choose Select and find Entourage in the resulting Open dialog box. Then close the Internet control panel, saving the settings if requested.

Creating reminders in Entourage

The addition of Entourage to the Office 2001 suite lets you add a dimension of time management to your Office 2001 documents. When working on a document in Word, Excel, or PowerPoint, you can schedule a reminder that will go into Entourage's Tasks list. Later, Entourage will remind you to follow up on the task.

To create a reminder for an Office 2001 document, follow these steps:

1. **Create or open a document in Word, Excel, or PowerPoint.**

2. **Choose Tools⇨Flag for Follow Up, or click the Flag for Follow Up button in the Standard toolbar.**

   The Flag for Follow Up dialog box appears, as shown in Figure 18-7.

Figure 18-7:
Use this
dialog box
to set your
reminder's
date and
time.

3. **Click on the month, day, or year to select them, and then change them using the small up or down arrows. Do the same for the hours and minutes. You can also select a date or time part with the Tab key, and use the up and down arrow keys on your keyboard for changes.**

4. **Click OK.**

The reminder goes onto Entourage's Tasks list, as shown in Figure 18-8.

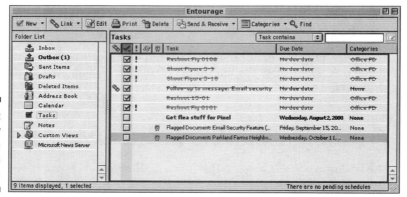

Figure 18-8:
The new
reminder, in
Entourage's
Tasks list.

Sharing Information with Word

A few lucky writers have the ability to write completely clean first drafts, with little or no revisions needed. Most of us aren't that fortunate, and we need to hone and polish our work in multiple drafts until it shines. Word 2001 has several tools to help with the revisions process. If your co-workers help with revisions, commenting and suggesting revisions for your work, Word 2001 makes tracking and incorporating changes from many people easy.

Making comments

Comments let co-workers and other editors, which I call *reviewers,* add notes to your work without changing your text. When a reviewer adds a comment, Word inserts an invisible *comment reference mark* and uses yellow shading to highlight the word closest to the insertion point. If you selected text before you added the comment, Word highlights all the selected text.

To add a comment to a document, follow these steps:

1. **Select the text you want to comment on.**

2. **Choose Insert⇨Comment.**

   The *comment pane* opens at the bottom of the document window.

3. **Type your comment into the comment pane.**

You can view comments other people have made in your document in one of two ways. The easiest way is to simply put your mouse cursor over some highlighted text. In a couple of seconds, the comment pops up in a ScreenTip above the text, as shown in Figure 18-9. The other way is to view the comments in the Comment pane of the document.

Comment in ScreenTip

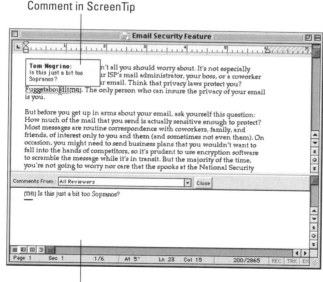

Figure 18-9:
Viewing
comments.

Comment in comment pane

Tracking changes

Besides simply commenting on your document, Word 2001 enables reviewers to edit the document, and Word keeps track of all the changes that were made. Word uses revision marks to show you the modifications in your document. *Revision marks* show where text is deleted, inserted, or otherwise changed. If a reviewer deletes some of your text, for example, that text shows up on-screen formatted as ~~strikethrough~~. Text inserted by reviewers is formatted as <u>underlined</u>. Word 2001 assigns a different color to each reviewer. All changes made by one reviewer might show up in red, and all changes made by another reviewer could appear in green.

Word 2001 doesn't show you the revision marks unless you ask it to. To see the revision marks in your document, follow these steps:

1. **Choose Tools⇨Track Changes⇨Highlight Changes.**

   The Highlight Changes dialog box appears, as shown in Figure 18-10.

2. **Click Track changes while editing.**

3. **Click Highlight Changes on Screen.**

4. **Click OK.**

   The revision marks appear in your document.

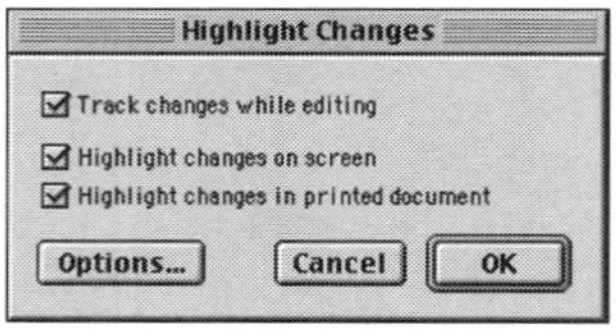

Figure 18-10:
Displaying
revision
marks
on-screen.

If you want to know who made a particular change to your document, rest the mouse pointer over a change. A ScreenTip appears, identifying the reviewer who made that change and identifying the kind of change, as shown in Figure 18-11.

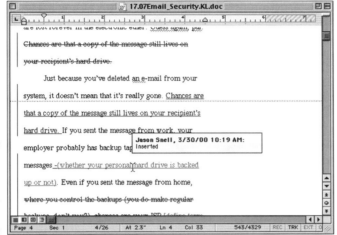

Figure 18-11:
Reviewing changes made by others.

After you have received all the changes from your co-workers, you can review the changes and accept or reject any suggested change. To review changes, follow these steps:

1. **Choose View⇨Toolbars⇨Reviewing.**

   The Reviewing toolbar appears, as shown in Figure 18-12.

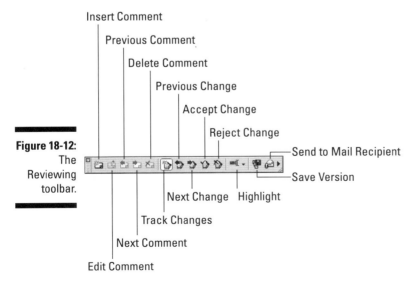

Insert Comment

Previous Comment

Delete Comment

Previous Change

Accept Change

Reject Change

Send to Mail Recipient

Save Version

Figure 18-12:
The Reviewing toolbar.

Next Change   Highlight

Track Changes

Next Comment

Edit Comment

2. **Click the insertion point before the revision you want to accept or reject.**

3. **On the Reviewing toolbar, click Next Change.**

   Word 2001 selects the changed text.

4. **If you want to keep the changed text, click Accept Change on the Reviewing toolbar. If you don't like the change that was made, click Reject Change.**

   Word 2001 automatically advances to the next change. If you accepted the change, the revision mark disappears from your screen. If you rejected the change, Word 2001 deletes the rejected text.

5. **Repeat Steps 3 and 4 until you have worked through all the changes in your document.**

Keeping track of versions

A nice feature in Word 2001 is its capability to store multiple *versions* of a document in one file. You can record snapshots of the changes made to a document by saving multiple versions. After you've saved versions of a document, you can go back and open, review, print, or delete earlier versions.

To save a version of your document, follow these steps:

1. **Choose File⇨Versions.**

   The Versions dialog box appears, as shown in Figure 18-13.

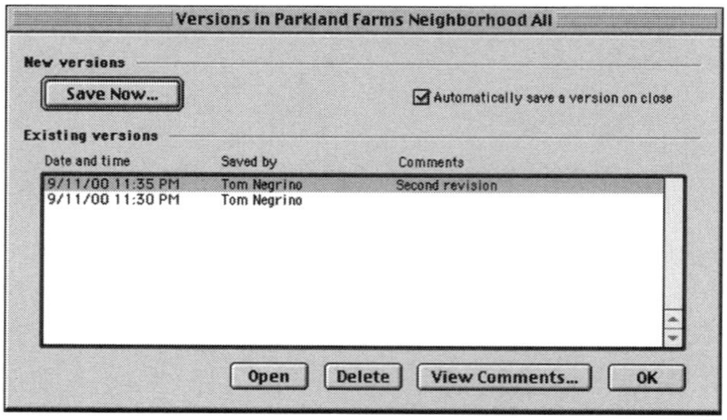

Figure 18-13:
Saving a
snapshot of
your
document
with the
Versions
feature.

Versions in Parkland Farms Neighborhood All

New versions

Save Now...   ☑ Automatically save a version on close

Existing versions

Date and time	Saved by	Comments
9/11/00 11:35 PM	Tom Negrino	Second revision
9/11/00 11:30 PM	Tom Negrino	

Open   Delete   View Comments...   OK

2. **Click the Save Now button.**

   The Save Version dialog box appears.

3. **If you want, type a comment in the Comments or Version box to identify the version.**

4. Click OK.

Word 2001 saves the version.

You might want to use the Versions feature only when a major revision to the document is complete, as having multiple versions in a file make it take up much more disk space. If your document contains big elements like graphics, the file size could get big enough so that it takes longer than usual to save the document.

Creating Excel worksheets in Word

Word enables you to create Excel spreadsheets from within Word. When you do so, you get all the power of Excel 2001. When you save your Word document, the Excel 2001 spreadsheet is also saved within your Word file.

To create an Excel worksheet in Word 2001, follow these steps:

1. In a Word document, click the insertion point where you want to create an Excel spreadsheet.

2. Click the More Buttons pop-up menu at the end of the Standard toolbar, and then click the Insert Microsoft Excel Worksheet button.

A spreadsheet grid appears, as shown in Figure 18-14.

Figure 18-14: Setting the size of an Excel worksheet within Word.

3. Click and drag in the grid to set the size of the spreadsheet in your Word document.

You're only setting the size of the spreadsheet's appearance in your Word document. You still have the full power of Excel, including the ability to use a bazillion cells.

4. Office 2001 switches to Excel, where you can type numbers, functions, or formulas in the usual manner. (To see how to use Excel, refer to Part IV.)

Sharing Information with Excel

Excel enables you to share spreadsheet and workbook information with other users. You can send workbooks to co-workers for review, much as you can with Word documents. You can also have a *shared workbook,* which is a workbook that has been set up to enable multiple users on a network to view and make changes at the same time. Because changes made to a shared workbook are live, each user sees the changes made by others.

Sharing workbooks

To set up a shared workbook on your company network, follow these steps:

1. **Choose Tools⇨Share Workbook.**

   The Share Workbook dialog box appears.

2. **Click the Editing tab.**

3. **Click the Allow Changes by More Than One User at the Same Time button.**

4. **Click OK.**

   Excel prompts you to save the workbook by displaying the Save dialog box.

5. **Give the shared workbook a name, and click Save.**

6. **Choose File⇨Save As, and then save the new shared workbook on a network server so that other users can access it.**

You can also use Personal File Sharing or Personal Web Sharing to share your files. See the Mac OS Help files for information on how to set up these services.

Using Word text in an Excel spreadsheet

Sometimes you want to use Word data inside an Excel spreadsheet. It could be that you have a fair amount of text you want to prepare in Word and then move into Excel, or you could copy a Word table and paste it into multiple spreadsheet cells.

When you link Word text to an Excel spreadsheet, any changes made to the Word document are reflected automatically in the Excel document. This automatic updating can save you a considerable amount of time and effort. One caveat: This technique won't work if the Excel workbook is shared.

To link Word text into Excel, follow these steps:

1. **In a Word 2001 document, select the text you want to link.**

2. **Choose Edit⇨Copy, or press ⌘+C.**

3. **Switch to Excel 2001.**

4. **Click the cell where you want the text to appear.**

5. **Choose Edit⇨Paste Special.**

   The Paste Special dialog box appears (refer to Figure 18-3).

6. **Click the Paste Link button.**

7. **In the As box, click Microsoft Word Document Object.**

8. **Click OK.**

Sharing Information with PowerPoint

PowerPoint shares information with Word and Excel in much the same way that those two programs share information with each other. You can copy, move, or link information among any of the three programs.

Building tables and charts from Excel information

To create a chart based on Excel data inside your PowerPoint presentation, follow these steps:

1. **Choose Insert⇨New Slide.**

   The New Slide dialog box appears.

2. **In the Choose a slide layout box, find and select the layout named Chart.**

3. **Click OK.**

   PowerPoint creates a new slide.

4. **On the Standard toolbar, click the Insert Chart button.**

   Microsoft Chart, a small helper application, appears, displaying a sample chart and datasheet.

5. **Open the Excel spreadsheet that you wish to chart.**

6. **In Excel, select and copy the data you wish charted.**

7. **Switch back to Microsoft Chart.**

8. **Click a cell in the datasheet and choose Edit⇨Paste.**

   The data from Excel will replace the sample data in the datasheet. The chart will also update.

9. **Choose File⇨Quit & Return to [the name of your presentation].**

   The worksheet closes, and you automatically switch back to PowerPoint 2001, where the chart you created from Excel data is inserted into your slide.

Linking Word text to your PowerPoint presentation

To copy Word text into PowerPoint, follow these steps:

1. **In a Word 2001 document, select the text you want to copy.**

2. **Choose Edit⇨Copy, or press ⌘+C.**

3. **Switch to PowerPoint 2001.**

4. **Click the text box of the slide where you want the text to appear.**

5. **Choose Edit⇨Paste.**

Chapter 19

Sharing Information Over the Internet

*O*ne of the things that the Internet revolution has taught us is the importance of sharing and collaboration. Actually, your Mom probably taught you that lesson long ago; it just took the computer industry years to figure out what Mom always knew: People work better when they work together.

Microsoft has responded to the increasing importance of collaboration and the Internet by building Internet integration features into all the Office 2001 programs — Word, Entourage, Excel, and PowerPoint can now save their documents as Web pages.

In addition, you can put hyperlinks in any Office document. A *hyperlink* connects to one part of your document to a Web page, to a different location in the same document, or to a different Office document on your hard disk. You can have a table of contents at the beginning of a long document, with each heading hyperlinked to the appropriate part of the document, for example. Clicking a heading in the table of contents takes you to that part of the document.

Besides working on the Internet, the Office 2001 applications also work better with each other, and the key to this new chumminess is Entourage 2001. Entourage is the shared address book and calendar for the other Office 2001 applications, so you can be working on any other Office 2001 document and bring in Entourage to remind you to follow up on some issue connected to that document. And, of course, you can use Entourage to e-mail any Office 2001 document from within any other Office application (for more on e-mailing documents, refer to Chapter 8).

Using Hyperlinks

Hyperlinks enhance the usability of your documents by enabling readers to get to related or supporting information easily. To insert a hyperlink, you have to tell whichever Office application you're working in where the link starts and what its destination is. By convention, hyperlinks are formatted in blue and are underlined, although Office 2001 enables you to change that formatting, if you want.

Linking to Web pages

To insert a hyperlink that points to a Web page, follow these steps:

1. **In your current document, select any text or picture you want to turn into a hyperlink.**

2. **Choose Insert➪Hyperlink, click the Insert Hyperlink button on the Standard toolbar, or press ⌘+K.**

   The Insert Hyperlink dialog box appears, set to the Web Page tab, as shown in Figure 19-1. The text you selected will be in the Display box.

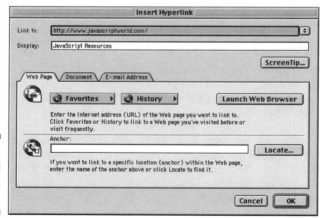

Figure 19-1:
The Insert Hyperlink dialog box.

3. **Do one of the following things:**

   • Type the URL of the Web page in the Link to box; then click the OK button.

- If you've already stored the URL of the Web page in Internet Explorer's Favorites list, click the Favorites pop-up menu, select the Web site from the list, and then click the OK button.

- If you have recently visited the target Web site, choose it from the pop-up menu accessed via the History button, and then click OK.

When you're typing a URL, it's important to type it exactly as it appears on the Web page. You can't change the capitalization or punctuation, add spaces, or change anything else. URLs aren't forgiving; if you mistype them, the hyperlinks just don't work.

The Office 2001 program you're working in creates the hyperlink, formatting it blue and underlined. This formatting makes it easy to tell where the links in your document are.

Office 2001 is smart enough to recognize all the standard forms of URLs (Universal Resource Locators, or Internet addresses) and can format them automatically as hyperlinks as you type them. To turn on automatic hyperlink formatting in Word 2001, follow these steps:

1. **Choose Tools⇨AutoCorrect.**

   The AutoCorrect dialog box appears.

2. **Click the AutoFormat As You Type tab.**

3. **In the Replace As You Type section, click the Internet Paths with Hyperlinks check box.**

4. **Click the OK button.**

Entourage does this a little differently. First, the Insert Hyperlink option (with submenu) is under the Message menu. Second, the menu options let you insert a link to a URL in the Internet Explorer window, its Favorites or History, but does not present the dialog box where you can type a URL.

Hereafter, whenever you type a URL in your document, Word 2001 turns it into a hyperlink. If the URL is for a Web page, when you're reading the document, clicking the hyperlink launches your Web browser (Internet Explorer or Netscape Navigator, for example), connects to the Internet, and loads the Web page. If the URL is an e-mail address, your e-mail program starts up, and a new e-mail message is created and addressed.

Which Web browser or e-mail program launches when you click a hyperlink depends on the settings in the E-mail or Web tabs of the Internet control panel, as shown in Figure 19-2. At the bottom of each of these tabs, you'll find a pop-up menu that lets you set the default program for that type of hyperlink.

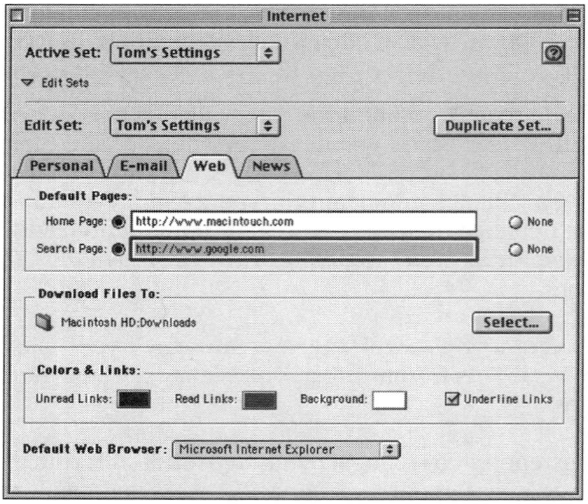

Internet

Active Set: Tom's Settings

▽ Edit Sets

Edit Set: Tom's Settings   Duplicate Set...

Personal \ E-mail \ Web \ News

Default Pages:

Home Page: ● http://www.macintouch.com   ○ None

Search Page: ● http://www.google.com   ○ None

Download Files To:

Macintosh HD:Downloads   Select...

Colors & Links:

Unread Links: Read Links: Background: ☑ Underline Links

Default Web Browser: Microsoft Internet Explorer

Figure 19-2:
Setting
Internet
Explorer as
your default
Web
browser.

Linking to other Office documents

To insert a hyperlink that points to another Office 2001 document (or actually, to any other document), follow these steps (except in Entourage; this section doesn't apply in that program):

1. In your current document, select any text or picture you want to turn into a hyperlink.

2. Choose Insert⇨Hyperlink, click the Insert Hyperlink button on the Standard toolbar, or press ⌘+K.

The Insert Hyperlink dialog box appears.

3. Click the Document tab.

The Document tab appears, as shown in Figure 19-3. The text you selected will be in the Display box.

4. Do one of the following things:

- If you have recently used the document, choose it from the pop-up menu accessed via the Recent Documents button, and then click OK.

- Click the Select button, find and double-click a file, and then click the OK button.

- If you've already stored the URL of the Web page in Internet Explorer's Favorites list, click the Favorites pop-up menu, select the Web site from the list, and then click the OK button.

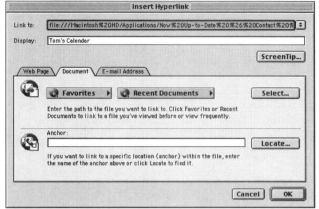

Figure 19-3:
The
Document
tab of the
Insert
Hyperlink
dialog box.

Inserting e-mail hyperlinks

It's just as common that you'll want to insert an e-mail address into your documents as a Web page, and Office 2001 has you covered. Follow these steps:

1. **In your current document, select any text or picture you want to turn into an e-mail hyperlink.**

2. **Choose Insert⇨Hyperlink, click the Insert Hyperlink button on the Standard toolbar, or press ⌘+K.**

   The Insert Hyperlink dialog box appears.

3. **Click the E-mail Address tab.**

   The E-mail Address tab appears, as shown in Figure 19-4. The text you selected will be in the Display box.

4. **Enter the e-mail address in the To box.**

   As you enter the address, the mailto: hyperlink appears in the Link to box.

   If you have recently used this e-mail address in Word, choose it from the pop-up menu accessed via the Recent Addresses button, and then click OK.

5. **Enter the Subject of the e-mail message (optional).**

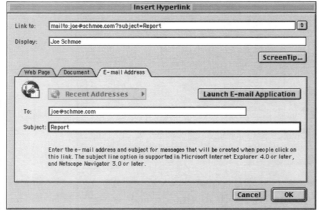

Figure 19-4:
The E-mail
Address tab
of the Insert
Hyperlink
dialog box.

Creating internal links

An *internal hyperlink* jumps the reader from one part of your document to another part of the same document. The procedure differs slightly in each of the Office programs: In Word, you link to a part of your document that you have defined as a bookmark; in Excel, you link to a range of cells to which you've given a name; in PowerPoint, you link to a particular slide; there aren't any bookmarks in Entourage. I've shown you how to create the internal link in Word, which is the most common example. Follow these steps to create an internal hyperlink in Word:

1. **Select the text or picture you want to make the destination of the hyperlink (the point in the document the reader sees after clicking the hyperlink).**

2. **Choose Insert⇨Bookmark.**

    The Bookmark dialog box appears, as shown in Figure 19-5.

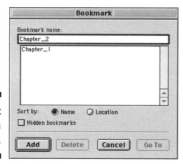

Figure 19-5:
Adding a
bookmark.

3. **In the text box, enter the name for your bookmark.**

   You can't include any spaces, slashes, or hyphens in a bookmark name. If you want to name a bookmark something like "Chapter 4," substitute the underscore character for the space, as in "Chapter_4."

4. **Click the Add button.**

5. **Select in your document the text you want to define as a hyperlink.**

6. **Choose Insert➪Hyperlink, click the Insert Hyperlink button on the Standard toolbar, or press ⌘+K.**

   The Insert Hyperlink dialog box appears.

7. **Click the Document tab.**

8. **Click the Locate button next to the Anchor text box.**

9. **The Select Place in Document dialog box appears.**

10. **Click the bookmark you want to make the hyperlink's destination.**

11. **Click the OK button to return to the Insert Hyperlink dialog box.**

12. **Click the OK button in the Insert Hyperlink dialog box.**

Removing hyperlinks

After working with a document for a while, you may want to eliminate a hyperlink. To remove a hyperlink, follow these steps:

1. **Select the offending hyperlink.**

   It can be difficult to select a hyperlink in your document without clicking and activating it. One way to work around this problem is to click near the hyperlink and then move the cursor into the hyperlink using the arrow keys on your keyboard.

2. **Choose Insert➪Hyperlink, or press ⌘+K.**

   The Insert Hyperlink dialog box appears.

3. **Click the Remove Link button.**

Using the Web Toolbar

The Web toolbar (see Figure 19-6) is available in all the Office 2001 applications except Entourage, and it enables you to integrate Web browsing into your work. You use the Web toolbar when you're working on a document and want to look up something on a Web site.

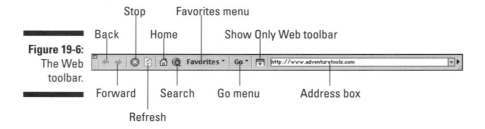

Figure 19-6:
The Web
toolbar.

Displaying the Web toolbar

To display the Web toolbar, do one of the following things:

- ✔ Choose View➪Toolbars➪Web.
- ✔ Control+click any toolbar, and then choose Web from the resulting short-cut menu.
- ✔ Choose Tools➪Customize to display the Customize dialog box, click the Toolbars tab, click the Web check box, and then click the Close button.

Browsing with the Web toolbar

When you make a choice from the Web toolbar, the Web page isn't displayed inside the Office program you're using. Rather, Office sends a message to whatever Web browser you set up as your default browser; that browser then launches and loads the Web page.

The Web toolbar has most of the same navigation buttons as Internet Explorer. Because Office uses the various settings you made when you set up Internet Explorer and Outlook Express, it inherits your home page and the search engine you prefer when you click the Search button. The toolbar also contains the Favorites menu, which contains all your Internet Explorer bookmarks.

To browse the Web with the Web toolbar, use the toolbar the same way you do in Internet Explorer.

Creating Web Pages with Office 2001

All the Office programs can save their documents in HTML format, which is Web format, but Word 2001 does a better job of it than Excel or PowerPoint do. Word 2001 has many features that help you create Web pages, and considering that Word is a word processor, you can use it to create surprisingly credible

Web pages. Although you probably won't turn to Word 2001 as your main Web-page-creation tool, it's definitely worth using to convert your Word documents to Web pages. After converting, you may want to touch up the pages by using a true Web page editor, such as Macromedia Dreamweaver or Adobe GoLive.

Excel and PowerPoint lack the editing capabilities needed to create Web pages. Your best bet is to use the HTML export capabilities of these programs as a starting point, knowing that you'll be editing the resulting pages with Word 2001 or another program for building Web sites.

Building Web pages in Word 2001

You can use Word 2001 to create Web pages in two ways. One way is to use Word from scratch to build the page, perhaps using the Word templates for assistance. The other way is to save an existing Word document in HTML format.

Using the Web templates

The Web templates installed with Office 2001 and the Value Pack on the Office 2001 CD-ROM provide a variety of pages, in a number of themes, that may be all you need for a simple Web site. The templates give you the page layout, icons, and background colors for Web pages. You just need to add your text and graphics to the page to finish it.

To use the Web templates to create a Web page, follow these steps:

1. **Choose File⇨Project Gallery.**

   The Project Gallery opens.

2. **Click the Web Pages category.**

3. **Choose one of the Web template themes.**

4. **Select the kind of Web page you want to create from the thumbnails on the right side of the window.**

5. **Click the OK button.**

   The new document appears, with the Web template applied and sample text (and possibly graphics) that will need to be replaced.

6. **Replace the sample text in the template with your own information.**

The page template appears in Word's Online Layout mode so that you can get a feel for how the page will look in a browser. That's no substitute, however, for looking at the page in a real Web browser; no exact correspondence exists between the way Word 2001 displays a page and the way the page looks in a browser. Always preview your pages in a browser before you publish them to the Web.

What's this HTML stuff?

HTML is an acronym for *HyperText Markup Language,* which is the format used to create Web pages. There's nothing special about an HTML file; it's just plain text surrounded by *markup tags,* which tell the Web browser how to interpret the text inside the tags.

Suppose that I want to display the phrase *Office 2001* in boldface on a Web page. The HTML code to do that looks like

```
<B>Office 2001</B>
```

The first tag, `<B>`, starts the boldface formatting; the end tag, `</B>`, ends the boldface. If you looked at the HTML *source,* the code that makes the whole Web page that has the above words on it, it would look something like this:

```
<HTML>
<HEAD>
<TITLE>Office 2001</TITLE>
</HEAD>
<BODY>
<B>Office 2001</B>
</BODY>
</HTML>
```

The page opens with the opening `<HTML>` tag, then the opening `<HEAD>` tag, which defines the header section of the page. Inside the header, there's a `<TITLE>` tag surrounding the title of the page, then the closing `</HEAD>` tag. The body of the document opens with the `<BODY>` tag, contains the "Office 2001" in boldface, then closes with the tag `</BODY>`. The page ends with `</HTML>`.

The nice thing about using Word 2001 to build Web pages is that you generally don't have to mess with HTML. Nothing stops you, however, from editing the HTML pages Word creates, at least theoretically. Practically, Word 2001 creates Web pages that are quite complex, using a lot of advanced Web building features, such as CSS (Cascading Style Sheets) and XML (Extended Markup Language). Word uses these to try to make the Web pages it creates look as close as possible to the way the pages look in Word. The results are generally good, but the source code needed can be awfully dense. If you want to learn more about HTML, you should pick up any of the three billion books about the subject. You may want to start with either of two books: *HTML 4 for the World Wide Web, Visual Quickstart Guide,* by Elizabeth Castro (published by Peachpit Press); or *HTML 4 For Dummies,* by Ed Tittel and Natanya Pitts (published by IDG Books Worldwide, Inc.).

Saving a document as HTML

To save an existing document as a Web page, follow these steps:

1. **Open the document you want to convert.**

2. **Choose File⇨Save as Web Page.**

   The Save As dialog box appears.

3. **In the text box, type the name of the new file.**

   For most Web servers to recognize the file, you have to add the `.html` extension to the filename. If you're writing about a bill that's moving through Congress, for example, you could name your file porkbarrel.html. It's also OK to use `.htm` as the file extension.

It's vital to name HTML files without spaces or slashes, which confuse the heck out of Web servers. Using all lowercase letters is also a good idea (but not mandatory).

4. **Click either "Save entire file into HTML" or "Save only display information into HTML."**

   The first choice saves extra information with your Word document that allows it to be more easily converted from a Web page back into a Word document, but that also adds a bit to the time it takes a Web page to be downloaded and displayed in a browser. The second choice strips away this extra material before saving. If your page will be on a one-way journey to the Web, choose the second option.

5. **Click the Save button.**

Adding flashy pictures to your Web pages

Most Word documents look fairly dull when you convert them into Web pages, and one good way to liven them up is to add pictures to the page. The Office 2001 CD-ROM comes with tons of clip art and photographs you can use on your Web pages.

To add pictures to a Web page, follow these steps:

1. **Put the insertion point where you want the picture to appear.**

2. **Do one of the following things:**

   - Choose Insert⇨Picture⇨ClipArt to pick a picture from the Office 2001 clip art library.

   - Choose Insert⇨Picture⇨From File to choose another picture on your hard disk.

   - Choose Insert⇨Picture⇨ClipArt, and then click the Online button, to connect to the Internet and check out the Web art at the Microsoft Web site.

3. **Select the picture you want to put on your page.**

4. **Click the Insert button.**

Turning Excel spreadsheets into Web pages

When Excel 2001 saves a spreadsheet as HTML, it turns the worksheet into an HTML table on an otherwise blank Web page. Excel attempts (and usually does a pretty good job) to maintain any special formatting that you've applied to the worksheet. If the worksheet contains a chart object, Excel exports it as a graphic, in GIF format. You can then "pretty up" this bare-bones Web page in a Web page editor or in Word 2001.

You can preview how your worksheet will look as a Web page by following these steps:

1. **Open an existing worksheet, or create and save a new one.**

2. **Choose File➪Web Page Preview.**

    Your Web browser launches and shows you how the Web page will look.

To save a spreadsheet as a Web page, follow these steps:

1. **Open an existing Excel 2001 spreadsheet, or create and save a new spreadsheet.**

2. **Select the part of the spreadsheet you want to convert to a Web page (optional).**

    If you don't select part of the worksheet, the entire worksheet will be saved.

3. **Choose File➪Save As Web Page.**

    The Save dialog box appears.

4. **Enter the name of the Web page in the text box.**

5. **Click the radio button labeled Workbook, Sheet or Selection: <range>, depending on what you want to save.**

6. **Navigate to where you want to save the Web page.**

7. **Click the Web Options button (optional).**

    The Web Options dialog box appears. In the General tab, enter the title of the Web page you're creating. In the Pictures tab, consider choosing "Allow PNG as an output format." The other two tabs can be ignored.

    The PNG (Portable Network Graphics) format is a relatively new Web graphics format that is smaller in size than the previously standard GIF or JPEG and has other useful characteristics. Be aware that although PNG is a superior format, people with some older Web browsers may not be able to view PNG files. These older browsers include older versions of the America Online browser, and Internet Explorer and Netscape prior to version 4.

8. **Click the Automate button (optional).**

    The Automate dialog box appears. Using this dialog box, you can set Excel 2001 to automatically save the worksheet as a Web page whenever you save the worksheet, or according to a timed schedule. You can use this cool feature to update information on a Web site periodically and automatically.

9. **Click the Save button.**

Publishing Entourage Calendars on the Web

If you want, you can share your Entourage Calendar with friends and co-workers by saving the Calendar as an HTML document and uploading it to a Web server. The Calendar will appear as a nicely-formatted Web page, with hyperlinks on the events in the Calendar that display the event's details in a list on the right side of the Web page.

To save your Entourage calendar as a Web page, follow these steps:

1. **In Entourage, click on Calendar in the Folder list.**

2. **Choose File⇨Save As Web page.**

3. **The Save as Web Page dialog box appears, as shown in Figure 19-7.**

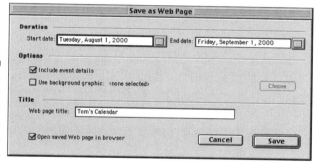

Figure 19-7:
Set up your
Calendar as
a Web page
here.

4. **In the Duration section, set the beginning and end dates for the Web calendar.**

5. **In the Options section, choose (optionally, of course) if you want to include the event details and include a background image. If you include the background image, you'll need to click the Choose button and find a graphic for the background of the calendar.**

Background graphics must be in Web-friendly formats (JPEG, GIF, or PNG), and will be tiled to fill up the calendar's space. In other words, if your graphic isn't big enough to fill up the space the whole calendar needs, it will be repeated as many times as needed to fill the space.

6. **In the Title section, enter a title that will appear at the top of the Calendar.**

7. **Click the Open saved Web page in browser button, so that you'll see a preview of how the page will look.**

8. **Click Save.**

A standard Save dialog box will appear.

9. **Enter a name for the calendar file.**

   You must follow the usual Web page rules for naming a Web page: just one word, no spaces or slashes in the name. Entourage will helpfully add the .htm file suffix for you.

10. **Click Save.**

    Entourage saves an HTML document with the name you gave it, plus a folder with supporting files, with the same name. If you clicked the Open saved Web page in browser button, you'll see the Calendar as Web page, as shown in Figure 19-8.

    In order for other people to see the Web page, you'll need to upload it to your Web server, in the usual fashion (slightly outside the scope of this book).

Previous month

Current month   Next month   Title

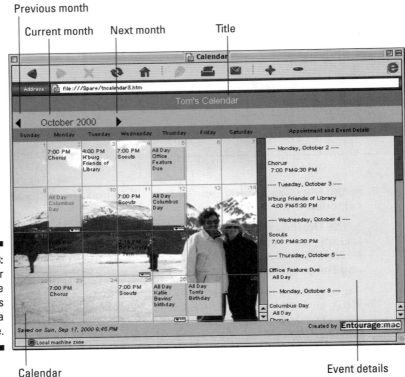

Figure 19-8: Your Entourage Calendar, as shown in a Web page.

Calendar

Event details

Part VII
The Part of Tens

In this part . . .

This part of the book is the one you should turn to when you want to polish your skills with Microsoft Office 2001. In the three chapters in this part, you find 30 ways to make working with Office faster, easier, and maybe even more enjoyable.

Chapter 20

Ten (Or So) Ways to Customize Office 2001

*M*icrosoft Office 2001 is an extremely powerful set of programs, enabling you to do practically anything you can imagine doing with a word processor, spreadsheet, and presentation program. All that power comes with the price of complexity, however. Sometimes, figuring out just how to do what you want to do can be difficult. You may disagree with the wizards at Microsoft about how to accomplish a particular task. No problem — the Office 2001 programs are customizable. If you don't like the Microsoft way of doing things, you can change the programs so that they make sense to you.

Add Custom Menu Commands

One of the best ways to customize the Office programs is to add commands to any of the menus. If your work requires a lot of scientific notation, for example, you may want to put Word's Equation Editor on the Insert menu.

To add a command to a menu, follow these steps:

1. **Choose Tools⇨Customize.**

   The Customize dialog box appears.

2. **Click the Toolbars tab.**

3. **Click the Menu Bar check box.**

   A customizable copy of the menu bar appears, as shown in Figure 20-1.

Figure 20-1:
A customiz-
able copy
of the
menu bar.

Copy of menu bar

The menu bar is just another customizable toolbar, as far as the Office programs are concerned.

4. **Click the Commands tab.**

5. **In the Categories box, click the category that contains the command you want to add to the menu.**

   If you can't find the command in a category, click the All Commands category.

6. **In the Commands box, click the command you want to add to the menu.**

7. **Drag the command to the name of the menu to which you want to add the command.**

   A horizontal line indicates where on the menu your command will appear.

8. **When the command is where you want it to be, release the mouse button.**

   The command appears on the menu.

9. **Press the Return key.**

   The Customize dialog box closes.

Rename Menu Commands

If you don't like the name of a particular menu command, change it! Follow these steps:

1. **Choose Tools⇨Customize.**

   The Customize window appears.

2. **Click the Toolbars tab.**

3. **Click the Menu Bar check box (if it isn't already checked).**

   A customizable copy of the menu bar appears (refer to Figure 20-1).

4. **On the copy of the menu bar, double-click the command you want to change.**

   The Command Properties window appears, as shown in Figure 20-2.

Figure 20-2:
Type the new menu command name into the Command Properties window.

Command Properties
Name: Word Count...
View: Default Style
☑ Begin a group
Keyboard...
Description
Word Count (Tools menu)
Counts the number of pages, words, characters, paragraphs, and lines in the active document. Punctuation marks and special symbols are also included in the word count.
Reset   Cancel   OK

5. **In the Name box, type the new name for the command.**

6. **Press the Return key to dismiss the Command Properties window.**

7. **Press the Return key again to dismiss the Customize window.**

There's an Achilles' heel of overzealous customization. For example, if you change the names of menus, you might have some trouble describing problems with telephone support technicians, since your program won't match theirs.

Add Your Own Shortcut Keys

Sometimes the shortcut keys that Microsoft thinks are logical make about zero sense to you. Again, you can change 'em if you don't like 'em. For example, I've been used to toggling the Show/Hide Paragraph Marks command by pressing ⌘+J since I started using Word 5.1. Word 2001 thinks that ⌘+J should mean Justify Text (it has a point — that does make more sense). But, heck, I've been doing it the old way for the last eight years, so I changed the shortcut key. Unfortunately, shortcut key customization is only available in Word; the other Office programs don't share in this particular bit of flexibility.

Follow these steps to assign shortcut keys any way you want:

1. **Choose Tools➪Customize.**

   The Customize dialog box appears.

2. **Click the Keyboard button.**

   The Customize Keyboard dialog box appears, as shown in Figure 20-3.

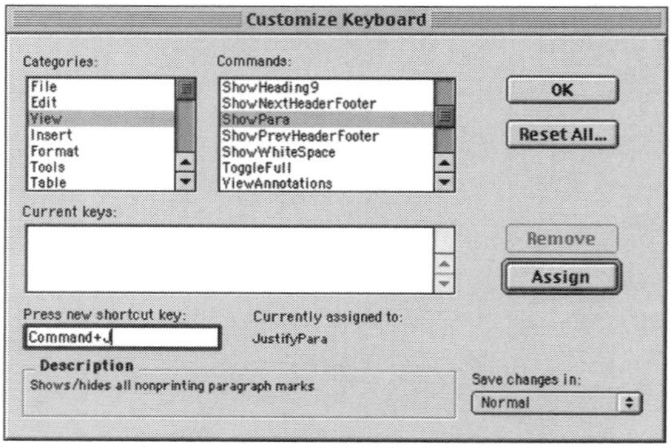

Figure 20-3:
Changing
shortcut
keys with
the
Customize
Keyboard
dialog box.

3. **In the Categories and Commands boxes, select the command for which you want to add or change the shortcut key.**

4. **Click the Press new shortcut key box.**

   If a shortcut key is already assigned for this command, it appears in the Current Keys box.

5. **Press on your keyboard the shortcut key combination you want to use.**

   If the combination is already in use, a message tells you which command now has it.

6. **Click the Assign button.**

7. **Click the OK button to close the Customize Keyboard dialog box and return to the Customize dialog box.**

8. **Click OK.**

Make a Custom Menu

You can create your own custom menus for particular projects and then hide or display them as needed. For example, suppose you do a lot of tables in Word, and you would like a custom menu that shows all of the table border styles.

To create a custom menu and add it to the menu bar, follow these steps:

1. **Choose Tools⇨Customize.**

   The Customize dialog box appears.

2. **Click the Toolbars tab.**

3. **Click the Menu Bar check box.**

   A customizable copy of the menu bar appears (refer to Figure 20-1).

4. **Click the Commands tab.**

5. **Scroll to the bottom of the Categories box and click New Menu.**

6. **Drag the New Menu item from the Commands box to where you want it to appear in the copy of the menu bar.**

   Next, you have to rename the new menu that's on the copy of the menu bar.

7. **Double-click the new menu on the copy of the menu bar.**

   The Command Properties window appears (refer to Figure 20-2).

8. **In the Name box of the Command Properties window, type the new menu's title, and then press the Return key.**

   Now you'll want to add commands to your new menu.

9. **Click (just once) the new menu name on the copy of the menu bar.**

   An empty box appears below the menu name.

10. **Drag to the Categories box of the Customize dialog box; then drag the command to the empty box on the new menu.**

11. **Repeat Steps 9 and 10 until you have added to the new menu all the commands you want to use, as shown in Figure 20-4.**

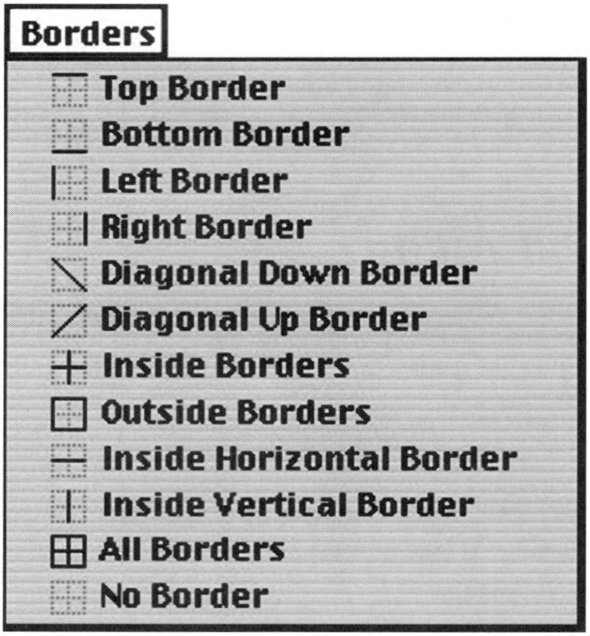

Borders

- Top Border
- Bottom Border
- Left Border
- Right Border
- Diagonal Down Border
- Diagonal Up Border
- Inside Borders
- Outside Borders
- Inside Horizontal Border
- Inside Vertical Border
- All Borders
- No Border

Figure 20-4:
The new
Borders
custom
menu.

12. **Press the Return key.**

13. **Click the Close button.**

Customizing Contextual Menus

Contextual menus contain commands that apply to the item the mouse pointer is on. You access them by holding down the Control key while clicking on something on the screen. In Chapter 5, you saw how to use contextual menus to move text and check and fix your spelling. You can modify a contextual menu to contain different commands from the ones that Microsoft includes with Office 2001.

To add a command to a contextual menu, follow these steps:

1. **On the Tools menu, click Customize, and then click the Toolbars tab.**

2. **Select the Shortcut Menus check box.**

   The Shortcut Menu toolbar appears, as shown in Figure 20-5.

Figure 20-5:
The
Shortcut
Menu
toolbar.

"Shortcut menu" is a term shared by the Windows version of Microsoft Office. In Office 2001, Microsoft has made a bigger effort to follow Mac terminology, but you'll still find some vestiges of the Windows terms. Just remember that a shortcut menu is a contextual menu, and you won't be confused.

3. **Click one of the categories (Text, Table, or Draw) on the Shortcut Menu toolbar, then click the shortcut menu you wish to change.**

4. **In the Customize window, click the Commands tab.**

5. **Choose a Category, and then drag a command from the Commands box to the shortcut menu.**

6. **Release the mouse button.**

7. **Press the Return key to accept the changes and close the Customize window.**

To delete an item from a contextual menu:

1. **On the Tools menu, click Customize, and then click the Toolbars tab.**

2. **Select the Shortcut Menus check box.**

3. **Click one of the categories (Text, Table, or Draw) on the Shortcut Menu toolbar, and then click the shortcut menu you wish to change.**

4. **Drag the offending command off the shortcut menu.**

5. **Press the Return key to accept the changes and close the Customize window.**

Record a Macro

All too often, people use their computers as barely smarter versions of objects they used before they had computers. Terrific programs such as Word 2001 are available, and most people use it as though it were a type-writer. Excel is used to add columns of numbers or handle simple lists — the least of its capabilities. Computers should be saving people from doing repetitive dogwork, thereby making it easier to do their jobs. That's the idea behind the Office 2001 AutoText, AutoFormat, and AutoCorrect features: trying to relieve people of some of the tasks that come up again and again.

Macros take this idea one step further. You can record a series of actions and commands as a macro and then play the macro to repeat the actions automatically.

Macros are programmed in Office 2001's internal scripting language, called Visual Basic for Applications (VBA). It's possible to program directly in VBA by choosing Tools⇨Macro⇨Visual Basic Editor, but you'll need some programming experience to do so. Describing how to program in VBA is beyond the scope of this book. Way beyond. Luckily, you don't need to know anything about programming to use macros, because Word and Excel have macro recorders that watch what you do and write the VBA code for you.

Suppose that you write a report every week. Although the beginning of the report has different text every week, it always has the same format. You can record a macro that assigns styles to the first several lines of your document and does the repetitive formatting for you. Any set of actions you perform more than once, you can record (and play back) as a macro. After you try macros a few times, you'll wonder how you got along without them.

The macro recorder does just fine with commands, menus, and text that you type, but it can't record mouse movements inside the document window. So you can't use the mouse to do things like select text or move the insertion point. Instead, use the keyboard to do those sorts of things, and your macro should record just fine.

After you record a macro, assign a toolbar button to it, assign a shortcut key to it, or add it to a menu.

Macros in Word 2001

To record a macro in Word 2001, follow these steps:

1. Choose Tools⇨Macro⇨Record New Macro.

The Record Macro dialog box appears, as shown in Figure 20-6.

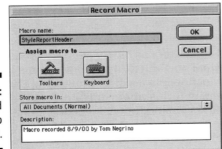

Figure 20-6:
The Record
Macro
dialog box.

2. Type a name for your macro in the Macro name box.

You can't have any spaces in the macro name; if you do, Word will give you the oh-so-helpful error message "Invalid procedure name."

3. (Optional) Assign the macro you're creating to a toolbar button or a shortcut key.

- To assign the macro to a toolbar button, click Toolbars. The Customize dialog box appears. In the Commands box, click the macro you're recording and drag it to a toolbar. Then click the Close button to begin recording the macro.

- To assign the macro to a shortcut key, click Keyboard. The Customize Keyboard dialog box appears. Click the Press New Shortcut Key box; then press the shortcut key you want to assign to the macro. Click the Assign button; then click the Close button to begin recording the macro.

The Stop Recording toolbar appears, as shown in Figure 20-7.

Figure 20-7:
The Stop
Recording
toolbar.

Stop button

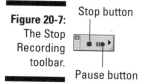

Pause button

4. Perform the actions you want to record in the macro.

5. Click the Stop Recording button when you're done.

To play back your macro, use the toolbar button or shortcut key you assigned in Step 3 or choose Tools⇨Macros. The Macros dialog box appears, as shown in Figure 20-8. Click the macro you want to run, and then click the Run button.

Figure 20-8:
Running a
macro from
the Macros
dialog box.

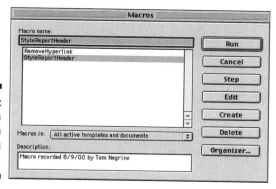

Macros in Excel 2001

Recording macros in Excel 2001 is somewhat different from recording them in Word 2001, although the basic idea is the same. Again, you use a macro to record a series of actions you want to repeat.

To record a macro in Excel 2001, follow these steps:

1. **Choose Tools⇨Macro⇨Record New Macro.**

   The Excel Record Macro dialog box appears, as shown in Figure 20-9.

Figure 20-9: The Excel 2001 Record Macro window.

2. **Type a name for your macro in the Macro name box.**

3. **(Optional) If you want to run the macro with a shortcut key, type the letter of the key in the Shortcut key box.**

   Excel 2001 isn't as flexible as Word 2001 when it comes to assigning shortcut keys. The only acceptable key combination is ⌘+Option+*letter,* in which *letter* is any lowercase letter on the keyboard.

4. **Click the OK button.**

   A Stop Recording toolbar appears (refer to Figure 20-4).

5. **Perform the actions you want to record in the macro.**

6. **Click the Stop Recording button when you are done.**

To play back your macro, use the shortcut key that you assigned in Step 3 or choose Tools⇨Macros.

Macros in PowerPoint and Entourage

This topic is a bit of a sore point. Microsoft generally did a good job of updating the programs in Office 2001 so that they're equivalent to their Windows 98/2000 counterparts in Office 2000. Unfortunately, PowerPoint 2001 for the

Mac got shortchanged: Significant capabilities are lacking on the Mac side, and one of those is the capability to record macros. If you want to use macros in PowerPoint 2001, you must program them yourself by using the Microsoft programming language, Visual Basic for Applications.

Entourage 2001 has fared even worse; you can't record macros, and you can't program them with VBA, either. But it does have something that the other Office 2001 applications lack: a Scripts menu. Scripts (they're much like macros) for Entourage 2001 are written in Apple's system-level scripting language, AppleScript. Many add-on scripts for Entourage are available on various Web sites. Two to check out for Entourage scripts are Microsoft's MacTopia site, at `www.mactopia.com`, and The Unofficial Microsoft Outlook Express Page (remember that Entourage is based on Outlook Express, so many of the same scripts that work on OE will work with Entourage), at `www.macemail.com/oe/`.

Helping the Visually Impaired

With so many icons, toolbars, and other interface widgets in the Office 2001 programs, your screen often seems to be cluttered. If you happen to be visually impaired, the problem is even worse. This section describes two ways to take the strain off your eyes.

Blow up those buttons

You can make the buttons in the toolbars big — really big. First, choose Tools⊅Customize to display the Customize dialog box. Click the Appearance tab. Click the Large Icons check box. Then click the Close button.

Zoom in for a better view

All the Office programs enable you to magnify (or shrink) the document window. This capability is especially useful if you're using small-point-size fonts in your document. You can zoom in while you're working on the document without messing up page breaks and margins. To zoom in, follow these steps:

1. **Choose View⊅Zoom.**

   The Zoom dialog box appears.

2. **Click the radio button for the magnification you want to use or enter a custom magnification in the text box.**

If you want to zoom in on one small portion of the document window, select it first and then click the Fit Selection button in the Zoom dialog box. Just that portion of your document zooms to be as large as necessary to fit on your screen.

3. **Click the OK button.**

The Standard toolbar also has a Zoom menu. Some people find using this menu to be faster than using the Zoom dialog box.

Customize the Recently Used File List

If you tend to work with and switch among many documents, you'll appreciate the capability to expand the Recently Used File List on the File menu. To do so, follow these steps:

1. **Choose Edit⇨Preferences.**

   The Preferences dialog box appears.

2. **Click the General tab.**

3. **Adjust the number in the Recently Used File List box.**

   Acceptable numbers are 0 through 9.

4. **Click the OK button.**

Eliminate Automatic Grammar Checking

By default, Word 2001 corrects your spelling and grammar as you type. If you find this feature to be annoying and would rather have the program check only when you ask it to do so, follow these steps:

1. **Choose Tools⇨Preferences.**

   The Preferences dialog box appears.

2. **Click the Spelling & Grammar tab.**

3. **Clear the check box labeled Check Grammar As You Type.**

4. **Click the OK button.**

Chapter 21

Ten Tips to Tune Up Your Toolbars

. . . .

In This Chapter

▶ Showing and hiding toolbars

▶ Adding buttons to toolbars

▶ Removing buttons from toolbars

▶ Adding menus and macros to toolbars

▶ Creating a toolbar for AutoText

▶ Creating a button for text formatting in Excel

▶ Moving and copying buttons

▶ Creating separators in toolbars

▶ Turning a toolbar into a floating palette

▶ Moving your toolbars where you want them

. . . .

Toolbars in the Office 2001 applications are amazingly useful; because of toolbars, access to virtually all the power of Office 2001 is literally just a click away. Can you make those toolbars work harder to help you? Sure, you can! You can customize toolbars to a fare-thee-well, and this book is just the thing to show you how.

Here are ten useful ways to get your toolbars working both smarter and harder. By the time you're done with this chapter, you'll have your toolbars begging for mercy.

Toolbars: Now You See Them, Now You Don't

Not all the toolbars show up on-screen at the same time, and that's a good thing. Figure 21-1 shows what happened to Floyd Robbins, of West Alpaca, New York. It seems that all of Floyd's toolbars decided to party on his screen at the same time. Because Floyd didn't have this book, he didn't know how to break up the gathering.

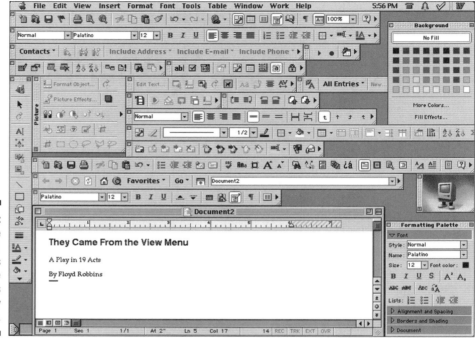

Figure 21-1:
All the
Word 2001
toolbars
have come
to roost. It's
not a pretty
sight.

Scary, no? This situation won't happen to you, though. To hide (or show) any toolbar, follow these steps:

1. **Control+click any toolbar.**

   A pop-up menu appears, with the active toolbars checked.

2. **Check (to show) or uncheck (to hide) the toolbar name on the pop-up menu.**

Adding a Button to a Toolbar

Adding a button to a toolbar is easy. Suppose that you often want to get synonyms for words as you write, so you want to add a Thesaurus button to the Standard toolbar. Follow these steps:

1. **Display the toolbar to which you want to add a button (in this case, the Standard toolbar is already displayed).**

2. **Choose Tools⇨Customize.**

   The Customize dialog box appears.

3. **Click the Commands tab.**

4. **In the Categories box, click the category for the command for which you want to create a button.**

   For Thesaurus, for example, click the Tools category.

5. **Scroll through the Commands box until you find the command you want, and drag it to the toolbar you displayed in Step 1.**

   If the command has an icon associated with it (not all commands do), the icon for the command will appear in the toolbar. If no icon exists, the name of the command will appear as text in the toolbar.

If you can't seem to find a command in a particular category, click All Commands in the Categories box.

Removing a Button from a Toolbar

To remove a button from a toolbar, follow these steps:

1. **Display the toolbar you want to modify.**

2. **While holding down the ⌘ key, drag the button off the toolbar.**

3. **Release the mouse button.**

   The toolbar button disappears.

You can't Undo the deletion of a toolbar button. If you make a mistake, add the button back to the toolbar, as described in the section "Adding a Button to a Toolbar," earlier in this chapter.

Adding Menus and Macros to a Toolbar

If you want to get ambitious about customizing toolbars, you can add any menu or macro to any toolbar. You're not limited to the menus that come with the Office programs; you can create your own custom menus and add them to toolbars too.

Putting one of the built-in menus on a toolbar

Follow these steps to add one of the built-in menus to a toolbar:

1. **Display the toolbar to which you want to add a menu.**

2. **Choose Tools⇨Customize.**

   The Customize dialog box appears.

3. **Click the Commands tab.**

4. **In the Categories box, click Built-in Menus.**

5. **Drag the menu you want to use from the Commands box to the toolbar.**

Creating a custom menu on a toolbar

If you have created any custom menus (refer to Chapter 20 to learn how), you can add them to toolbars. Follow these steps:

1. **Display the toolbar to which you want to add a menu.**

2. **Choose Tools⇨Customize.**

   The Customize dialog box appears.

3. **Click the Commands tab.**

4. **In the Categories box, click New Menu.**

5. **Drag the New Menu item from the Commands box to the toolbar.**

   Next, you have to rename the New Menu item that's on the toolbar.

6. **Double-click the New Menu item on the toolbar.**

   The Command Properties window appears, as shown in Figure 21-2.

Command Properties

Name: Writing Tools

View: Default Style

☑ Begin a group

Keyboard...

Description
Custom

Choose a new button image for the selected toolbar button.

Reset   Cancel   OK

Figure 21-2:
Naming a
custom
menu on a
toolbar.

7. **In the Name box, type the new menu's title. Click OK.**

Now you can add commands to your new custom menu.

8. **Click (just once) the custom menu's name on the toolbar.**

An empty box appears below the menu name.

9. **Drag a command from the Categories box of the Customize dialog box to the empty box on the custom menu.**

10. **Repeat Steps 8 and 9 until you've added all the commands you want to use on the custom menu.**

11. **Press the Return key.**

Adding a macro to a toolbar

To add a macro to a toolbar, follow these steps:

1. **Display the toolbar to which you want to add a macro.**

2. **Choose Tools⇔Customize.**

The Customize dialog box appears.

3. **Click the Commands tab.**

4. **Click Macros in the Categories box.**

5. **Drag the macro from the Commands box to the toolbar.**

Because macros have long, geeky names, you may want to rename the new macro on the toolbar.

6. **Double-click the custom menu on the toolbar.**

   The Command Properties window appears (refer to Figure 21-2).

7. **In the Name box, type the macro's new title, and then click OK.**

Letting Those Toolbars Float

Some people prefer toolbars; others prefer floating palettes. Office 2001 can accommodate both sorts in perfect harmony. At the left edge of any toolbar is the move handle. Click the move handle and drag downward to turn the toolbar into a palette. You can also use the move handles to rearrange the toolbars. Just drag the toolbars where you want them.

Making an AutoText Toolbar

AutoText stores text or graphics you want to use again, whether those elements are boilerplate language, your signature, or your letterhead. You can save time and effort by creating a new toolbar for your AutoText entries. Follow these steps:

1. **Choose Tools⇨Customize to display the Customize dialog box.**

2. **Click the Toolbars tab.**

3. **Click the New button.**

   The New Toolbar dialog box appears.

4. **Type a name for the new toolbar.**

5. **Click the OK button to close the New Toolbar dialog box and return to the Customize dialog box.**

   You can't name the new toolbar AutoText because a built-in toolbar already has that name. Choose another name.

   A new, empty toolbar will appear.

6. **Click the Commands tab.**

7. **Click AutoText in the Categories box.**

8. **Drag the AutoText items you want to use from the Commands box to the toolbar.**

Adding the Style Menu in Excel 2001

Excel 2001 enables you to create text and number styles, but because the Style menu isn't part of the Standard toolbar, you have to make a trip to the Format menu and the Style dialog box, or to the Formatting Palette, whenever you want to format your text. To fix this hideous oversight, follow these steps:

1. **Choose Tools⇨Customize to display the Customize dialog box.**

2. **Click the Commands tab.**

3. **Click Format in the Categories box.**

4. **Drag the Style Menu command from the Commands box to the Formatting toolbar.**

   This command, the one that reads Style, has a blank box to the right of it — not the one that simply reads Style.

 Though it might make sense to add a Style menu to the Formatting Palette, rather than a toolbar, you can't; unfortunately, the Formatting Palette in the Office 2001 applications isn't customizable.

Moving and Copying Toolbar Buttons

You can rearrange toolbar buttons to your heart's content. If you want to move a button from one toolbar to another, first make sure that both toolbars are displayed. Then, to move the button, hold down the ⌘ key and drag the button to its new home — on the same toolbar or on a different toolbar. To copy the button, hold down the Option key while you drag.

Separating Those Toolbar Buttons

If you create your own toolbars, you may notice that the buttons all seem to run together. To create a separator bar between buttons, ⌘+click a button and drag it just a little to the right or left. When you release the mouse button, the separator bar appears.

 If you drag the button too far, you end up moving the button to another toolbar or to a different place on the same toolbar. Just drag the button back to where you started and try again.

Putting Your Toolbars Where You Want Them

Toolbars don't have to stay at the top of the screen. You can turn a toolbar into a floating palette and then drag the floating palette to any edge of the screen to dock it as a toolbar.

Chapter 22

Ten Quick Time-Saving Tips

*M*icrosoft Office 2001 is so chock-full of features and capabilities that I had a problem trimming the number of cool tips to only ten. Luckily, I was able to sprinkle throughout the rest of the book most of the tips I couldn't fit into this chapter.

Here are ten interesting tips, each one of which is guaranteed to save you time and effort. As a bonus, you can use these tips to amaze your friends and leave your office rivals in the dust.

Paint Your Formats

In all the Office 2001 programs, it's a snap to copy character and paragraph formatting from one place in your document to another. Just click the Format Painter button on the Standard toolbar.

To use the Format Painter, follow these steps:

1. **Format some text the way you like it.**
2. **Select the text you just formatted.**
3. **Click the Format Painter button.**
4. **Select the text to which you want to apply the formatting.**

You can quickly apply the same formatting to several locations in your document by double-clicking the Format Painter button; this action locks the formatting on. Click the button again when you're done formatting.

Flash Your Formulas

When you work in Excel 2001, you often want to check out formulas in different cells. You can click each cell in turn and look at the formula on the formula bar. Alternatively, you can choose Tools➪Preferences to display the Preferences dialog box, click the View tab, click the Formulas check box, and then click the OK button.

That procedure is way too much work, though, if you ask me. Instead, press Control+~ (tilde) to display formulas in the cells, as shown in Figure 22-1.

Figure 22-1:
When you toggle Display Formulas on by pressing Control+~, your spreadsheet's cells expand to display the formulas.

	16.06 Web Biz Comparisons			
	A	**B** **Dedicated Server**	**C** **Shopping Cart**	**D** **Hosted Store**
1				
2			CheckItOut	Yahoo! Store
3				
4	**Startup Costs**			
5				
6	Hardware	=1199+199	0	0
7	Software	=(3489-B6)+40	40	40
8	Internet Service Provider Startup	200		0
9	Domain Registration	70	70	70
10	Banking/Merchant Account Fees	125	125	125
11				
12	Total Startup	=SUM(B6:B10)	=SUM(C6:C10)	=SUM(D6:D10)
13				
14				
15	**Monthly Fees**			
16				
17	Server space/connectivity	300	39	100
18				
19	Merchant account statement fee	25	25	25
20	Lease for authorization software	0	40	40
21	Discount rate	=0.025*H6	=0.025*H6	=0.025*H6
22	Per-transaction charges	=0.3*H4	=0.3*H4	=0.3*H4
23				
24				
25	Total Monthly Fees	=SUM(B17:B22)	=SUM(C17:C22)	=SUM(D17:D22)

Sheet1 / Sheet2 / Sheet3 /

Ready

Save 'Em All, Close 'Em All

If you've used a computer for more than about a day, you've learned an unpleasant fact: Computers crash, and when they do, you lose all the work you did since the last time you saved. If you regularly work with more than one document open, the problem can be even worse because you have to keep switching among documents to save them all. Here's a better solution. Holding down the Shift key in Word 2001 changes File⇨Save to File⇨Save All. (You have to use the mouse to choose Save All.)

A similar trick works in both Word 2001 and Excel 2001 to close all open windows. Holding down the Shift key changes File⇨Close to File⇨Close All.

Have AutoCorrect Do It for You

The Word 2001 AutoCorrect feature is terrific for fixing misspelled words on the fly, but did you know that it can automatically insert symbols (called *dingbats*) for you? Suppose that you can never remember the right key combination for the copyright symbol (©). Just type **(c),** and Word 2001 automatically replaces it with ©. Table 22-1 shows you the other symbol shortcuts.

Table 22-1	Automatic Symbol Replacements
What You Type	*Word 2001 Replacement*
(c)	©
(r)	®
(tm)	™
...	... (true ellipsis)
:(	☹
:-(	☹
:)	☺
:-)	☺
:|	☺
:-|	☺

(continued)

Table 22-1 *(continued)*	
What You Type	**Word 2001 Replacement**
<--	←
<==	⬅
-->	→
==>	➡
<=>	⇔

You can also use AutoCorrect for bold and italic formatting on the fly. If you type ***bold*** and **_italic_**, Word changes them to the real formatting (**bold** and *italic*). You can use this technique with entire phrases as well as with individual words.

Select Just One Part

Although this trick has been around since Word 5.1, it's still a good one: You can draw a selection box in Word, just like you can in a graphics program. This capability is great when you want to copy a column of numbers that is in a tabbed list rather than in a table. Normally, you would have to copy the entire list and then laboriously edit each line. Not with this trick. Just click at the beginning of the text you want to select, hold down the Option key, and drag a selection box around the text, as shown in Figure 22-2. Then copy, cut, format, or do whatever else you want.

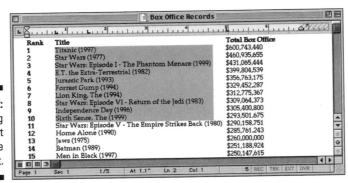

Figure 22-2: Selecting just a part of the document.

Insert Alternate Rows or Columns

You're probably used to adding single rows or columns to your Excel spreadsheets; all you have to do is select a row (or column) and make a trip to the Insert menu. But let's say that you want to add multiple rows (or columns) at once, interspersed between the existing ones?

You can do it. Just select the beginning row by clicking its row number. Hold down the Command key, and click on each of the rows that you want to insert a new row between. Then choose Insert⇨Rows. Excel puts a new blank row between each of the selected rows. See Figure 22-3.

Figure 22-3:
Inserting multiple rows between existing rows. The first screen shows multiple selected rows; the second shows the new inserted rows.

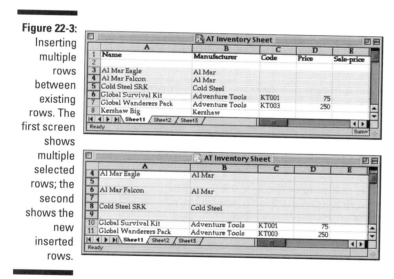

Give an Automatic List a Break

When you use automatic numbering (or automatic bullets) in a Word document, a new number or bullet appears whenever you press the Return key. You've probably wanted to put a blank line between groups of numbered or bulleted lines. You can stop the auto-numbering or auto-bulleting by pressing Return twice and then restart the process by choosing Format⇨Bullets and Numbering. No need, however; Office 2001 has an easier way: Just press Shift+Return to insert the blank line; then press Return again to continue with the numbers or bullets.

Use the Spike

Chances are that you've never heard of the Word 2001 Spike. I hadn't either, until I started researching this book. The Spike is a way to move a group of text or graphics between nonadjacent locations. This feature is kind of like a Clipboard you can keep adding stuff to, except that you always cut items to the Spike; you can't copy them. The Spike (which was also in Word 98) is definitely a carryover from the Windows version of Word, but it's a useful one (I guess that Microsoft got some things right!).

To use the Spike, follow these steps:

1. **Select text or a graphic.**

2. **Press ⌘+F3.**

   The selected item disappears from the document and goes to the Spike.

3. **Repeat Steps 1 and 2 for other items you want to move.**

4. **Click where you want to insert the Spike's contents.**

5. **Press ⌘+Shift+F3.**

   The Spike's contents spew out to the new location, in the order in which you put them on the Spike. The Spike is now empty; items don't stay on the Spike, as they do on the Clipboard. Weird, huh? — but still useful.

You can insert the contents of the Spike without emptying it: Cut items to the Spike, choose Insert⇨AutoText⇨AutoText, and then click the AutoText tab. Click Spike in the Enter AutoText Entries Here box, and then click the Insert button.

Quick Selections in Excel

The fastest way to select a row in Excel is to select any cell in the row and press Shift+Spacebar. If you want to select a whole column, click into any cell in the column and press Control+Spacebar. And the quick way to select the entire worksheet is to press Control+Shift+Spacebar.

Of course, the old-fashioned ways to make the selections with the mouse still work: For a row, click its number header at the left edge of the worksheet; for a column, click the letter header at the top of the worksheet; and for the entire worksheet, click the blank cell at the upper-left corner of the worksheet. But in terms of speed, the keyboard shortcuts rule.

Move It, Mr. Paragraph!

You can rearrange paragraphs quickly by selecting the paragraph you want to move and then pressing Control+Shift+↑ to move it above the preceding paragraph or Control+Shift+↓ to move it below the next paragraph. You can also hold down the Control and Shift keys and repeatedly press an arrow key until the paragraph moves to the position you want.

Index

• *V* •

Notes

Notes

Notes

Notes

Notes

Notes

Notes

Notes

Dummies Books™
Bestsellers on Every Topic!

🤓 GENERAL INTEREST TITLES

INESS & PERSONAL FINANCE

Title	Author	ISBN	Price
ing For Dummies®	John A. Tracy, CPA	0-7645-5014-4	$19.99 US/$27.99 CAN
Plans For Dummies®	Paul Tiffany, Ph.D. & Steven D. Peterson, Ph.D.	1-56884-868-4	$19.99 US/$27.99 CAN
Writing For Dummies®	Sheryl Lindsell-Roberts	0-7645-5134-5	$16.99 US/$27.99 CAN
ng For Dummies®	Bob Nelson & Peter Economy	0-7645-5034-9	$19.99 US/$27.99 CAN
r Service For Dummies®, 2nd Edition	Karen Leland & Keith Bailey	0-7645-5209-0	$19.99 US/$27.99 CAN
ing For Dummies®	Dave Thomas & Michael Seid	0-7645-5160-4	$19.99 US/$27.99 CAN
Results For Dummies®	Mark H. McCormack	0-7645-5205-8	$19.99 US/$27.99 CAN
uying For Dummies®	Eric Tyson, MBA & Ray Brown	1-56884-385-2	$16.99 US/$24.99 CAN
elling For Dummies®	Eric Tyson, MBA & Ray Brown	0-7645-5038-1	$16.99 US/$24.99 CAN
Resources Kit For Dummies®	Max Messmer	0-7645-5131-0	$19.99 US/$27.99 CAN
g For Dummies®, 2nd Edition	Eric Tyson, MBA	0-7645-5162-0	$19.99 US/$27.99 CAN
Dummies®	John Ventura	1-56884-860-9	$19.99 US/$27.99 CAN
hip For Dummies®	Marshall Loeb & Steven Kindel	0-7645-5176-0	$19.99 US/$27.99 CAN
g For Dummies®	Bob Nelson & Peter Economy	1-56884-858-7	$19.99 US/$27.99 CAN
ng For Dummies®	Alexander Hiam	1-56884-699-1	$19.99 US/$27.99 CAN
Funds For Dummies®, 2nd Edition	Eric Tyson, MBA	0-7645-5112-4	$19.99 US/$27.99 CAN
ting For Dummies®	Michael C. Donaldson & Mimi Donaldson	1-56884-867-6	$19.99 US/$27.99 CAN
Finance For Dummies®, 3rd Edition	Eric Tyson, MBA	0-7645-5231-7	$19.99 US/$27.99 CAN
Finance For Dummies® For Canadians, 2nd Edition	Eric Tyson, MBA & Tony Martin	0-7645-5123-X	$19.99 US/$27.99 CAN
peaking For Dummies®	Malcolm Kushner	0-7645-5159-0	$16.99 US/$24.99 CAN
osing For Dummies®	Tom Hopkins	0-7645-5063-2	$14.99 US/$21.99 CAN
ospecting For Dummies®	Tom Hopkins	0-7645-5066-7	$14.99 US/$21.99 CAN
or Dummies®	Tom Hopkins	1-56884-389-5	$16.99 US/$24.99 CAN
siness For Dummies®	Eric Tyson, MBA & Jim Schell	0-7645-5094-2	$19.99 US/$27.99 CAN
siness Kit For Dummies®	Richard D. Harroch	0-7645-5093-4	$24.99 US/$34.99 CAN
01 For Dummies®	Eric Tyson & David J. Silverman	0-7645-5306-2	$15.99 US/$23.99 CAN
nagement For Dummies®, 2nd Edition	Jeffrey J. Mayer	0-7645-5145-0	$19.99 US/$27.99 CAN
Business Letters For Dummies®	Sheryl Lindsell-Roberts	0-7645-5207-4	$16.99 US/$24.99 CAN

TECHNOLOGY TITLES 🤓

ERNET/ONLINE

Title	Author	ISBN	Price
Online® For Dummies®, 6th Edition	John Kaufeld	0-7645-0670-6	$19.99 US/$27.99 CAN
Online Dummies®	Paul Murphy	0-7645-0458-4	$24.99 US/$34.99 CAN
or Dummies®, 2nd Edition	Marcia Collier, Roland Woerner, & Stephanie Becker	0-7645-0761-3	$19.99 US/$27.99 CAN
or Dummies®, 2nd Edition	John R. Levine, Carol Baroudi, & Arnold Reinhold	0-7645-0131-3	$24.99 US/$34.99 CAN
gy Online For Dummies®, 2nd Edition	Matthew L. Helm & April Leah Helm	0-7645-0543-2	$24.99 US/$34.99 CAN
Directory For Dummies®, 3rd Edition	Brad Hill	0-7645-0558-2	$24.99 US/$34.99 CAN
Auctions For Dummies®	Greg Holden	0-7645-0578-9	$24.99 US/$34.99 CAN
Explorer 5.5 For Windows® For Dummies®	Doug Lowe	0-7645-0738-9	$19.99 US/$28.99 CAN
hing Online For Dummies®, 2nd Edition	Mary Ellen Bates & Reva Basch	0-7645-0546-7	$24.99 US/$34.99 CAN
rching Online For Dummies®	Pam Dixon	0-7645-0673-0	$24.99 US/$34.99 CAN
g Online For Dummies®, 3rd Edition	Kathleen Sindell, Ph.D.	0-7645-0725-7	$24.99 US/$34.99 CAN
lanning Online For Dummies®, 2nd Edition	Noah Vadnai	0-7645-0438-X	$24.99 US/$34.99 CAN
t Searching For Dummies®	Brad Hill	0-7645-0478-9	$24.99 US/$34.99 CAN
For Dummies®, 2nd Edition	Brad Hill	0-7645-0762-1	$19.99 US/$27.99 CAN
rnet For Dummies®, 7th Edition	John R. Levine, Carol Baroudi, & Arnold Reinhold	0-7645-0674-9	$19.99 US/$27.99 CAN

RATING SYSTEMS

Title	Author	ISBN	Price
r Dummies®, 3rd Edition	Dan Gookin	0-7645-0361-8	$19.99 US/$27.99 CAN
For Linux® For Dummies®	David B. Busch	0-7645-0650-1	$24.99 US/$37.99 CAN
For Dummies®, 2nd Edition	John Hall, Craig Witherspoon, & Coletta Witherspoon	0-7645-0421-5	$24.99 US/$34.99 CAN
S 9 For Dummies®	Bob LeVitus	0-7645-0652-8	$19.99 US/$28.99 CAN
e® Linux® For Dummies®	Jon "maddog" Hall	0-7645-0663-3	$24.99 US/$34.99 CAN
usiness Windows® 98 For Dummies®	Stephen Nelson	0-7645-0425-8	$24.99 US/$34.99 CAN
or Dummies®, 4th Edition	John R. Levine & Margaret Levine Young	0-7645-0419-3	$19.99 US/$27.99 CAN
ws® 95 For Dummies® 2nd Edition	Andy Rathbone	0-7645-0180-1	$19.99 US/$27.99 CAN
ws® 98 For Dummies®	Andy Rathbone	0-7645-0261-1	$19.99 US/$27.99 CAN
ws® 2000 For Dummies®	Andy Rathbone	0-7645-0641-2	$19.99 US/$27.99 CAN
ws® 2000 Server For Dummies®	Ed Tittle	0-7645-0341-3	$24.99 US/$37.99 CAN
ws® ME Millenium Edition For Dummies®	Andy Rathbone	0-7645-0735-4	$19.99 US/$27.99 CAN

Dummies Books™
Bestsellers on Every Topic!

GENERAL INTEREST TITLES

FOOD & BEVERAGE/ENTERTAINING

Title	Author	ISBN	Price
Bartending For Dummies®	Ray Foley	0-7645-5051-9	$14.99 US/$21.99 CA
Cooking For Dummies®, 2nd Edition	Bryan Miller & Marie Rama	0-7645-5250-3	$19.99 US/$27.99 CA
Entertaining For Dummies®	Suzanne Williamson with Linda Smith	0-7645-5027-6	$19.99 US/$27.99 CA
Gourmet Cooking For Dummies®	Charlie Trotter	0-7645-5029-2	$19.99 US/$27.99 CA
Grilling For Dummies®	Marie Rama & John Mariani	0-7645-5076-4	$19.99 US/$27.99 CA
Italian Cooking For Dummies®	Cesare Casella & Jack Bishop	0-7645-5098-5	$19.99 US/$27.99 CA
Mexican Cooking For Dummies®	Mary Sue Miliken & Susan Feniger	0-7645-5169-8	$19.99 US/$27.99 CA
Quick & Healthy Cooking For Dummies®	Lynn Fischer	0-7645-5214-7	$19.99 US/$27.99 CA
Wine For Dummies®, 2nd Edition	Ed McCarthy & Mary Ewing-Mulligan	0-7645-5114-0	$19.99 US/$27.99 CA
Chinese Cooking For Dummies®	Martin Yan	0-7645-5247-3	$19.99 US/$27.99 CA
Etiquette For Dummies®	Sue Fox	0-7645-5170-1	$19.99 US/$27.99 CA

SPORTS

Title	Author	ISBN	Price
Baseball For Dummies®, 2nd Edition	Joe Morgan with Richard Lally	0-7645-5234-1	$19.99 US/$27.99 CA
Golf For Dummies®, 2nd Edition	Gary McCord	0-7645-5146-9	$19.99 US/$27.99 CA
Fly Fishing For Dummies®	Peter Kaminsky	0-7645-5073-X	$19.99 US/$27.99 CA
Football For Dummies®	Howie Long with John Czarnecki	0-7645-5054-3	$19.99 US/$27.99 CA
Hockey For Dummies®	John Davidson with John Steinbreder	0-7645-5045-4	$19.99 US/$27.99 CA
NASCAR For Dummies®	Mark Martin	0-7645-5219-8	$19.99 US/$27.99 CA
Tennis For Dummies®	Patrick McEnroe with Peter Bodo	0-7645-5087-X	$19.99 US/$27.99 CA
Soccer For Dummies®	U.S. Soccer Federation & Michael Lewiss	0-7645-5229-5	$19.99 US/$27.99 CA

HOME & GARDEN

Title	Author	ISBN	Price
Annuals For Dummies®	Bill Marken & NGA	0-7645-5056-X	$16.99 US/$24.99 CA
Container Gardening For Dummies®	Bill Marken & NGA	0-7645-5057-8	$16.99 US/$24.99 CA
Decks & Patios For Dummies®	Robert J. Beckstrom & NGA	0-7645-5075-6	$16.99 US/$24.99 CA
Flowering Bulbs For Dummies®	Judy Glattstein & NGA	0-7645-5103-5	$16.99 US/$24.99 CA
Gardening For Dummies®, 2nd Edition	Michael MacCaskey & NGA	0-7645-5130-2	$16.99 US/$24.99 CA
Herb Gardening For Dummies®	NGA	0-7645-5200-7	$16.99 US/$24.99 CA
Home Improvement For Dummies®	Gene & Katie Hamilton & the Editors of HouseNet, Inc.	0-7645-5005-5	$19.99 US/$26.99 CA
Houseplants For Dummies®	Larry Hodgson & NGA	0-7645-5102-7	$16.99 US/$24.99 CA
Painting and Wallpapering For Dummies®	Gene Hamilton	0-7645-5150-7	$16.99 US/$24.99 CA
Perennials For Dummies®	Marcia Tatroe & NGA	0-7645-5030-6	$16.99 US/$24.99 CA
Roses For Dummies®, 2nd Edition	Lance Walheim	0-7645-5202-3	$16.99 US/$24.99 CA
Trees and Shrubs For Dummies®	Ann Whitman & NGA	0-7645-5203-1	$16.99 US/$24.99 CA
Vegetable Gardening For Dummies®	Charlie Nardozzi & NGA	0-7645-5129-9	$16.99 US/$24.99 CA
Home Cooking For Dummies®	Patricia Hart McMillan & Katharine Kaye McMillan	0-7645-5107-8	$19.99 US/$27.99 CA

TECHNOLOGY TITLES

WEB DESIGN & PUBLISHING

Title	Author	ISBN	Price
Active Server Pages For Dummies®, 2nd Edition	Bill Hatfield	0-7645-0603-X	$24.99 US/$37.99 CA
Cold Fusion 4 For Dummies®	Alexis Gutzman	0-7645-0604-8	$24.99 US/$37.99 CA
Creating Web Pages For Dummies®, 5th Edition	Bud Smith & Arthur Bebak	0-7645-0733-8	$24.99 US/$34.99 CA
Dreamweaver™ 3 For Dummies®	Janine Warner & Paul Vachier	0-7645-0669-2	$24.99 US/$34.99 CA
FrontPage® 2000 For Dummies®	Asha Dornfest	0-7645-0423-1	$24.99 US/$34.99 CA
HTML 4 For Dummies®, 3rd Edition	Ed Tittel & Natanya Dits	0-7645-0572-6	$24.99 US/$34.99 CA
Java™ For Dummies®, 3rd Edition	Aaron E. Walsh	0-7645-0417-7	$24.99 US/$34.99 CA
PageMill™ 2 For Dummies®	Deke McClelland & John San Filippo	0-7645-0028-7	$24.99 US/$34.99 CA
XML™ For Dummies®	Ed Tittel	0-7645-0692-7	$24.99 US/$37.99 CA
Javascript For Dummies®, 3rd Edition	Emily Vander Veer	0-7645-0633-1	$24.99 US/$37.99 CA

DESKTOP PUBLISHING GRAPHICS/MULTIMEDIA

Title	Author	ISBN	Price
Adobe® In Design™ For Dummies®	Deke McClelland	0-7645-0599-8	$19.99 US/$27.99 CA
CorelDRAW™ 9 For Dummies®	Deke McClelland	0-7645-0523-8	$19.99 US/$27.99 CA
Desktop Publishing and Design For Dummies®	Roger C. Parker	1-56884-234-1	$19.99 US/$27.99 CA
Digital Photography For Dummies®, 3rd Edition	Julie Adair King	0-7645-0646-3	$24.99 US/$37.99 CA
Microsoft® Publisher 98 For Dummies®	Jim McCarter	0-7645-0395-2	$19.99 US/$27.99 CA
Visio 2000 For Dummies®	Debbie Walkowski	0-7645-0635-8	$19.99 US/$27.99 CA
Microsoft® Publisher 2000 For Dummies®	Jim McCarter	0-7645-0525-4	$19.99 US/$27.99 CA
Windows® Movie Maker For Dummies®	Keith Underdahl	0-7645-0749-1	$19.99 US/$27.99 CA

Dummies Books™
Bestsellers on Every Topic!

GENERAL INTEREST TITLES

JCATION & TEST PREPARATION

T For Dummies®	Suzee Vlk	1-56884-387-9	$14.99 US/$21.99 CAN
Financial Aid For Dummies®	Dr. Herm Davis & Joyce Lain Kennedy	0-7645-5049-7	$19.99 US/$27.99 CAN
Planning For Dummies®, 2nd Edition	Pat Ordovensky	0-7645-5048-9	$19.99 US/$27.99 CAN
ay Math For Dummies®	Charles Seiter, Ph.D.	1-56884-248-1	$14.99 US/$21.99 CAN
AT® For Dummies®, 3rd Edition	Suzee Vlk	0-7645-5082-9	$16.99 US/$24.99 CAN
E® For Dummies®, 3rd Edition	Suzee Vlk	0-7645-5083-7	$16.99 US/$24.99 CAN
For Dummies®	Ann DeLaney	1-56884-381-X	$19.99 US/$27.99 CAN
T I For Dummies®, 3rd Edition	Suzee Vlk	0-7645-5044-6	$14.99 US/$21.99 CAN

TOMOTIVE

epair For Dummies®	Deanna Sclar	0-7645-5089-6	$19.99 US/$27.99 CAN
A Car For Dummies®	Deanna Sclar	0-7645-5091-8	$16.99 US/$24.99 CAN

ESTYLE/SELF-HELP

For Dummies®	Dr. Joy Browne	0-7645-5072-1	$19.99 US/$27.99 CAN
Marriage Work For Dummies®	Steven Simring, M.D. & Sue Klavans Simring, D.S.W	0-7645-5173-6	$19.99 US/$27.99 CAN
ing For Dummies®	Sandra H. Gookin	1-56884-383-6	$16.99 US/$24.99 CAN
s For Dummies®	Zig Ziglar	0-7645-5061-6	$19.99 US/$27.99 CAN
gs For Dummies®	Marcy Blum & Laura Fisher Kaiser	0-7645-5055-1	$19.99 US/$27.99 CAN

TECHNOLOGY TITLES

TES

oft ® Office 2000 For Windows® For Dummies®	Wallace Wang & Roger C. Parker	0-7645-0452-5	$19.99 US/$27.99 CAN
oft® Office 2000 For Windows® For Dummies® k Reference	Doug Lowe & Bjoern Hartsfvang	0-7645-0453-3	$12.99 US/$17.99 CAN
oft® Office 97 For Windows® For Dummies®	Wallace Wang & Roger C. Parker	0-7645-0050-3	$19.99 US/$27.99 CAN
oft® Office 97 For Windows® For Dummies® k Reference	Doug Lowe	0-7645-0062-7	$12.99 US/$17.99 CAN
oft® Office 98 For Macs For Dummies®	Tom Negrino	0-7645-0229-8	$19.99 US/$27.99 CAN
oft® Office X For Macs For Dummies®	Tom Negrino	0-7645-0702-8	$19.95 US/$27.99 CAN

RD PROCESSING

2000 For Windows® For Dummies® Quick Reference	Peter Weverka	0-7645-0449-5	$12.99 US/$19.99 CAN
WordPerfect 8 For Windows® For Dummies®	Margaret Levine Young, David Kay & Jordan Young	0-7645-0186-0	$19.99 US/$27.99 CAN
2000 For Windows® For Dummies®	Dan Gookin	0-7645-0448-7	$19.99 US/$27.99 CAN
For Windows® 95 For Dummies®	Dan Gookin	1-56884-932-X	$19.99 US/$27.99 CAN
97 For Windows® For Dummies®	Dan Gookin	0-7645-0052-X	$19.99 US/$27.99 CAN
erfect® 9 For Windows® For Dummies®	Margaret Levine Young	0-7645-0427-4	$19.99 US/$27.99 CAN
erfect® 7 For Windows® 95 For Dummies®	Margaret Levine Young & David Kay	1-56884-949-4	$19.99 US/$27.99 CAN

READSHEET/FINANCE/PROJECT MANAGEMENT

For Windows® 95 For Dummies®	Greg Harvey	1-56884-930-3	$19.99 US/$27.99 CAN
2000 For Windows® For Dummies®	Greg Harvey	0-7645-0446-0	$19.99 US/$27.99 CAN
2000 For Windows® For Dummies® Quick Reference	John Walkenbach	0-7645-0447-9	$12.99 US/$17.99 CAN
oft® Money 99 For Dummies®	Peter Weverka	0-7645-0433-9	$19.99 US/$27.99 CAN
oft® Project 98 For Dummies®	Martin Doucette	0-7645-0321-9	$24.99 US/$34.99 CAN
oft® Project 2000 For Dummies®	Martin Doucette	0-7645-0517-3	$24.99 US/$37.99 CAN
oft® Money 2000 For Dummies®	Peter Weverka	0-7645-0579-3	$19.99 US/$27.99 CAN
Excel 97 For Windows® For Dummies®	Greg Harvey	0-7645-0138-0	$22.99 US/$32.99 CAN
en® 2000 For Dummies®	Stephen L. Nelson	0-7645-0607-2	$19.99 US/$27.99 CAN
en® 2001 For Dummies®	Stephen L. Nelson	0-7645-0759-1	$19.99 US/$27.99 CAN
ooks® 2000 For Dummies®	Stephen L. Nelson	0-7645-0665-x	$19.99 US/$27.99 CAN

Dummies Books™
Bestsellers on Every Topic!

GENERAL INTEREST TITLES

THE ARTS

Title	Author	ISBN	Price
TArt For Dummies®	Thomas Hoving	0-7645-5104-3	$24.99 US/$34.99 CA
Blues For Dummies®	Lonnie Brooks, Cub Koda, & Wayne Baker Brooks	0-7645-5080-2	$24.99 US/$34.99 CAN
Classical Music For Dummies®	David Pogue & Scott Speck	0-7645-5009-8	$24.99 US/$34.99 CAN
Guitar For Dummies®	Mark Phillips & Jon Chappell of Cherry Lane Music	0-7645-5106-X	$24.99 US/$34.99 CA
Jazz For Dummies®	Dirk Sutro	0-7645-5081-0	$24.99 US/$34.99 CAN
Opera For Dummies®	David Pogue & Scott Speck	0-7645-5010-1	$24.99 US/$34.99 CAT
Piano For Dummies®	Blake Neely of Cherry Lane Music	0-7645-5105-1	$24.99 US/$34.99 CAN
Shakespeare For Dummies®	John Doyle & Ray Lischner	0-7645-5135-3	$19.99 US/$27.99 CAN

HEALTH

Title	Author	ISBN	Price
Allergies and Asthma For Dummies®	William Berger, M.D.	0-7645-5218-X	$19.99 US/$27.99 CAN
Alternative Medicine For Dummies®	James Dillard, M.D., D.C., C.A.C., & Terra Ziporyn, Ph.D.	0-7645-5109-4	$19.99 US/$27.99 CAN
Beauty Secrets For Dummies®	Stephanie Seymour	0-7645-5078-0	$19.99 US/$27.99 CAN
Diabetes For Dummies®	Alan L. Rubin, M.D.	0-7645-5154-X	$19.99 US/$27.99 CAN
Dieting For Dummies®	The American Dietetic Society with Jane Kirby, R.D.	0-7645-5126-4	$19.99 US/$27.99 CAN
Family Health For Dummies®	Charles Inlander & Karla Morales	0-7645-5121-3	$19.99 US/$27.99 CAN
First Aid For Dummies®	Charles B. Inlander & The People's Medical Society	0-7645-5213-9	$19.99 US/$27.99 CAN
Fitness For Dummies®, 2nd Edition	Suzanne Schlosberg & Liz Neporent, M.A.	0-7645-5167-1	$19.99 US/$27.99 CAN
Healing Foods For Dummies®	Molly Siple, M.S. R.D.	0-7645-5198-1	$19.99 US/$27.99 CAN
Healthy Aging For Dummies®	Walter Bortz, M.D.	0-7645-5233-3	$19.99 US/$27.99 CAN
Men's Health For Dummies®	Charles Inlander	0-7645-5120-5	$19.99 US/$27.99 CAN
Nutrition For Dummies®, 2nd Edition	Carol Ann Rinzler	0-7645-5180-9	$19.99 US/$27.99 CAN
Pregnancy For Dummies®	Joanne Stone, M.D., Keith Eddleman, M.D., & Mary Murray	0-7645-5074-8	$19.99 US/$27.99 CAN
Sex For Dummies®	Dr. Ruth K. Westheimer	1-56884-384-4	$16.99 US/$24.99 CAN
Stress Management For Dummies®	Allen Elkin, Ph.D.	0-7645-5144-2	$19.99 US/$27.99 CAN
The Healthy Heart For Dummies®	James M. Ripple, M.D.	0-7645-5166-3	$19.99 US/$27.99 CAN
Weight Training For Dummies®	Liz Neporent, M.A. & Suzanne Schlosberg	0-7645-5036-5	$19.99 US/$27.99 CAN
Women's Health For Dummies®	Pamela Maraldo, Ph.D., R.N., & The People's Medical Society	0-7645-5119-1	$19.99 US/$27.99 CAN

TECHNOLOGY TITLES

MACINTOSH

Title	Author	ISBN	Price
Macs® For Dummies®, 7th Edition	David Pogue	0-7645-0703-6	$19.99 US/$27.99 CAN
The iBook™ For Dummies®	David Pogue	0-7645-0647-1	$19.99 US/$27.99 CAN
The iMac For Dummies®, 2nd Edition	David Pogue	0-7645-0648-X	$19.99 US/$27.99 CAN
The iMac For Dummies® Quick Reference	Jenifer	0-7645-0648-X	$12.99 US/$19.99 CAN

PC/GENERAL COMPUTING

Title	Author	ISBN	Price
Building A PC For Dummies®, 2nd Edition	Mark Chambers	0-7645-0571-8	$24.99 US/$34.99 CAN
Buying a Computer For Dummies®	Dan Gookin	0-7645-0632-3	$19.99 US/$27.99 CAN
Illustrated Computer Dictionary For Dummies®, 4th Edition	Dan Gookin & Sandra Hardin Gookin	0-7645-0732-X	$19.99 US/$27.99 CAN
Palm Computing® For Dummies®	Bill Dyszel	0-7645-0581-5	$24.99 US/$34.99 CAN
PCs For Dummies®, 7th Edition	Dan Gookin	0-7645-0594-7	$19.99 US/$27.99 CAN
Small Business Computing For Dummies®	Brian Underdahl	0-7645-0287-5	$24.99 US/$34.99 CAN
Smart Homes For Dummies®	Danny Briere	0-7645-0527-0	$19.99 US/$27.99 CAN
Upgrading & Fixing PCs For Dummies®, 5th Edition	Andy Rathbone	0-7645-0719-2	$19.99 US/$27.99 CAN
Handspring Visor For Dummies®	Joe Hubko	0-7645-0724-9	$19.99 US/$27.99 CAN

Discover Dummies Online!

The Dummies Web Site is your fun and friendly online resource for the latest information about *For Dummies*® books and your favorite topics. The Web site is the place to communicate with us, exchange ideas with other *For Dummies* readers, chat with authors, and have fun!

Ten Fun and Useful Things You Can Do at www.dummies.com

1. Win free *For Dummies* books and more!
2. Register your book and be entered in a prize drawing.
3. Meet your favorite authors through the Hungry Minds Author Chat Series.
4. Exchange helpful information with other *For Dummies* readers.
5. Discover other great *For Dummies* books you must have!
6. Purchase Dummieswear® exclusively from our Web site.
7. Buy *For Dummies* books online.
8. Talk to us. Make comments, ask questions, get answers!
9. Download free software.
10. Find additional useful resources from authors.

Link directly to these ten fun and useful things at
http://www.dummies.com/10useful

For other technology titles from Hungry Minds, go to
www.hungryminds.com

Not on the Web yet? It's easy to get started with *Dummies 101*®: *The Internet For Windows*® *98* or *The Internet For Dummies*® at local retailers everywhere.

Hungry Minds™

Find other *For Dummies* books on these topics:
Business • Career • Databases • Food & Beverage • Games • Gardening
Graphics • Hardware • Health & Fitness • Internet and the World Wide Web
Networking • Office Suites • Operating Systems • Personal Finance • Pets
Programming • Recreation • Sports • Spreadsheets • Teacher Resources
Test Prep • Word Processing

HUNGRY MINDS
BOOK REGISTRATION

We want to hear from you!

Visit **dummies.com** to register this book and tell us how you liked it!

✔ Get entered in our monthly prize giveaway.

✔ Give us feedback about this book — tell us what you like best, what you like least, or maybe what you'd like to ask the author and us to change!

✔ Let us know any other *For Dummies®* topics that interest you.

Your feedback helps us determine what books to publish, tells us what coverage to add as we revise our books, and lets us know whether we're meeting your needs as a *For Dummies* reader. You're our most valuable resource, and what you have to say is important to us!

Not on the Web yet? It's easy to get started with *Dummies 101®: The Internet For Windows® 98* or *The Internet For Dummies®* at local retailers everywhere.

Or let us know what you think by sending us a letter at the following address:

For Dummies Book Registration
Dummies Press
10475 Crosspoint Blvd.
Indianapolis, IN 46256

BESTSELLING
BOOK SERIES